Math Coach

A PARENT'S GUIDE
TO HELPING CHILDREN
SUCCEED IN MATH

Wayne A. Wickelgren, Ph.D.,
and **Ingrid Wickelgren**

B

BERKLEY BOOKS NEW YORK

B

A Berkley Book
Published by The Berkley Publishing Group
A division of Penguin Putnam Inc.
375 Hudson Street
New York, New York 10014

Copyright © 2001 by Wayne A. Wickelgren, Ph.D., and
Ingrid Wickelgren
Book design by Richard Oriolo
Cover design by Jill Boltin

PRINTING HISTORY
Berkley trade paperback edition / July 2001

The Penguin Putnam Inc. World Wide Web site address is
www.penguinputnam.com

LIBRARY OF CONGRESS CATALOGING-IN-PUBLICATION DATA

Wickelgren, Wayne A., 1938–
Math coach : a parent's guide to helping children
succeed in math / Wayne A. Wickelgren & Ingrid
Wickelgren.—Berkley trade pbk. ed.
p. cm.
Includes bibliographical references and index.
ISBN 0-425-17983-4
1. Mathematics—Study and teaching.
I. Wickelgren, Ingrid. II. Title.

QA11.W54 2001
510'.71—dc21

2001025497

PRINTED IN THE UNITED STATES OF AMERICA

10 9 8 7 6 5 4 3 2 1

For Peter, Kirsten, and Jeanette,
to whom I taught math and for whom
I coached math teams

Contents

The ideas and experiences described in this book come virtually exclusively from the first author, Dr. Wayne Wickelgren, and the parts of this book written in first person are from his perspective. The second author, Wayne's daughter Ingrid, is responsible for much of the book's phrasing and structure.

Acknowledgments

Both authors are grateful for the efforts of their editor at Berkley Books, Bret Witter, who felt passionately about *Math Coach* despite having inherited it from another editor and worked extremely hard to make it the best it could be. After reading the first version of the book, Bret responded promptly with an impressively detailed blueprint for how to tighten its structure, eliminating many digressions and repeated points. His talent, thoughtfulness, and clarity were essential to the authors' ability to create what you are about to read.

Ingrid and Wayne would also like to thank Ingrid's husband, Bob Langreth, who lent his considerable skills as a writer and editor to help improve the final version of *Math Coach* and provided much encouragement throughout its writing. In addition, this book would never have existed were it not for the support and efforts of Ingrid's talented agent, Albert Zuckerman, and for the enthusiasm for the book displayed by Berkley's president and publisher, Leslie Gelbman, and the book's first editor, Lisa Considine.

Wayne thanks Katherine Newman and Paul Attewell for their continual encouragement to write this book. He also wishes to recognize two scholarly figures whose writings helped inspire many of his educational ideas. First is Eric Hirsch, author of the courageous and enlightening book, *The Schools We Need and Why We Don't Have Them*. Second is the late, great, Albert Shanker, former president of the American Federation of Teachers and math teacher, whose weekly "Where We Stand" columns Wayne read for eight years.

Wayne's admiration of Shanker's intellect, knowledge, independence of mind, and good judgment grew with every column he read. To him, Shanker was a hero, someone who cut through all the educational fads, faulty claims, and faulty criticisms to zero in on both what is good in education, and ought not be eliminated by a new fad, and what is in dire need of improvement. "I wish I had written to Albert Shanker before he died to tell him how much I admired what he wrote," Wayne later mused. "I hope he would have liked this book."

For her part, Ingrid would like to acknowledge the remarkable efforts of her father in completing this book. Wayne began writing *Math Coach* and went through the extensive editing process while in the throws of a devastating illness called Amyotrophic Lateral Sclerosis (ALS), also known as Lou Gehrig's disease. ALS causes progressive paralysis by gradually weakening nearly all of the body's muscles, including those essential to breathing. Victims of this disorder are usually given two to five years to live at the time of diagnosis.

When Wayne could no longer breathe on his own he still continued to work on his computer, optimistically striving to achieve his goals as he has done all his life. At one point in the book he admonishes parents: "Be a good model for your child. Reach for the stars yourself, but set realistic goals too. And set a good example when life kicks *you* in the teeth."

Ingrid cannot imagine a better model than her father in this regard. Life has dealt him a powerful blow, and he has proven himself a formidable adversary. Indeed, Wayne has practiced nearly all of the myriad pieces of advice he gives in this book. He is an extremely dedicated parent who paid very close attention to his children's education, allowing no assignment to be forgotten and no educational opportunity to be missed.

For Ingrid, her dad has always been a source of optimism and advice that she has sorely needed time and again. It is her great privilege to share her secret source of inspiration and success with you.

As a final note, both Ingrid and Wayne owe a deep debt of gratitude to Wayne's wife, Norma Graham, without whom this book could never have been completed. Norma's incredible can-do spirit, organization, and tireless effort have kept her entire family sane and able to go on with their regular lives despite the extremely difficult circumstances brought on by Wayne's illness. This is all the more impressive given that Norma juggles her extraordinary family responsibilities along with those of her job as a psychology professor at Columbia University.

f you think your child should be learning math better or faster than she or he has been, this book is for you. Whether your child is struggling with math or finds it too easy, you can use the advice, activities and strategies in this book to improve your child's math skills far beyond what they would be with ordinary schooling.

The tips and tools I describe in the following chapters are derived from my studies of learning, memory, and mathematical problem-solving as well as my hands-on teaching of math to children, both my own and others. As a cognitive psychologist, I have spent over four decades pursuing a deeper understanding of how people think, learn, and remember, a quest I began at

Harvard and continued at the University of California (Berkeley), MIT, the University of Oregon, and Columbia University. This work, documented in scores of papers and two textbooks, underlies my philosophy toward math education and informs my judgment on the most effective and efficient ways of teaching math to children.

I have put my ideas about, and techniques for, teaching math to the test in numerous ways. At MIT and the University of Oregon I taught classes in mathematical problem solving incorporating innovative methods that I later published in a popular book titled *How to Solve Problems* (now reprinted under the title *How to Solve Mathematical Problems*). I have been a volunteer math teacher in my children's schools and spent seven years coaching winning math teams in several of those schools. I have also tutored all five of my children in math, accelerating them three years to five years ahead of their classmates in the standard math curriculum.

As a parent I have put most of my energies into math education in part because I knew a solid grounding in math would benefit my children's future careers. So far, it has, and in unpredictable ways. My daughter Ingrid, a writer and journalist, uses her math background to help her understand the statistics in the scientific reports she covers. My son Abe, an economist, also uses math extensively in his research, which involves constructing mathematical models in economics and law.

And, despite the importance of math to future success, I knew that the quality of math instruction in schools was far more variable than for other school subjects. Indeed, math is the subject I most wished I had mastered better before college. So I vowed that none of my children would leave home wanting for a better background in math.

I began teaching math to my children when Ingrid, my oldest, was in the third grade. One week in the spring when she was out of school sick, I brought her assignments, books, and workbooks home. I realized that her class was never going to finish the math workbook at the rate they were going, so I had Ingrid do as much as she could. She got far ahead of the rest of the class—in one week!

After that, I began teaching math to both Ingrid and Abe at home on a regular basis, to see how much they could learn. I acquired math workbooks and textbooks, and they sped through them, working just three hours per week. A year and a half later, at ages 10 and 8, they knew all the math taught before algebra and were placed into seventh-grade honors math at the local junior high. Ingrid and Abe then simply moved ahead in math at the usual pace, finishing calculus at ages 15 and 13 respectively.

When my other three children came along years later, I knew that they too could learn math much faster than it is taught in school. Their school system, in New York City, wasn't flexible enough to enable them to jump any grade-levels in math in elementary school, so I taught them at home until they knew enough to qualify for accelerated math at their future middle schools. The oldest of these children, Peter, was allowed to take algebra as a sixth grader. But I ended up having to teach algebra to his younger sisters myself because their schools did not permit them to take it in the sixth grade, which was when they were ready for it.

Kirsten, the older of the two, eventually completed high school calculus in tenth grade, as her brother Peter had, and both Peter and Kirsten took advanced math courses at their high school in eleventh grade and at local universities in twelfth grade. Kirsten went on to study math, and Peter, physics at Harvard. After intensive home schooling in math from second through sixth grade, my youngest daughter, Jeanette, was placed in ninth-grade honors math (known as geometry or second-year integrated math) as a seventh grader and continues to do well in her advanced high school math classes.

In attending to my own children's math education, I also developed a passion for improving the math skills of other children. I nurtured talent as well as helped children who were struggling with the subject. I started this in Ingrid's second-grade math class, in which I gave instruction once a week to children working on problems. After that I tutored various schoolchildren in math and even taught a few supplementary math classes in schools. But my most extensive efforts to teach math to kids occurred as a math team coach in New York City elementary and middle schools. In this role I helped groups of children solve difficult math problems during weekly team practices to prepare them for competition.

Being a math team coach was probably my most exciting and rewarding teaching experience. For one thing, my teams did well. Over the years they finished first in New York State twice and second three times. They took first in New York City twice and first in Manhattan five times, among other achievements. Individuals I coached finished first in the nation five times, took five New York State championships, and won numerous city- and Manhattan-wide contests.

Students on my math teams learned a lot of math they weren't taught in school and developed great confidence in their math abilities. In fact, one year I taught some of my math team members an entire course of algebra after I learned their school had dropped its accelerated math program. My instruction enabled these kids to learn a valuable subject when it was most appropriate for them to do so.

From all this experience I have learned many lessons about how to best help children master mathematics and even excel in the subject. Among them: Most children can learn math much faster than the school system prescribes. That means that even if your child is currently behind, there is plenty of wiggle room for catching up, especially if you start early. Math education proceeds slowly in school before eighth or ninth grade, so those are the ideal years to improve your child's mastery of math or speed him or her ahead through the curriculum (though starting later is okay too).

Whatever your child's current level in math, you can boost your child's math skills enormously using the advice in this book. On the following pages you will learn how to ensure that your child benefits from the best possible math instruction throughout the school years and how to give your child the supplemental help he or she needs to master the math curriculum.

My advice comes in two parts. Part 1 will help you determine your child's current level and ability in math and evaluate the math instruction he or she is getting in school—essential steps to understanding how, and how much, to supplement his or her math instruction. Part 1 also presents various strategies for helping your child succeed in math, both in and outside of school.

Part 2 is geared toward parents who would like to teach their children math themselves. It includes general teaching tips as well as instructions for teaching specific math topics, from arithmetic to algebra. The book ends with a chapter on math teams, a marvelous activity that many parents should consider for their children.

Whatever approach you take toward your child's math education, of one thing you can be sure: By taking the steps prescribed herein, your efforts will change your child forever. Investing time in your child's education—whether it's tutoring, consulting with educators, or helping your child set goals—will show your child that you think education is important. Even when your child complains about doing extra schoolwork, rest assured that he or she is learning, however unconsciously, to value learning. It is a value your child will carry throughout life and, in all likelihood, into the next generation.

Part I

Chapter 1

Setting Goals for Your Child

As a parent you may wonder what you should expect from your child in math. What is a reasonable rate of progress in this notoriously difficult subject? Though the speed of math learning varies with the child, with the right instruction your child can very likely learn math much faster than you imagine. That means that even if your child is behind in math now, you can get him or her back on track with only moderate effort. If your child is not behind, you can propel him or her substantially ahead in math. And don't be afraid to push your child to achieve more in math than his or her teachers expect.

What most American educators, and parents, consider a "normal" rate of progress through the math curriculum is actually too slow for the vast majority of children. Take the guideline that most college-bound students should proceed through the K–12 math curriculum—a hierarchy of classes stepping from simple arithmetic to calculus—at a pace that lands them in algebra in ninth grade. This is too easy for most children. In a regular middle school two of my children attended, all of the students took algebra in or before *eighth* grade and over 80 percent mastered it, putting them one or more years ahead in math.

Entire *countries* of students accomplish this routinely. The Third International Mathematics and Science Study, conducted in 1996, found that the material taught in U.S. eighth-grade math classes was taught in the seventh grade in many other developed countries and even earlier in Japan and Germany. As a result, U.S. eighth graders performed significantly poorer on a standardized math test than eighth graders in twenty other countries, and far poorer than Japanese students, who scored highest. Overall, U.S. elementary and middle school math education lags a full year behind that in dozens of countries and one and a half years behind Japan and Germany.

There's no reason American children shouldn't keep up with their peers in foreign nations. So strive to get your child into algebra by eighth grade, not later. In the U.S., this requires preparing your child to qualify for "honors math," a math track that now admits just one fifth of American students, and usually starts in seventh grade with pre-algebra.

Algebra by eighth grade is a completely realistic goal as long as your child has no unusual learning or emotional disabilities and has at least a couple of years to work toward this objective. (If your child is older, don't despair. You can still radically speed your child's progress in math.) It's okay if your child is already a fifth or sixth grader and is a little behind in math. There is still time to make the goal. And if your child is younger than that, he or she should have little trouble achieving it, since you have years before honors math begins in which to employ the tips and tools in this book. Indeed, algebra in eighth grade might be conservative for your child, depending on his or her ability and motivation—a subject I address later on.

Why do I frame the goal with algebra? It is the math prior to algebra that is taught especially slowly in the U.S. Thus, the pre-algebra years are the ones in which you can most easily speed your child ahead, or help him or her catch up in math, giving the child a chance to learn as much math as possible.

That is likely to be critical for your child's future success. The more math your child knows by the end of high school, the more math he or she will be able to use all his or her professional life. Math is obviously essential in most fields of science, engineering and computers. But it's also increasingly valued on Wall Street in investment banking and in management consulting, as well as at high-tech companies in Silicon Valley and elsewhere. After high school it is usually too late to catch up to those with better math skills. That's because competing responsibilities and activities limit time for math later on, when math also becomes more difficult and time-consuming to master.

In addition, it is during the slow, pre-algebra years that your child is most at risk of becoming bored with math and unmotivated to study it. Worse, if your child earns high grades with little effort, he or she might well conclude that studying hard in math is unnecessary, becoming lazy and failing to develop good work habits. This can be harmful later on when your child inevitably runs up against students who have been studying hard all along, and finds that he or she can't compete. Such experiences can be so discouraging, even for gifted math students, that they drop mathematics altogether. So it's very important to keep your child challenged in math and encourage him or her to work hard from an early age.

This requires some studying outside of school, but not a lot. A student can learn a year of pre-algebra math in three to six months studying three to ten hours per week, depending on the child's math aptitude. It also requires your involvement with your child's schools. For one thing, be sure your child's schools offer the appropriate honors-track classes. In a middle school, look for algebra or first-year "integrated math," or a similar math series that includes (in its first two years) algebra, a lot of geometry, and usually extras like logic, statistics, and probability. And check that the high school offers an Advanced Placement (AP) calculus course to twelfth graders, ideally a choice between less advanced "AB" calculus and more advanced "BC" calculus.

If you find that one of your child's schools does not offer the math classes he or she needs, organize parents to demand that it does. Many of the schools lacking advanced math courses are in low income or minority areas. This kind of discrimination should not be tolerated. Find out what your child needs to do to qualify for the honors track—pass a test, get high grades in math, obtain teacher recommendations—and using the advice in this book, prepare your child to satisfy those requirements.

BRAIN DEVELOPMENT AND MATH

You may wonder whether there are biological limits to how fast your child can learn math. This is a reasonable concern. Indeed, educators often cite such limits as a reason for delaying the teaching of various math concepts, such as algebra.

It's true that the human brain is far from being completely formed at birth, and the brain continues to mature until about age sixteen, with some individual variation. Reading, for example, requires the maturation of a brain area, a part of the cerebral cortex, that represents words as single chunks. Before that area matures between the ages of five and eight, children may learn to pronounce words phonetically, but cannot read them fluently.

When my first child, Ingrid, was about seven months old, I began teaching her to tell letters apart in hopes this would help her learn to read early. Crawling on the floor with Ingrid, I would hold up two letters, A and B, for example, and say, "Ingrid, which one is the B?" She would grab one of the letters. If she took the wrong letter, I wouldn't let go and would repeat the instruction. When she took the correct letter, I let her have it and showered her with kisses.

After three months of playing this game, Ingrid became quite good at it, and our friends were very impressed. When she learned to talk, she could name these letters. As a toddler in preschool, Ingrid learned to sound out words. But even after lots of practice, she still had to sound out every word she encountered, even those she had "read" tens or hundreds of times before.

Then, almost miraculously, one day when Ingrid was about five and a half, she began to read whole words fluently. Suddenly she only had to sound out a word once before reading it by sight. Then and only then did she start to read avidly on her own. My second child, Abe, also learned to read at five and a half, despite a three-year effort to teach him earlier, using phonics, with which he too learned to sound out words.

So there are limits to what a young child's brain can comprehend. Sometimes no matter how hard one tries, the brain resists learning something because it is not ready, and one simply has to wait. As I taught my kids math, I was ever watchful for such biological blockades. To my surprise, I couldn't find any.

For example, educators typically delay teaching basic addition and subtraction until elementary school, but children as young as three can learn these operations. Both Ingrid and Abe learned all basic addition and subtraction facts, and some multiplication facts, at ages three, four, and five. At the same ages, they also learned what these operations meant. Many of their Montessori school classmates accomplished the same thing.

Was this because Ingrid, Abe, and their classmates were exceptionally bright? The best evidence suggests no. In a recent study, psychologists Janellen Huttenlocher and Susan Levine, and their colleagues at the University of Chicago, found that children's ability to perform nonverbal addition and subtraction developed between ages two and a half and three. To show this, they hid a set of objects under a box and then either added objects to or took them away from the box while the child watched. The child then assembled a set of objects corresponding in number to the set under the box. By age three, most of the children could perform this task accurately, showing that they understood the concept of number and the operations of addition and subtraction. The children studied came from a wide variety of backgrounds including disadvantaged ones, and many lacked the language skills necessary to do conventional classroom mathematics.

This is not to say that there are *no* age-related limits to math learning. In particular, before a child can read simple sentences fluently, the child will not be able to do story problems by himself or herself or learn from a textbook. It's also highly unlikely that a toddler's brain could handle calculus or even algebra. But such limits are irrelevant because, with very rare exceptions, toddlers haven't mastered the prerequisite math that would enable a person of *any* age to learn algebra or calculus. So the relevant question is whether there are biological barriers to processing the math that one would teach a child next. And for children over age three, there may not be any. (Research supporting maturational limits done by a famous developmental psychologist, Jean Piaget, has been contradicted by later studies in the field.)

Of course, your child may have temporary trouble understanding certain math concepts, but the reason for that is unlikely to be a maturation issue. It could be lack of verbal skills. Indeed, Huttenlocher and Levine conclude that it is the verbal encoding of addition and subtraction that is often lacking in young children and not the nonverbal understanding of these concepts. In such a case, you might present the problem in a way that requires fewer verbal skills, say, by reading a story problem aloud. An even likelier reason: Your child hasn't adequately learned some important background ideas in math. Try to home in on the ideas that were not learned and explain them more clearly. None of the children I have taught had any persisting difficulty comprehending any math concept. When they forgot some concepts more quickly than I expected, this signaled a need for more practice and instruction with these concepts, rather than a maturational limit.

ASSESSING ABILITY

Even if there are no universal biological barriers blocking math learning, your child's progress in math may be hindered—or helped—by his or her natural math aptitude. Differentiating children by their abilities and skills is a controversial subject, but math aptitude can vary greatly among children, just as children differ in their ability to run, jump, give speeches, draw, sing, comfort others, tell jokes, or lead a group. And though it's generally impolite to speak of such differences, it is important to recognize that they exist—and for parents to have a sense of where their children rank among others.

Having a sense of your child's math ability can help you set realistic goals for your child in math. It can help you decide whether your child is progressing in math as fast as he or she can or whether you need to push a little harder or do something different—such as provide supplementary math education. For example, you probably want to supplement your child's math education if

- Your child has a very high ability in math—that is, appears to be among the best 10 percent of students in his or her class

- Your child is at least average in math and has career ambitions in math or a math-related field

- Your child scores in the range of college-bound kids, but his or her school math training is inadequate for admission to the college-prep math track or for scoring at the child's ability on the math portion of the Scholastic Aptitude Test (SAT)

- Your child is of normal intelligence, but isn't mastering the basics of arithmetic in school—a necessity for independent living

One way to assess your child's math ability is to have him or her take an IQ test (see box on page 10), but a simpler and probably more accurate method is to observe his or her learning rate relative to that of other children. If your child catches on to math concepts quickly compared to others the same age, he or she is probably a fast learner. Similarly if lots of other kids seem to catch on to math concepts more quickly than your child does, he or she may be of only average math ability. If you can't observe your child's learning rate directly, you can get some clues from the child's teacher, from performance in school, and sometimes even from the child, if that child seems good at assessing his or her abilities.

My daughter Ingrid says she was well aware of the differences in math ability between herself and her brother Abe, from the time I began teaching them at home at ages eight (Ingrid) and six (Abe). Ingrid remembers times when I would pose a problem to the two of them, and Abe would soon begin scribbling on his paper to come up with the correct answer. Ingrid, meanwhile, would look puzzled, wondering how Abe had figured it out so quickly. She knew she wasn't stupid, but it was obvious to her that her younger brother had a gift for numbers she could not claim.

Still, Ingrid took algebra in the seventh grade (when she was just eleven) without much difficulty. She learned plenty of math to complete a fast-paced college physics sequence and the curriculum required for a biology major. She is now a successful writer specializing in scientific and medical topics.

Meanwhile, Abe wanted to become a professional basketball player as a child and for years worked incredibly hard at improving his basketball skills. After first grade he played in a league every winter and went to as many as three basketball camps in the summer. Year round, he practiced basketball for an hour a day or more. As a result, he was named the starting point guard for his seventh-grade team. But after that, his tiny stature and limited natural ability made him less attractive to coaches than kids who were bigger and learned new skills much faster. While his accomplishments in basketball diminished—he did not make the high school basketball team—his success in math continued unabated. He excelled in his advanced classes and remained five years ahead of grade-level in math.

IQ Tests

One way to assess a child's ability in math is to have the child take an intelligence, or IQ, test. These tests aim to measure a person's mental aptitude as inscribed in his or her genes. They don't really do that, as discussed below. But like simple observation, such tests can give you a rough idea of your child's math aptitude and thus help you determine whether or not to provide supplementary math education.

If you want your child to take the so-called Stanford-Binet IQ test or Wechsler intelligence scale, you will probably have to pay a psychologist to administer it. The SAT can also be used to assess IQ, but is only suitable for doing so in math if a student has had first-year algebra and geometry, since the test assumes that knowledge. Copies of old SATs are available in books, and for a modest fee a child of any age can take an SAT. The results are not sent to colleges if the test is taken before the ninth grade.

Your child's score on an IQ test will often be given as a percentage relative to others the same age. For instance, a child ranked at the 90th percentile scored higher than 90 percent of age-mates, while a child ranked at the 10th percentile scored better than just 10 percent.

Whatever your child's score, be aware that no intelligence test measures genetic ability in math or any other mental skill isolated from environmental factors such as education, nutrition, and health care. Those who design intelligence tests attempt to

It was clear from watching this drama unfold that Abe's natural talents lay more in math (and other school subjects) than in playing basketball. Similarly, it should quickly become apparent to you from your child's experiences whether your child is very talented at math or has lesser abilities in this area. But remember: Even if your child's natural talents in math do not suggest he or she should become a mathematician, your child could still use his or her math skills to become very successful—perhaps as an engineer or financial manager. My son did, after all, develop a helluva basketball game, making him a top player in the adult recreational leagues he later joined.

assess IQ by limiting the knowledge tested to the basics everyone should know and by giving problems that require insights to solve. However, not everyone has the basic knowledge, and people can learn things that will help them solve "insight" problems. More prosaically, any child who is sick or hungry the day of the test may perform poorly, no matter what his or her intelligence.

Given such caveats, if your child takes an IQ test, something that can be helpful but is not essential, interpret the result intelligently. In addition to your child's health and general well-being on the test day, consider these factors:

- The IQ scores of children who've had lots of expert math training often overestimate innate math ability, and those of children from disadvantaged backgrounds generally underestimate it.

- Under normal conditions, IQ scores are less reliable if a child is younger than seven years old, but their reliability increases with age. That's because young children's brains do not all develop at the same rate or in the same way and these differences even out over time.

- Early intelligence measures may be *more* accurate than later ones for children from educationally disadvantaged backgrounds, as poor learning environments can cause a steady decline in IQ scores.

ASSESSING SKILL

Though assessing your child's natural math ability can help you set realistic goals for him or her, it will not tell you specifically what math he or she is ready to learn. For that, you need to determine what your child actually knows in mathematics regardless of intelligence. So, for instance, while you may strive to put your child in algebra by eighth grade, you should realize that your child is, in fact, ready for algebra only when he or she has mastered all the preceding math.

Indeed, evaluating your child's current knowledge and skill is the only way to ensure your child gets the math instruction he or she needs. That's because mathematics is a hierarchical subject—that is, more advanced ideas are built upon more elementary ideas that should be taught first. For instance, addition is taught before multiplication, because multiplication is defined as repeated addition. And since abstract ideas are built upon concrete ones in math, a child must master equivalent fractions in arithmetic before trying to tackle them in algebra. So be sure your child has mastered each topic in math before moving on to the next one.

The only way to know that: Have your child take a test that covers the math he or she should know. Tests measure math skill and knowledge far more accurately than they measure intelligence. Indeed, measuring knowledge is what all tests do. Even the best IQ tests measure intelligence only indirectly, as intelligence is just one factor that contributes to the knowledge that enables the test taker to correctly solve the test problems.

In math, by far the most efficient and accurate kinds of tests are objective ones—those on which the questions have one correct answer, or occasionally two or more correct answers. Common forms include multiple choice, fill-in-the-blank, and true-false. By contrast, essay tests are more subjective. Because there is a simple formula for grading objective tests—using an answer key, the grader (or a computer) marks every answer correct or incorrect and tallies the correct answers—grader biases cannot unfairly influence the score. And objective tests can assess a variety of math problem-solving skills in a short period of time, yielding a comprehensive evaluation of a child's math skills. Decades of objective testing in math demonstrate the validity and reliability of objective tests in assessing mathematical knowledge and problem-solving skill.

Opportunities for your child to take objective math tests abound. They include relatively easy school-administered math tests that compare students and schools across the nation; moderately challenging state tests like the New York State Regents Exams, which cover each of the first three years of high school math; and the more advanced College Board Achievement and Advanced Placement (AP) math tests. The many exams found in textbooks or prepared by teachers for their classes are other sources of objective information about your child's math knowledge.

Bear in mind however that such tests are accurate only if your child is not more advanced in math than the level of problems on the test. If the test is too easy, your child's score may be spuriously low relative to other students (if he or she makes lots of careless mistakes), and won't reflect your child's true math knowledge. Only difficult math tests on

Objective Tests and Admissions Policies

The use of objective admission tests for colleges, specialized K–12 schools, and "gifted" programs protect against important biases that have unfairly deprived many students of equal opportunity for education. They remain our best protection against such prejudice. Objective tests can also protect against favoritism. For example, it is widely assumed that a child whose parent is a teacher or administrator in the New York City public schools will have a vastly better chance of being admitted to a desirable public school than a child without such a connection. One popular public magnet school in New York City supposedly admitted students only by random lottery. But the school system's Special Commissioner of Investigation found that 52 percent of one year's incoming students had parents who worked for the school system or the city government.

Such favoritism does not determine who is admitted to the three specialized science high schools in New York City. Why? By New York State law, admission to these high schools must be based solely on each student's score on an objective test.

which no one gets a perfect score can accurately measure the highest levels of math skill.

Are there downsides to objective tests? Some people think so. Many educators for instance do not like the idea of scoring some children better than others. Some also oppose objective tests out of fear that the scores of children in their class or school might reflect badly on them, the educators. Parents too often complain about objective tests—almost always after a child scores poorly on one. After all, it's much easier to blame the test than the child's lack of knowledge. That's especially true when the stakes are high, as with important school admissions tests like the SAT.

In short, objection to tests—or the scores they yield—rests largely on fear or denial of failure. The reaction is natural, but it's one we would all be wise to overcome. Objective tests are an invaluable source of information for individuals, institutions, and society. In particular, they are the best way for you and perhaps your child's teacher to determine what your child knows and doesn't know, and thus, what instruction the child needs to make optimal progress. The ability to objectively monitor learning is also a great motivator for both students and teachers—as is any competitive spirit engendered by an objective test.

Embrace every appropriate opportunity to rigorously test your child on his or her math skills. If there are things you want your child to learn that aren't on any test, go ahead and teach your child those things. But if possible, find an objective way to measure what your child has learned or you may be deceiving yourself. And if your child scores poorly on a test, don't blame the test. Be thankful for it. You and your child now know exactly on what skills or concepts he or she must work harder to master. Not knowing is the greatest danger of all.

PERSONALIZING YOUR GOALS

As you monitor your child's progress in math, use it to guide your expectations of him or her. Over time, your child's achievements in math and other areas will provide a realistic view of your child's strengths and weaknesses. And it is important to tailor your child's ambitions to his or her talents—both in terms of education and in the careers you encourage the child to pursue.

Your child's talents may or may not be in math. So do all you can to motivate your child to learn math and provide the best teaching possible, but as only one part of a well-rounded life. When you've done that, you've done your best and should accept your child's progress in math at school.

Despite what my dad told me, it is not true that you can do anything if you work hard enough. But if you temper your ambition with realism, you can derive enormous satisfaction from the truly spectacular results of hard work coupled with excellent instruction.

Chapter 2

Evaluating Schools

Nothing is more important to a child's math education than the school he or she attends. Even among otherwise good schools, the math instruction can vary from poor to excellent, depending on both the skill of the teachers and the math-teaching philosophy at that school. You as a parent need to know how to assess the math education your child will get. This assessment may help you select a school for your child, or, if that is not possible, find creative ways—within or outside the school— of ensuring that your child gets the math education he or she deserves before it is too late.

It can, in fact, be dangerous to assume that a reputably good school is offering excellent math instruction. One sixth grader I coached—I'll call him Jim—was the victim of such an assumption. Jim had just transferred from a highly regarded elementary and middle school where he had been a top math student. Even so, he was woefully ignorant compared to many other children in his grade who had learned math at other elementary schools.

Why? Jim's old math teachers used teaching methods that produce only very slow learning of math. Jim's parents apparently chose his old school because of its good reputation, but did not, or did not know how to, evaluate the kind of math education Jim received there. When they realized the problem, they switched Jim to a different school.

I encountered similar problems when my daughter Kirsten's school abruptly changed its math program just before she entered the sixth grade. But I knew the warning signs of inferior math education—despite the claims of the teachers that this new program would be superior to the previous one. At first I tried to counter the new math agenda; when that failed, I implemented a plan to teach Kirsten the math she would suddenly not be taught in school. My strong-headed daughter was enraged by the school's plan, but our stopgap measures prevented any long-term damage.

Oddly, the methods that so frustrated Kirsten and left Jim far behind are part of the latest fashion in math education, one based on the 1989 Standards of the National Council of Teachers of Mathematics (NCTM)—which I call Standards math. Virtually all parents of children going to school in the present era will encounter teachers and other educators influenced by Standards math. Thus, it is critical to understand these methods and how they might shortchange your child's math education.

STANDARDS MATH

The Standards math movement began a decade ago to improve students' attitudes toward math and help them understand the subject more deeply. In crafting revolutionary new standards in math education, the NCTM aimed to introduce new teaching techniques and curricula that would eliminate fear of math and reach into the minds of thousands of children who struggled with mathematics taught by traditional methods. The California Board of Education first endorsed the Standards in 1992; since then, they've been adopted in part or in whole by forty-nine states. Indeed, the Standards document is the closest thing this country has to a national math curriculum. (In the year 2000, the Standards were modified, but only subtly, and the moderate changes are not yet reflected in schools; this text refers to the 1989 standards.)

The most pervasive theme echoed throughout the Standards is their emphasis on student exploration and discovery. Instead of presenting information to the class, Standards math teachers ask their students to discover mathematical concepts while solving math problems. Typically, students break up into small groups of four or so to solve a problem. The teacher circulates among the groups to observe the discussions, but otherwise does not interfere with their learning by providing too much information.

This framework is intended to let each child's natural creativity in math blossom, enabling children to discover important concepts and problem-solving methods on their own. At the same time, it's supposed to elicit everyone's participation, teach children to work with others, and help them communicate effectively about math. Teachers encourage students in the groups to do a lot of talking and writing about the thinking process that led to a solution as well as actually solving the problem and understanding it in mathematical terms.

To facilitate discussion, the groups are often working on math problems that are somewhat different from traditional computational or story problems. These nontraditional problems are typically grounded in real-world situations. They are open-ended and contain many parts and many possible answers—and so are good fodder for discussion. One example from the 1989 Standards: A middle school math teacher demonstrates a pendulum made from a string and a weight and asks students to construct a pendulum, investigate how it functions, and formulate questions that arise. Traditional problems, by contrast, have a single correct answer and focus on closely related mathematical ideas and facts.

Hands-on, real-world activities dominate Standards math classrooms. Students learn addition, subtraction, multiplication, and division facts by manipulating objects instead of working with pencil and paper. To learn the fact **5 x 4**, children might be asked to create five sets of four beads (or four sets of five beads) and then count the total number of beads. They do this for each kind of fact, instead of memorizing them symbolically. Memorization is regarded as dull for kids and also ineffective as a learning method, as it seems at odds with really understanding the material.

The emphasis on real-world examples rears its head in the larger scale organization of the material. Rather than dividing a year by topics such as long division, fractions, and decimals, the year is organized by group projects that often mix math with language arts or social studies to create interdisciplinary studies organized around real-world scenarios. A year's worth of mathematics might look like this: A Wagon Train's Journey West, A Genetic Study of Fruit Fly Reproduction, Managing a Supermarket, A Month in the Life of a Real Estate Broker, A Voyage to Mars.

Such "concrete" learning activities are designed to avoid abstractions that children might have trouble grasping. Standards math teachers believe that prior to adolescence, children's minds can handle concrete mathematical concepts but are not mature enough to handle abstract numbers and operations. This argument is used to justify slow progression in mathematics for students. The Standards math document advocates avoiding algebra before ninth grade, and it discourages students from taking calculus in the twelfth grade, even if they intend to go to college.

In their effort to make math more accessible and fun for everyone, Standards math teachers often cut back the amount of mathematical material they present in a class, and instead include "motivational" nonmath activities in math class. They may ask students to illustrate math assignments, bundle homework into a pretty portfolio with an attractive binding, cut out pictures of geometric shapes, or write essays describing how they feel about math. Teachers may even base a student's math grade in part on such subjective evaluations so that more students can get good grades in math, ensuring no one's confidence in math is shattered. Similarly, they rally against objective tests on the grounds that scores foster unhealthy competition.

PERILS OF DISCOVERY

The Standards have a number of positive features, including their emphasis on understanding, solving more challenging problems, enriching the math curriculum with more probability and statistics, early use of calculators, and extensive early study of coordinate geometry. However, the aspects of the Standards described above have had unfortunate consequences for math education. Indeed, many parents and teachers around the nation have concluded that implementing the Standards has decreased the quality and quantity of math learned by all students.

After endorsing Standards math in 1992, the California Board of Education rejected almost all of its principles in late 1997, and at least one California parent group—dubbed Mathematically Correct—has formed to oppose the Standards. In Plano, Texas, parents have sued the school district for refusing to provide an alternative to that district's version of Standards math. And in late 1999, a group of nearly 200 scholars and mathematicians wrote a letter to U.S. Secretary of Education Richard Riley criticizing many of the tenets of the approach.

Why the uproar? There are numerous complaints against Standards math and its most common implementations. Among them: It dumbs down class content and lowers expectations for all kids. It doesn't adequately test kids' knowledge. It wastes far too much time on activities that have little to do with math. And despite good intentions, it can actually decrease student participation.

But the most important downfall of the approach is that it often results in only cursory knowledge of the nuts and bolts of math—including basic arithmetic facts, such as $5 - 3 = 2$ and $3 \times 4 = 12$, and how to solve a variety of math problems. This severely weakens the math curriculum because basic mathematical knowledge and problem-solving skill are the key ingredients of math proficiency. Mastering basic facts early is critical because they form the basis for a huge amount of mathematics that follows. A child who doesn't know those facts by heart—and how to use them in problems—is at a serious disadvantage, even if he or she understands the concepts of addition, subtraction, multiplication and division.

The primary reason for the downfall: excessive reliance on student discovery of facts and principles instead of explicitly teaching them. Discovery sounds good on paper. In practice, it is time-consuming, inefficient, and results in little learning.

For one thing, it's simply not possible to discover much of the important math learned in elementary school. A child can't deduce that the phrase "three to the fourth power" means $3 \times 3 \times 3 \times 3$, that "of" can mean x, or that there are 5,280 feet in a mile. These essential facts must be directly taught and memorized by students. While Standards math teachers don't completely deprive their classes of such basic information, they often give it short shrift.

Even for facts that students could conceivably discover, asking students to do so through largely unsupervised discussion is very inefficient. Using the discovery method, students are given very little of the information necessary to solve problems. Solving problems thus requires gigantic leaps of intuition that virtually no students possess, so they flounder. A class typically spends half an hour—and sometimes as long as *two and a half hours*—on a single problem. At the extreme, one child complained to me that his class spent an entire week on one problem before the teacher told the students how to solve it.

By contrast, in a class taught by direct instruction, students have been given most of the information necessary to solve the problems. The amount of insight necessary is relatively small, so at least some students solve the problems quickly. Problems are typically answered in 5 minutes or less, and a teacher steps in with the answer if kids take too long.

To add to the inefficiency, students in Standards math classes are asked to do more than just solve each problem. They are supposed to discuss in detail how they solved the problem and even write essays about it. This takes even more time, especially since the discussion often wanders due to lack of a teacher's direction.

The consequence? Very few problems get solved and very little information is transmitted from the teacher to the students—to the great detriment of the students' mathematical proficiency. Exposing children to a large number of problems of various types is essential to developing their problem-solving ability, because each time a person learns something, that learning is specific to a particular context. Children will only learn to apply more general mathematical rules or ideas to different problems after being exposed to lots of problems for which those rules or ideas are relevant. Intensively analyzing a small number of problems will not accomplish the same thing, and children's problem-solving skills will remain weak.

The organization of Standards math around interdisciplinary projects, such as planning family food budgets, is another weakness masquerading as strength. The traditional approach, in which classes are arranged by topics such as arithmetic, fractions, algebra, and geometry that build from one level to the next, has been used for decades for good reason. The material within each subject hangs together in logical ways, and is typically broken down into smaller units within which knowledge is even more tightly linked. Teaching students to hang together closely related pieces of knowledge makes sense and produces a deep understanding of a subject.

By contrast, teaching across subject boundaries lacks depth. It may be fun for the students, but it doesn't help the mind organize the knowledge in a logical way, making it harder to remember. What's more, teaching by projects is far more likely to cause a teacher to overlook some important basic fact or principle that is ordinarily taught in the more tightly structured approach.

Using small groups as a vehicle for discovery also has drawbacks. Though small-group learning is designed to encourage participation from everybody, it often fails to do so. In my children's experience, the most knowledgeable child or two in each group typically figured out the answers while the others socialized. So the students who needed to learn the math didn't, and the kids who knew the math largely wasted their time.

If a problem required a lot of student discovery, a group typically succeeded in solving it *because* one of the children already knew—from outside instruction perhaps—what the group was supposed to discover. Little or no learning took place. Often this happened with very little discussion, except when the teacher dropped by, so the students didn't really learn to work together either. Indeed, the best possibility for student interaction is a scenario in which the knowledgeable students teach the necessary math to the others. That doesn't happen often, and when it does, it's less efficient than if the trained teacher were doing that instead.

The Standards-sanctioned practice of discouraging students from taking advanced math classes—or indeed forbidding them to do so—means that most students learn less math than they could. Similarly, cutting back the amount of material presented so that more students can master it results in a significant dumbing down of the curriculum. This hurts the majority of kids who could master more math. And despite the intention, which is to leave no one behind, this approach also hurts the weakest math students, who need educators to make sure they learn all the material necessary to advance to the next level—not some watered-down amount.

Padding classes with nonmath activities such as artwork and essays further dilutes the amount of math learned. The goal of such exercises—to improve students' liking for math and confidence in their ability to do math—is a worthy one. But this is not the way to foster such positive attitudes. Making kids happy by having them draw pictures and write about "why I like or dislike math" in math class teaches them that it's okay to avoid something important if it's hard. That is not a good lesson. The only way to really increase kids' confidence in math is to teach them more math, so they get better at it.

When grades are largely based on such nonmath activities, another huge problem arises: Lower motivation to learn math. This problem is particularly severe when grades are based on portfolios—collections of math homework, essays, and artwork—which are subjectively graded and may depend only very little, if at all, on math knowledge. Producing nice artwork and verbiage will often compensate for poor math skills, and grades can be easily elevated with help and contributions from family members and friends, as many components of portfolios are done outside of class. Since students know their grade doesn't depend on mastering math, few bother to do so. Depressingly, those who do learn the math might find that they have been graded down for poor essays or artwork!

Teachers who disparage the practice of teaching different math to students of varying skill may use high portfolio grades to "demonstrate" that everyone in the class learned a lot and no student was much farther ahead than any other.

MYTHS AND FACTS

Underlying many of the facets of Standards math are myths about math learning. Recognizing them will help you better understand how to evaluate your child's math education and to counteract—at least in your own mind—arguments educators may make in support of the Standards math approach.

MYTH #1: Children under age twelve can learn math using concrete examples but are incapable of learning abstract concepts and operations.

FACT: Concrete and abstract ideas are not separated in the brain, but lie on a continuum. So the implied mental leap necessary to cross from concrete ideas to abstract ones is fictitious. What's more, a concept—such as the number 6—becomes more abstract the more that is known about it. It's not the age of children that determines whether they are ready to handle a more abstract level of understanding but their grasp of the more concrete levels that came before. Thus, with good instruction, children can gradually develop more abstract mathematical thought processes no matter their age.

Take the number 6. The first thing a child usually learns about it is the name *six*. After that, a child learns to count 6 objects—still, a fairly concrete understanding. The idea of 6 becomes more abstract, though, when the child understands that 6 is not specific to the number of discrete objects but can denote length, as 6 steps on a number line. The brain develops an even more abstract idea of 6 as it is extended to area, volume, speed, weight, and so on. The "abstractness" of 6 increases still further as the child learns facts such as $6 + 5 = 11$ or $42 \div 7 = 6$, and again as the child learns exponents and that the square root of 36 is 6. It increases once more when the child learns that 6 is not a prime number but a composite with prime factors 2 and 3.

Belief in this myth has had real effects in the classroom. One of the most important is the overuse of exercises that involve manipulating objects—such as counting beads—to teach arithmetic. Object-oriented activities are very useful for young children who are just getting a grasp of the concepts of number, addition, and subtraction. (See part 2.) But kids get a grip on such abstractions quickly, and they rapidly outgrow the need to manipulate beads and lay rods end to end every time they are asked to add and subtract. Once children are ready to start doing math on paper, such activities are a tedious waste of time. (They are also an ineffective way of teaching basic arithmetic facts for other reasons described later in this book.) If your child's teacher relies extensively on manipulatives for teaching arithmetic facts, your child is unlikely to learn these facts well.

MYTH #2: The brains of seventh and eighth graders are too immature to learn algebra, and elementary school students have a limited ability to solve story problems because they have trouble understanding the meaning of addition and subtraction.
FACT: As discussed earlier, over age three there are no known biological barriers to learning math. Age is not an important factor; knowledge is.

MYTH #3: A child needs a deep understanding of every piece of mathematical knowledge in the curriculum.
FACT: Many mathematical ideas and facts *are* learned better if one can understand them deeply, but this is not always true or practical. Memorization, or rote learning, should play a substantial role in math education.

Thinking Skills

Standards math teachers often emphasize "thinking skills" such as general problem-solving methods that are supposed to be applicable to any puzzle or problem, rather than only certain problem types. They include things such as working backward, a method some people use to solve mazes. (You start at the finish.) Another example is defining subgoals. The idea is to break a problem into smaller, intermediate steps that can be solved more easily and that lead to the final solution.

I described such methods in the book *How to Solve Problems*, and applied them mainly to problems requiring no more than a year each of algebra and plane geometry. I also taught them to bright math students at the Massachusetts Institute of Technology and was so enthusiastic about them that I challenged students to bring in problems to try to stump me. The problems could be tricky, but could not require specialized knowledge. I never failed to solve them, and the students were impressed. Enrollment soared from twenty to eighty in three years. Students claimed their grades in math and science went from Bs to As after taking my course.

Thus, I understand why Standards math proponents are eager to teach young students general problem-solving methods. However, their enthusiasm is largely unwarranted, especially because they advocate replacing math facts and *specific* problem-solving skills with these *general* methods. First of all, there aren't enough general problem-solving methods to fill a curriculum. Remember that my class at MIT was just *one* class, not an entire curriculum, and it was taught to students who had been, and

Although relating ideas in meaningful ways generally promotes far more effective learning than does rote repetition, some math facts and concepts must be memorized because nobody has found good ways to relate them to anything else the child knows and proving them is generally beyond the intellectual reach of children. Furthermore, it doesn't always make sense to try to explain why a mathematical statement is true, even though most people prefer to get such explanations when possible. The explanation is sometimes extremely time-consuming, and ultimately not helpful for problem solving, so it is better to simply explain how to do something and leave it at that. For instance, kids easily catch on to the technique for dividing a number by a fraction: Flip the fraction's numerator and denominator and then multiply by the flipped fraction. Why does this work? A formal proof is too difficult for most kids to understand and is irrelevant to using the rule were being, taught lots of specific math facts in other classes. General problem-solving methods were fun, additional tools for them, not a replacement for specific math knowledge.

Second, despite my own experience, there isn't strong evidence for the usefulness of general problem-solving methods. While some researchers have found hints that teaching some general problem-solving methods can be beneficial, most rigorous research has failed to find much support for the value of these methods.

One reason is probably that the methods are effective only when combined with specific, background knowledge, which MIT students have (but elementary and middle school children still need to learn). Over the past two decades, cognitive psychology researchers have repeatedly shown that problem-solving methods and other higher order thinking skills can be used effectively only when a person has a large body of knowledge on which the thinking skills can operate.

By the time I began coaching school math teams, years after I taught at MIT, I had learned that the best way to improve students' problem-solving skills was to teach them to solve *specific* types of problems, not general problem-solving techniques. At first I occasionally pointed out some general methods to my students, but as the years went by I did so less and less. Such methods should never fill a substantial portion of any math class for children or teens. The time spent on learning such methods is time lost from learning the math they need to know.

for dividing by a fraction. A short plausibility argument is the most a teacher should do.

MYTH #4: Whenever a student uses mathematical ideas, he or she must review his or her basic understanding of why those ideas are true.

FACT: This is a waste of time. Gaining a deep understanding is ideal for *learning* many math concepts, but once something is learned, you want to be able to use it automatically. It's like driving a car. When a person first learns to drive, he or she must think carefully about all the rules of the road, how far to rotate the wheel when turning the car left or right, how many feet to trail the car ahead, and so on. But after driving becomes routine, the reactions on the road are automatic and it is not necessary to continually review the conscious learning process that went on in the beginning.

Similarly, once math rules and methods are learned well, they become automatic and can be used without continually rewinding the learning process. Indeed, one wants learning by understanding to ultimately lead to direct associations in the mind, because that produces more efficient problem solving. It allows one to concentrate on what's new in a problem, not what one already knows.

For example, solve these problems:

$$5 + 4 = \underline{\hspace{1cm}} \qquad\qquad \frac{3}{7} \times \frac{5}{8} = \underline{\hspace{1cm}}$$

$$15 - 7 = \underline{\hspace{1cm}} \qquad\qquad \frac{3}{7} \div \frac{5}{8} = \underline{\hspace{1cm}}$$

$$35 \div 7 = \underline{\hspace{1cm}}$$

For the problems you knew how to solve, did you think about why your answer was correct? (The solutions are 9, 8, 5, $\frac{15}{56}$, $\frac{24}{35}$.) I never did, not in the tens of thousands of simple problems I have done as a mathematical psychologist. I was happy to know what to do and not concerned about why it was the correct thing to do. Similarly, any engineer or scientist may use many mathematical principles every day in his or her work without ever needing to contemplate why these principles are true.

M Y T H   # 5 : Understanding is all or none. Either you understand something or you don't.
F A C T : Understanding comes in types and degrees. Consider the concept of parallel lines. One child might know a definition of parallel lines, and that's all. Another child might understand how to use the concept of parallel lines to solve problems. A third child may have only a partial understanding of parallel lines, and a weaker ability to apply the concept. A fourth child might be able to construct proofs involving parallel lines. These are all different types and degrees of understanding, and a teacher should value all of them.

M Y T H   # 6 : Too much explaining by a teacher produces passive learning.
F A C T : This is nonsense. *All* learning is active, whether it occurs by listening to a lecture, reading a book, answering a question, or solving a problem. For example, to learn the meaning of this sentence, a person must pay atten-

tion to the sentence, think about its meaning, and perhaps recall related ideas related to that meaning. There is nothing passive about this.

MYTH #7: Developing creativity involves freeing a child to let his or her thoughts blossom into a thousand questions.

FACT: Creativity is an outgrowth of learning, and a lot of it. The past twenty-five years of cognitive psychology research has shown that the more a person knows about a subject, the more creative he or she can be in it. No question an adult poses is considered creative if someone else has already asked it. Thus, an adult must know what has come before to ask creative questions. This is true more generally as well. A student's ability to be creative in any area of knowledge increases with his or her knowledge of that area. Knowledge forms the fodder for creative new ideas.

Thus, a desire to enhance creativity should not move a curriculum away from the math basics—but closer to them. Indeed, achieving many of the goals of Standards math educators—whether they know it or not—requires helping children master the nuts and bolts of mathematics. That's true for increasing motivation, improving problem-solving skills (see box), augmenting understanding, and, of course, developing creativity.

MYTH #8: Calculators can replace the need to learn arithmetic facts well.

FACT: It's very difficult to learn or do any type of more advanced math without having completely mastered the basic arithmetic facts. For instance, to find the greatest common factor of 63 and 49, a child must recognize that $63 = 9 \times 7$ and $49 = 7 \times 7$ to see that 7 is the greatest common factor. Or take the basic algebra problem $9x - 3 = 24$. If a child has these facts memorized, he or she quickly adds 3 to both sides to come up with $9x = 27$. Then the child divides by 9 to get $x = 3$. The solution will come far more slowly to a child who must punch each step into a calculator. And the increased difficulty will only increase the child's frustration with math—frustration that will mount as the child faces similar difficulties again and again on many types of problems. The examples given here are truly just the tip of the iceberg.

MYTH #9: Math essay tests in which students write or speak their thoughts as they solve problems paint a more complete picture of what math concepts a student understands and the nature of any misunderstandings.

Subjective Standardized Math Tests

Surprisingly, subjective math tests have found their way outside of individual class-rooms and into standardized testing. Take the Performance Assessment in Mathematics, or PAM. It consists of a tiny number of questions, three, I believe, too few to cover any substantial amount of math. In addition, the scoring criteria have been so lenient that students' scores are extremely poor reflections of their mathematical knowledge. For instance, according to Manhattan math teacher Mark Sacerdote, writing in the April 14, 1993, *New York Times*, the following PAM problem was distributed to teachers to explain how to assign grades to answers on a scale from 1 to 6: "Sue has two cats, Bo and Rusty. She needs to buy a sixty-day supply of cat food for them. Bo finishes three-quarters of a can of food each day. Rusty finishes half a can of food each day. Cat food costs $1 for three cans. What would be the cost of this supply of cat food for Bo and Rusty?"

The correct answer is $25. But Sacerdote noted that the 1993 scoring guidelines suggest that a student who answers $40 (figuring a full can of food per day for each cat) will earn 5 points if the graders decide the student made only a "minor computational error." And any answer earns 3 points if graders determine that "enough of the calculation is shown to demonstrate some understanding of the process . . . but the work shown is confusing because of a major error." Sacerdote concludes: "Scoring criteria like these should guarantee heartening results."

Indeed. And what could be a motivation for such leniency? Since such tests are often used to evaluate teachers or teaching methods, educators may want to cover up their failure by easy grading. Unless the grading is done by a professional testing agency hired by a level of government, such as federal, far removed from the graded school system, the risk of such a cover-up using tests like the PAM is substantial. After all, teachers in the school can grade their own tests and allocate points generously.

FACT: If that were true, such tests would be useful. However, verbal reports are an extremely poor way to test understanding of mathematics. One reason is that the words used to describe human thinking are vague. Even verbally adept students have a lot of trouble communicating what they understand and don't, let alone the specific nature of their misunderstandings. No one understands the nature of thinking well enough to interpret such descriptions unambiguously.

Moreover, many gifted math students use nonverbal thought processes, including visualizing spaces and shapes, in solving math problems. This makes verbal communication close to impossible. Such students often perform terribly on such tests, even though they understand the math and solve the problems correctly. The test can turn these students' best subject into one of their worst.

Thinking-aloud math tests also limit the breadth of math knowledge that can be taught and tested. Since each student generates the equivalent of a short essay for every problem, students can answer, and teachers can grade, only about one or two problems per day from each student instead of the ten or twenty needed to develop and test adequately a student's problem-solving skills.

THE BEST FOR YOUR CHILD

The first step to combating Standards math and making sure it does not compromise your child's education is to understand its deficiencies. Then you will know how to recognize inferior math education and improve upon it. You may, for example, want to supplement your child's math education using the tips and tools presented in the rest of this book. If your community allows some school choice, you can also vote against Standards math. Using the information in this chapter, you can knowledgeably choose a school whose math teachers do not use the Standards to guide their teaching—and thereby insure that your child gets a good math education. You might also be able to push for change within your child's school, as discussed below.

But what specific features of math instruction should you look for in a school? Here are some of the most essential:

- A curriculum that includes advanced math classes such as algebra in middle school and Advanced Placement (AP) calculus in high school, and a flexible policy governing admission to those classes. Schools should leave advanced classes open to any student who earns a good grade in the prerequisite courses no matter the student's age, grade, or previous placement in a math track. To earn the qualifying grade, students should even be allowed to take a course again. In that way, hard-working students are not shut out from any course they are qualified to take. This encourages students to challenge themselves academically.

An AP math class *should* be restricted to students who have mastered all the prerequisites to ensure that students succeed in AP classes. The same is true for other difficult classes, such as first-year algebra, that many students struggle with or fail when they have not mastered what came before. In addition, the prerequisite classes must be challenging enough to prepare students for more advanced math. That means teachers must not cut back on the amount of math they teach but instead pack their classes with information.

Ask educators what math classes are offered at their school and about the criteria for admitting students to them. When do they think most students should take algebra? What about calculus? Do they believe in challenging students in math and in allowing each child to proceed through the curriculum at a rate dictated by his or her own motivation and skill?

- Extensive, if not exclusive, use of traditional teaching methods instead of discovery. That is, teachers should present information to the class, but stop every minute or two to ask questions or pose problems based on this information. This produces far faster learning than asking students to discover answers with little help. It is also much more effective than straight lecturing, as most kids will not pay attention to a long lecture—but they will if forced to respond frequently to the information given.

The benefits of balancing questioning and information delivery in learning are underscored by a classic study by psychologist A. I. Gates. In that study people spent different proportions of time reading (absorbing) information versus attempting to recall what they read. People learned the most when they spent about 80 percent of their time trying to answer questions about the material. If they spent less time recalling facts, they learned less. But if they spent more time in recall, their learning also tapered off.

A similar ratio should be employed in the classroom. Math teachers can query students in a variety of ways. They can pose general questions about a math concept to test students' understanding of it. They may explain a problem-solving method using an example problem and then ask the students to solve similar problems. Teachers may even give students a chance to figure out the answer to a new type of problem while providing feedback and hints, and ultimately the answer when none is forthcoming. Using such methods, which also include homework and class work that cement ideas taught in class, kids learn the math they need to know and develop good problem-solving skills. They even learn to talk effectively about math. Ask your child: How many problems did you solve during class? Are you learning a lot? If possible, observe part of a class and make your own judgments.

- Occasional use of group learning exercises—perhaps to give students a chance to work together on special research or engineering problems or more complex math problems. Such activities can be beneficial when teachers also use the direct teaching method described above because teachers provide enough relevant instruction ahead of time to allow more of the students to participate. The problem of unequal participation is further minimized if a teacher calls on *individuals* within a group to answer questions rather than relying solely on group output. That way, every student has a big incentive to strive to understand the solution.

  Most of the time, however, your child's teacher should address the entire class at once, a method that can better ensure equal participation, and that is more efficient than doling out instructions to small groups separately. Ask your child whether the teacher breaks the class into small groups or speaks to the entire class, and what happens during any group learning that does occur in class.

- Lots of practice with the basic arithmetic facts as numbers—not as beads, rods, or tick marks. Any child who has mastered the art of counting objects should be moved at once to pencil-and-paper representations of addition and subtraction facts. When these are mastered, teachers should explain multiplication and division abstractly as repeated addition and subtraction, and illustrate them only briefly with objects. Later, fractions may be introduced using objects and pictures, but children should rapidly be taught to manipulate them symbolically on paper. As with whole numbers, fractions can be added, subtracted, multiplied and divided far faster on paper than any other way, and even the meaning of these basic operations on fractions is easier to understand that way. Ask your child's teacher about his or her approach to teaching arithmetic facts and test your own child's knowledge of them.

- Inclusion of negative numbers early in the elementary school math curriculum rather than delaying their introduction until first-year algebra. Learning about negative numbers and how to add, subtract, multiply and divide those numbers is part of arithmetic, and it makes sense to include them along with positive numbers when arithmetic is taught. (Part 2 demonstrates how.) In addition, teaching negative numbers early helps even out the information load in math, adding material to the slow, early math curriculum and taking it away from algebra, which is often overwhelming for students. Ask elementary school educators when and what students are taught about negative numbers.

- Occasional use of motivational activities geared toward helping children understand why math is useful and valuable (rather than other types of art and writing projects). Teachers might, for instance, describe a variety of careers that require math training and explain what training is needed for each. They might initiate a discussion or assign readings about the role of math in managing one's personal finances and other aspects of life. You could even offer to design a lesson that would give kids a broader view of the usefulness of math. Such activities should not be frequent, however, because they take time away from math instruction. To check that your child's teacher is focusing on math fundamentals, look at your child's math homework. It should include lots of math problems to which there are single correct answers, and no artwork or writing.

- Math classes whose titles or units reflect traditional topics such as arithmetic, fractions, algebra, and geometry. So-called integrated math—which includes traditional topics plus probability, statistics, and transformational geometry and other extras—is a fine approach too.

- Use of objective tests whose problems have one correct answer. Objective tests are by far the most efficient and accurate way of evaluating math skill and they are the best way to motivate kids in math. Most students will study because they realize it will have a direct impact on their grade. They also know how to study: Solve math problems in the textbook or workbook. Teachers can be even more explicit about what students must learn by teaching directly to an objective test. That is smart as long as the test measures a significant body of knowledge, and many standardized tests do, including the SAT and AP tests. Look at your child's math tests to be sure the questions are problems with right and wrong answers rather than essays. If there are no tests, that is a bad sign and you should find out why.

REAL SELF-ESTEEM

Rather than making math less stressful with easy testing and art projects, math teachers must, in effect, make it more so. That is, they must set high goals for students and push them to achieve those goals. That will promote real self-confidence, the kind acquired by accepting a difficult challenge and succeeding.

Indeed, one of the primary aims of Standards math educators—to create a totally noncompetitive environment in which all children are judged successful and equal—can have deleterious psychological consequences for children. Why? It is a lie and can give children who believe it an unrealistic view of their abilities. Misleading children to think they have skills they lack and have acquired without work can ruin their lives. Such children may not do the hard work necessary to succeed later in life.

On the other hand, educators who reward students for their real achievements can boost children's confidence in lasting and important ways, even though that means praising different students for different things and at different times. My son Peter's second-grade teacher was one such educator. She thoughtfully picked out three students—Peter among them—to study a more challenging math curriculum than the rest of the class, because she felt these children could handle it.

Peter was thrilled. Unlike praise from his parents, which Peter knew could be biased, his teacher's actions told him he was good at math; this was a huge boost to his self-confidence. Even more important were the effects on another little boy in the group, who had discipline problems at the time. Because the teacher's judgment was good, this child was able to solve the problems she gave him, showing him that he could succeed in math by working hard. This experience was perhaps pivotal in this boy's decision years later to attend a challenging and academically selective high school rather than continue to be a serious behavior problem in school. I know the boy remembered this for a long time, because years later I overheard him speak of it to Peter.

Some people might protest such special treatment, thinking it would hurt the self-esteem of the other kids in the class. But that isn't inevitable. A teacher can minimize general awareness of the treatment by delivering it unobtrusively. More importantly, a teacher can give *every* child special projects and feedback in an area in which he or she is especially skilled, boosting each child's confidence in a realistic way.

Nothing surpasses such thoughtful self-esteem building by a teacher, because it teaches kids that talent combined with hard work can lead to success. Every child needs guidance and encouragement to develop his or her particular talents. That's the kind of experience that provides children with truly justified self-esteem. Unjustified self-esteem is worth less than nothing; justified self-esteem is the stuff dreams are made of.

YOU CAN MAKE A DIFFERENCE

If the math education your child is getting at school is inadequate in any way, push for change. If major policy changes aren't forthcoming, talk to receptive educators about offering more advanced classes for small groups of children, or about making an exception and admitting your child to a more advanced math class if your child is ready. If certain math teachers make their classes too easy or fill them with activities that distract from learning the nuts and bolts of mathematics, find a teacher who favors rigor and focuses on the teaching of specific math facts, concepts, and principles.

Watch out for discipline problems too, which are common in American classrooms and exact a high social cost. If riotous behavior is preventing your child from learning, demand that the school remove the disruptive students from your child's class.

Research Shows?

Educators often attempt to close off debate by claiming that "research shows," something. What do you do when you hear that? Listen carefully. Do you fully understand the study? Does it, and the conclusions the educator has drawn, make sense to you? Can the educator supply a reference that will allow you to look up the actual study? If these answers are all no, be wary. The study is probably not a good basis for making a decision.

Why? First, the study itself can be flawed, and thus the conclusions drawn from it are not justified. In educational research, for example, studies typically attempt to compare two real-life situations to determine the cause of their different outcomes. But very often the situations are different in so many ways that it is next to impossible to determine which difference was the critical one. Second, the person describing the study— assuming it is not the same person who actually did the study—could very well be misinterpreting it, an important reason to take a look at the study yourself. (Another cautionary comment on "research has shown" can be found on pages 265–266 of E. D. Hirsch's magnificent book, *The Schools We Need and Why We Don't Have Them*.)

Because I am a cognitive psychology researcher, I rely primarily on findings from studies of basic learning and memory from which valid conclusions can be drawn because the experiment is controlled. That is, the situations being compared only differ in one aspect at a time. The downside of controlling conditions, of course, is that they are less realistic: What the people in the experiment are asked to learn or consider, for instance, is quite different from the material taught in real-life educational settings. So when you hear about new research, don't simply accept it at face value. Think about it carefully. Read more about it, and ask a lot of questions.

You might want to organize other parents to back your efforts for change. If the school refuses to help you fix the problem, you may have to find math instruction outside of the school, or if possible, switch your child to a different school. But to take appropriate action, you must be aware of the education your child is getting. Using this book, you will have the tools to evaluate it intelligently. The rest is up to you.

Chapter 3

Strategies for Excellence

O nce you've set goals for your child in math, how do you ensure these goals are met? One crucial element is, of course, evaluating your child's math instruction in school and acting to remedy any deficiencies. Assuming you are doing what you can in that vein, consider other avenues for helping your child make optimal progress in math, both in and outside of school.

If your child is now struggling with math or scoring only in the average range in his or her classes, focus on helping your child master the math taught in each grade. Mastery means getting As or the equivalent in math. If your child is already doing well in math at school, help the child progress through the math curriculum as rapidly as possible, while still mastering the material. This chapter will provide optimal strategies for achieving these things. A child of any skill level can benefit from math "enrichment" activities to enhance problem-solving proficiency and math appreciation. Other ways of improving your child's math education might include enrolling the child in a nonstandard type of school or encouraging the child to skip a grade. This chapter will discuss such options.

PREVIEW

One way of helping your child master math in an upcoming grade is to provide a preview of difficult material so that when that material is taught, the child will already be somewhat familiar with it and will therefore learn it faster and better.

Preview is a good idea whenever a future course is likely to contain more material than your child can learn in the time allotted. This will be true frequently for a child who learns math slowly. If your child is in this category, you might want to regularly preview the next year's math the summer before. Unfortunately, parents rarely use preview for this purpose, because of the misconception that starting next year's math is "getting ahead." It's not. (Indeed, preview is not a good idea for students who will have no trouble learning the math they will be taught in the coming year.)

Even very able math students occasionally face extremely difficult courses for which a preview would be helpful. A child may face such difficulty, for example, if he or she is placed in a math class one or more math levels ahead of his or her previous class. Learning some of the math in the advanced class ahead of time can substantially ease the transition. And some math or math-related courses—including serious college introductory physics courses and college-level pure math classes—are difficult for virtually everyone. Previewing the material in those courses is almost always a good idea.

Often preview can occur at home under conditions that are less threatening than a competitive, crowded classroom. The more concepts your child learns in advance, the more likely he or she is to succeed later on in the classroom setting. Your child will also feel like he or she is keeping up rather than catching up.

If your child has failed to master the math taught in prior grades, you have a bigger challenge, because your child also has to catch up to grade-level. Diagnose your child's problem. Is it poor instruction, lack of motivation, or does your child really need more time to learn than other kids?

If possible, get a tutor to help your child learn the math in his or her current grade simultaneously with the math not yet mastered in prior grades. The tutor might need to start the review one or more grades back. If your child is an average or fast learner who has simply lacked motivation or good instruction, it should be no problem to cover all this material at once. More extensive tutoring outside of school, perhaps including preview, may be necessary if your child tends to learn math slowly. In rare cases, you might need to bring your child back a year. But remember that no matter what your child's skill level, you can speed his or her progress much faster than educators' guidelines suggest, so don't panic just because your child is behind.

ENRICHMENT

No matter how much math your child knows, provide enrichment. Enrichment activities expand your child's knowledge and appreciation of math without overlapping with the math taught in school. Here are several valuable math enrichment activities:

Books

Reading to your children when they are young is a magical activity. Among your reading materials, include some about math, science, mathematicians, or scientists. Your children can read to you after they learn to read, but you don't have to stop reading to them. I love to read things to my kids that I enjoyed. It's like sharing a favorite movie, only more active.

Independent Study

To foster independence and self-motivation, provide materials for your child to study on his or her own. Give your child math books and other math-related materials, explain their usefulness, and ask the child to read the materials and solve the problems they include. Help your child make a schedule for reading parts of the book and solving problems in those parts.

Bring up the possibility of doing an independent math or science research project. Brainstorm ideas. Discuss how a project might be approached and how long it might take. In doing so, your child will learn what it means to commit to a long-term project. Don't be concerned, however, if a young child or teenager is not highly motivated to pursue independent intellectual projects, such as completing a study or learning algebra. Before high school, very few kids pursue such projects without a lot of adult supervision.

Math Contest Problems

A particularly valuable enrichment activity is solving problems from math contests. You can purchase books of these problems for all grades beginning with second from the organizations that run the contests (listed in the appendix). These problems test and teach elegant mathematical concepts and principles that never appear in most math classes. They are far more difficult than those used in math courses, often including more steps and requiring insights into new aspects of the problem. They can even lead your child to think of similar or more general math problems. Being more like the complex problems solved by professionals who use math, contest problems provide important experience missing from most math classes.

In addition, solving contest math problems will help your child immensely on the math parts of important aptitude tests, such as admission tests for selective high schools, the SAT, and math-related achievement tests. Indeed, this enrichment activity will give your child a critical edge, because most parents (and many teachers) are unaware that these problems exist. Order the problem books and assign your child problems at home. You may also want to assign other kinds of recreational math problems, such as logic puzzles, not covered in the curriculum.

To boost your child's motivation, encourage him or her to solve these problems as part of a math club or team. These fun and extremely valuable activities are described in more detail in part 2 of this book.

Math Pullout

Another way to enrich your child's school math experience, and that of other kids, is by volunteering to "pull out" five to eight children from the child's class to help them solve specially designed math problems once a week during the class or at another time. You will enhance the math problem-solving skills of these children and provide social support for their interest in math. You will also have fun and learn firsthand about the difficulties of teaching.

Here are tips for doing this. The children, who will be chosen by the teacher, should have similar math skills, whether above or below average. For average or above average students, use books of math contest problems. Since these problems are difficult, start with problems a grade or two below your child's class—without telling the kids you are doing that. When they master problems for that grade, advance to the next. You will have to teach them a lot of math along the way. For below-average students, ask the teacher what types of instruction and problems would be best. Pull out a smaller number of students—say three or four—than you would more skilled students, because they are likely to need more help and may present greater discipline problems. Do not force any reluctant child to participate.

Research

Get your child involved in a research project that interests him or her. If your child is sufficiently motivated, you could start as early as fourth grade. For example, a young child could grow plants from seeds and study how the height of the plants is influenced by the amount of water they get each day and the amount of time they spend under a sunlamp. If possible, find a researcher who is willing to be an advisor on the project.

Ask teachers and other parents if there are math or science fairs in your region to which your child might submit a research article or poster. In the article or poster, your child will include background information on the topic (say, plant growth), questions he or she attempted to answer (the role of water and light in the growth of a particular plant species), research methods (number of plants used, how they were grown), results of the study (the heights of different plants given different treatments), and its conclusions.

Your Child As Tutor

As captains of their high school math team, my children Peter and Kirsten taught math concepts and problem-solving methods to a class of about thirty of their fellow math-team members. They planned the content for the forty-minute daily class, choosing example problems to explain, constructing practice tests, and grading them. This was an extremely valuable experience for them, since they both aspired to be professors of math-related subjects. For a year and a half, Kirsten ran an after-school math club for grades 2 through 6 at an elementary school near her high school. Then for a year and a half, she and two classmates ran a weekly after-school supplementary math-team practice at their former middle school.

Opportunities to teach a class in school are rare, but students do occasionally run after-school math clubs, math-team practices, or workshops for younger math students. And there are plenty of opportunities for students to tutor others one-on-one. If your child is good at math, encourage him or her to help tutor peers or younger children, because the experience has many advantages for the tutor. For one thing, it can help your child learn math. Teaching requires the teacher to rethink the information he or she already knows, cementing the knowledge in the brain. This same process also spawns new insights about the material, such as how to use it in new types of problems or other situations the tutor hasn't encountered before.

Tutoring can also boost your child's self-esteem and verbal skills. As long as your child never acts superior to others or puts them down, helping peers in math can also help forge friendships.

Tutoring should not replace any studying of advanced math. But if your child is stuck in a math class that is largely review and the teacher won't supply more advanced problems, offer your child's services as a tutor. That way, your child will learn something, and won't become bored.

ACCELERATION BEYOND THE HONORS TRACK

In addition to enrichment, some degree of acceleration—that is, proceeding through the math curriculum faster than average—is important for many children. As discussed earlier, keeping your child challenged in math is critical so the child learns as much as possible and doesn't get bored or lazy.

Achieving any degree of acceleration requires two steps: Ensuring that your child knows the math he or she plans to skip and then convincing educators to place your child in the appropriate advanced math class. The latter is often very difficult to do in elementary school, so during those years, plan to teach your child additional math outside of school (or hire a tutor to do so) to prepare him or her to accelerate in sixth or seventh grade. Another option: Ask your child's elementary school teacher to provide advanced work in math.

Most advanced placement in math occurs in a jump of one year in sixth to ninth grade (depending on the school), when children are "tracked," that is, divided into groups based on a one-time measure of ability. Some end up in the honors math track; most don't. Once placed in a track, a child can be demoted to a lower track, but cannot generally be promoted to a higher one.

As long as your child's school has an honors track and your child knows the math required for getting into it, accelerating your child by one year in math should not be a problem. Accelerating more than that, however, can be difficult, since many educators are reluctant to place children farther ahead in math than their school's tracking system allows. But it's important to try anyway, if your child is especially bright in math and needs the challenge. Here's what to do:

Find Out What Your Child Knows

You must be confident that your child knows the material he or she plans to skip. So if you don't already know, find out exactly what your child knows in math. If you can't determine this yourself, hire someone to determine it for you. You also need to know the school's math curriculum for the math levels to be skipped and for the level in which you want your child placed. Again, you may need to hire someone, ideally a knowledgeable teacher in your school system, to explain this to you and act as your adviser. At some point, you may need to make a convincing case that your child is far enough ahead to justify skipping to an advanced grade in math, even though your child will undoubtedly also be tested. Don't let a strenuous testing process dissuade you. After all, you want to be sure you are making the right decision.

Jump Early

I'll assume your school begins the honors track in seventh grade. If your child is entering middle school, the easiest two-year jump is from grade-6 math into grade-7 honors math (pre-algebra). This is also the jump most likely to be approved. Even if your child is a little weak in some aspect of arithmetic, the pre-algebra class will provide an opportunity to make up the deficiency before algebra. Jumping to grade-8 honors math—algebra—as a seventh grader requires more extensive preparation because algebra is less forgiving. The same is true if a child who is slated to enter grade-8 honors wants to jump to grade-9 honors. It's even better if your child can officially jump to a higher grade in math in elementary school, though that is rarely possible.

Be Conservative

Prepare your child for a bigger jump in math than he or she actually makes. Such a conservative approach will make the transition easier on the child, who will soon have to compete with much older children. When my youngest daughter, Jeanette, skipped two grades of math to enter ninth grade math as a seventh grader, she knew another year and a half of math beyond the level she skipped to. As a result, she had no trouble with the transition. For a jump of two or more years, your child should know at least one third of the math to be covered in the advanced class.

Resolve Other Uncertainties

Resolve any other uncertainties you might have about placing your child in an advanced math class before you seek approval. That way, you can be confident in your decision and show that you are aware of the risks and have taken steps to minimize them. If you voice reservations, or seem unsure, educators are likely to use that to justify denying your request.

Consider whether your child would be discouraged by the greater competition he or she will face in the advanced class. Could this undermine your child's self-confidence in a favorite subject? Or is your child confident enough to handle, or even enjoy, the new competition? Will your child still be at the top of the class? Ask your child how he or she feels. Not jumping ahead may be riskier for kids who could become overconfident, bored, or lazy.

Think about the common beliefs and values, described in other parts of this book, of today's educators so you are prepared to counter them. Plan arguments to support your beliefs and values concerning acceleration.

Prepare your child to handle the social challenges of being in an advanced math class. Counsel your child against acting superior or putting others down. Such behavior is immoral, inappropriate, and against the child's best interests. I know one student who was expelled from an advanced class because he was so obnoxious. Short of that, a child who acts like a big shot will make lots of enemies and few friends. Avoid such problems by teaching your child to be kind and respectful toward others.

Take Care of Logistics

When an educator objects to your proposal on the basis of logistical problems, be ready with a solution. Consider schedule conflicts. If you want your second grader to take fourth-grade math, find out if the fourth- and second-grade math classes are at the same time. If so, fine; your child will not miss other parts of second grade. If not, work out a way of minimizing the disruption. For example, suggest that your child make up the work in the missed second-grade classes during the second-grade math periods.

Account for the time it takes your child to travel between classrooms and try to minimize this by choosing a nearby fourth-grade class, for example, or a math class next to lunchtime or at the beginning or end of the day. This is a bigger problem, of course, when the class is in a different building. Arrange travel to a different school for math to minimize the time lost from the child's other school classes. Again, beginnings and ends of days or lunchtime are best. Ideally the schools will coordinate this for you, but you should have a plan too.

There may be a safety issue. Depending on where you live and how old your child is, traveling between two schools may carry some risk. You might find a friend or an adult chaperone to walk with your child.

Educators might also object that the math teacher in the higher grade is taking on a greater workload with the addition of your child. There may be administrative costs connected with giving credit for a more advanced class. Think of ways you would be willing to help compensate for these inconveniences with your own help or money.

Solicit Advice

Ask other parents, friendly teachers, and your children if any other student at your child's school has taken math classes in an advanced grade. If so, ask the student's parents how to go about arranging it, including with whom you need to discuss this option. If you find that no precedent exists, being prepared is even more important.

Seek Approval

From whom should you seek approval for this jump? If your child would be jumping into a math class taught at a middle school, ask the middle school's math department head, if there is one. Similarly, for a high school math class, talk to the high school math department head. His or her approval is likely to be necessary and once it's given, also sufficient. The fewer people who have to give permission, the better your chances of approval.

If your child's jump requires going to a new school for math, you also need permission from the lower school the child attends. The principal of that lower school is probably the appropriate person to approve this, but your child's elementary teacher can help coordinate the class schedules.

If your child has officially skipped math levels at an elementary school, be sure the grade-levels of the completed math classes are recorded on your child's school records, so a middle school will honor them. Check on this after the year's grades are recorded (perhaps the following September). When your child is ready to take math at a middle school, make arrangements the spring before your child would enroll. To prove your child's readiness, have your child's fall elementary school math grade and level sent to the middle school in spring and the spring grade sent when it's available.

Advice for Negotiating with Educators

To make all your negotiations with educators as smooth as possible, heed this advice:

- Familiarize yourself with the concepts, beliefs, and values of educators in general and the ones you're dealing with in particular.

- Respect their expertise, dedication, and right to differ with you, but don't be intimidated.

- Know exactly what you want and why; prepare your proposal carefully in advance.

- If possible, have alternative proposals.

- Accept rejections gracefully and try to achieve the goal another way.

- It's your child. It's their school. You can try to fight a negative decision by taking your case to the superintendent or the school board, but you're unlikely to prevail unless you have the support of a large group of parents or other adults in your community.

Once you succeed in getting your child placed in a school math class one or more years ahead of his or her age, the schools will almost always take over math instruction from there. They will keep the child the same number of grades ahead in math as long as your child is doing well in his or her advanced classes. The parent no longer needs to do the instruction or find someone else to do it, saving lots of time and perhaps money too.

SHOULD YOUR CHILD SKIP A GRADE?

One way to move ahead in math is to skip an entire grade in school, which also moves the child to the next grade for every subject and activity. My oldest child, Ingrid, skipped first grade, and though she had no major academic or social troubles resulting from the skip, I do not advocate skipping a grade and did not want any of my other children to skip. Why? For one thing, skipping a grade made Ingrid likely to leave home for college a year earlier than she would have otherwise, reducing the number of years I would spend with her. Somehow I failed to realize this problem until many years after the deed was done, and it was too late to change it.

In addition, I don't think skipping a grade is good for a child's self-confidence. After a child skips a grade, he or she is now competing in nearly every aspect of life with older children—and so, inevitably, cannot compete as well as the child could against age-mates. Parents of children born near the end of the year often hold them back a year in school to increase the odds their children will be successful academically, socially, and athletically. When your child skips a grade, you've done the reverse.

As I write this book, I think about all the little and not-so-little triumphs and failures that occur in life—a compliment, a completed project, a good grade, a date, a snub, a frustration. If you want your child to experience as many triumphs as possible, skipping a grade is not a good idea. Of course, the child feels good about being able to skip at first; after that, your child's family, friends, and teachers may occasionally mention it. But the significance of the achievement dims over time. Meanwhile, experiences such as getting the highest grade on a spelling test, being your school's fourth-grade 50-yard dash champion, being asked to the seventh-grade dance by the boy or girl you have a crush on, assume great prominence in a child's life. These triumphs are less likely to occur when your child is competing against and socializing with kids who are a year older.

Jumping ahead in math without skipping a grade is a much better option. Your child is then equally able to succeed in all areas except in the advanced math class. Your daughter is third-grade spelling champion, wins the fifty-yard dash in fourth grade, and goes to a seventh-grade dance with the boy she has a crush on. And your child can still participate in math contests at his or her age level. This means that, while your child's grades may be slightly lower in the advanced math class, he or she will be more than compensated by far better contest scores. (For your child to participate in math contests, you may have to volunteer to coach a math team, or perhaps pay someone else to do so. It's worth it, as described in part 2 of this book.)

ATYPICAL SCHOOLS

If you are finding it difficult to implement your math education strategies in the local public school, look for an alternative school. One possibility is a school for gifted students. Another is a school that enables complete class choice unhampered by age and grade.

Gifted Schools

Whether an elementary or high school, a gifted school is a good option for many bright children. Typically, children are selected on the basis of an IQ test or a similar test of verbal and math skill, although occasionally admission also depends on teacher recommendations or other subjective evaluations. A policy of admitting only dedicated students permits more advanced instruction than would be possible without such a selection process. In math, it often permits acceleration or enrichment. Accelerating your child in math through a gifted school will enable your child to take additional math classes—say, at a local college—in his or her final high school years, augmenting his or her math education.

In addition to offering a higher level of instruction, gifted schools provide a more competitive intellectual environment for children. In such an environment, your child's academic standing is likely to be lower than it would in a mixed ability school. At the high school level, this could be a significant problem for students whose class standing at a gifted school might be too low for admittance to an elite college. Such students might stand a much better chance if they attended a school in which they could get top grades. It's true that colleges admit students with lower class standing from gifted schools, but that bias does not fully compensate students whose grades are in the bottom half at a gifted school.

However, gifted schools may beef up rewards for intellectual achievements, for example, by encouraging participation in academic contests, that *can* compensate for a decrement in standing within a class. They also offer social and extracurricular rewards. Many regular classrooms harbor anti-intellectual attitudes and hostility toward students who work hard in their classes. Being surrounded by classmates who share your values can be far more rewarding than being the "class brain." My son Peter loved the three-day national MATHCOUNTS competition in Washington, D.C., because he was surrounded by kindred spirits. As a seventh grader, he came to me in tears at the end of the competition, saying he'd miss his friends from it. Sure, he liked his friends at school, but they were not really like him. The MATHCOUNTS kids, he said, "are just like me."

Similarly, many of the kids who attend the gifted summer camps run by Johns Hopkins University, among others, find friends and social acceptance for the first time in their lives. As Charlie Brown said: "Happiness is being one of the gang." At a gifted school, your child could feel like one of the gang.

If you decide to look for a gifted school for your child, here are a few hints. First, take your child's age into account. While some gifted programs select kids as young as three based on IQ tests and other evaluations, these selections are not very accurate because intelligence measures in children under seven are inaccurate. For that reason, gifted programs that start below the second grade aren't the most productive. Of course, if a desirable gifted program admits children only at a very young age, you will have to apply early if you want your child admitted. If admission is more flexible, try to find out the proportion of applicants admitted at each age—but all else equal, apply when your child is at least seven. If you apply when your child is younger, and your child is rejected, do not conclude your child is not gifted. Just try again when your child is older.

Second, try to find a gifted elementary or middle school that feeds into a middle or high school amenable to advanced placement. Accelerating students in math at the gifted school only makes sense if students can keep their lead—by entering more advanced classes—when they graduate. Otherwise, there is not much point to it (unless you plan to provide supplementary education in later grades) and teachers at the gifted school will probably not attempt to accelerate children. (If you can't find a school that accelerates students, your child can still garner other benefits from a gifted environment.)

Third, investigate the intellectual and social environment of a gifted school. Some gifted programs are tiny islands inside large, low performing, regular schools. I opted against such programs because I was concerned about my children's safety and happiness in such a situation. What's more, I was not favorably impressed with the intellectual level of the classes I visited.

Fourth, be prepared to expend great effort to find a good gifted school or program. Even after an extensive investigation of New York City schools, I somehow missed one, a school with two large, high-performing gifted elementary programs. In retrospect, one of these would probably have been a better choice for my children than the school they attended because of its more challenging intellectual environment and greater acceptance of accelerated math placement.

Schools That Offer Class Choice

If you are dissatisfied with traditional schools, there are alternative schools that provide more freedom and flexibility for students. Perhaps you'd like a school whose educators believe that instruction should proceed at different rates for different children, depending on their skill rather than their age. In this vein, consider a school that offers students complete class choice regardless of their age or grade.

Eastside Elementary School

Imagine not having to choose between forcing a child to repeat a grade, separating the child from friends, and advancing that child to a grade that is too difficult. Imagine every child working at his or her own rate until he or she masters a topic, with no grade except "mastery." Imagine children of many ages mixing in classes organized only by topic. By some miracle, an alternative elementary school of this type appeared near my office at the University of Oregon in Eugene just as I realized the limitations of conventional schooling. That school was Eastside Elementary School.

Eastside had no grades—not in its classes, not in the entire school. A child could sign up for any class regardless of his or her grade. Since a first grader, say, could sign up for a class conducted at a third, fourth, or even sixth grade level, Eastside provided ample opportunities for acceleration. So if your six-year-old, say, had mastered second-grade math, he or she could take third-grade math in first grade, a two-year jump. Advancing a grade a year, the child would complete fifth-grade math in third grade. Then the child might learn sixth-grade math at the elementary, at a middle school, or from a parent, tutor, or distance-learning course.

Eastside also provided a number of advanced and challenging classes. For instance, at ages eight and ten, my children Abe and Ingrid took "Mathematical Physics," a class with wonderful experiments timing balls rolling down inclines, graphing the data, and describing it with a mathematical function. And since parents were allowed to teach, I gave an algebra class for advanced fifth and sixth graders.

The main drawback of Eastside was that, while classes were supposed to be chosen by children with advice from their parents, Eastside teachers allowed children to choose classes totally on their own. The theory was that children would autonomously choose a balanced educational diet.

It didn't work out that way. Left to their own devices, most children chose pottery over addition, baseball over creative writing. And most *were* left to their own devices because their parents accepted the idealism the school propounded and did not pay close attention to what classes their children took. With so many students and course decisions to make, the teachers really couldn't adequately fill the vacuum, and there was no system for relaying recommendations to parents or children.

As a result, after a year or two many parents found that their children had taken few, if any, math classes. Not surprisingly, this left their children far behind in math.

That didn't happen with my children, who benefited greatly from Eastside's flexibility because I monitored their curriculum closely. I learned about the various classes offered and scoured the course lists to assure that my kids took challenging, valuable courses. If you decide on a school like Eastside, be prepared to provide similar guidance. Consider your child's choices, but don't leave your child's education up to either the child or the school, because both are likely to drop the ball.

Sudbury Valley School

There are schools with even less structure than Eastside. Take the Sudbury Valley School, a private K–12 school in a Boston suburb. This school gives each child complete freedom to choose how they spend their time at school. There are no classes except those specifically requested by a group of students. Children learn largely on their own, reading books, talking to each other and to teachers or outside experts, solving problems, playing games and sports, practicing musical instruments, doing arts and crafts, and anything else that can be done on the school grounds.

While you can read at length about the school's strengths on its web site, one of its biggest potential benefits is that every child can proceed at his or her own pace, in math and in other subjects as well.

There are also potential drawbacks. Since young children are not generally highly motivated to learn math, they may choose not to study much of it. In a school such as Sudbury your child is likely to choose a pace of math learning that is far below what his or her intellect would allow. Even if you plan to "motivate" your child, be wary. If the teachers at the school suspect that your child's requests for math instruction stem from you, they may *not* give your child what he or she requests and you may end up educating your child in math yourself. So ask the school's educators about whether they will object to your pushing your child to learn math (and other important subjects), before enrolling the child. Be up front about it. Don't bank on fooling teachers into thinking a child's requests to learn math are self-motivated if they aren't. It won't work.

Even if your child is motivated in math, or school officials are willing to provide math instruction in any case, you'll need to determine what kind of instruction that might be. The Sudbury School seems to expect children to learn largely on their own, but math and mathematical science are far harder to learn on one's own than other subjects. So find out how easy it is to get a teacher to teach a course at the school. Ask school officials questions such as:

What is the highest level of math instruction the school's teachers are qualified to provide?

What are the areas of expertise of the school's teachers in math?

What math-teaching experience do they have?

What courses of math instruction or study do skilled, motivated students undertake at the school?

Will the school find somebody to guide my child's independent study of math and answer his or her questions?

On Sudbury's web site, one teacher described how a dozen nine- to twelve-year-old students asked him to teach them arithmetic, so he did, along with fractions, decimals, percents, and square roots in only twenty hours of class time spread over twenty weeks. That's very fast, and shows how rapid learning can be when the students are highly motivated (and older). Still, elements were missing. The students undoubtedly lacked the experience with a wide variety of word problems necessary to fully master arithmetic problem solving. What's more, the teacher claimed his course covered all the math in grades 1–6. It didn't, though it covered a good chunk of it. And one wonders why nine- to twelve-year-olds are still learning basic addition, indicating a lack of previous math instruction. You don't want your child to start this late.

Do children usually know the best path for themselves? Maybe you, like Sudbury officials, believe they do. Of course, too much pushing from parents or the wrong type of pushing can turn off, or hurt, kids. But I believe some direction setting from parents is very important. It not only helps children make decisions, but lets them know you care. And I think parents do often know what's best for their young children and even for their teenagers (though it's a good idea to respect your teenager's judgment). But parents aren't perfect, and we should all be sure our goals for our children are based on their abilities and interests and not our own frustrated ambitions.

Start Your Own School

One way to find the perfect school for your child is to start your own. You could fashion your school just as you wish, with perhaps an emphasis on enriched and accelerated math. The Sudbury Valley School sells information relevant to starting your own private school. Another option is to start a charter school. Many states now permit a limited number of such schools, which are public because they are supported by tax dollars based on the number of students enrolled. Charter schools are regulated by the state or by a local school district, but within those regulations, a charter school's founders can specify (through its charter) the kind of school they want it to be.

Starting any kind of school is extremely time-consuming, unless you have lots of money to hire others to do the work. And your school could go out of business, as most small businesses do in the first few years. Some time ago, three staff members at one of New Jersey's thirteen charter schools suddenly resigned in midyear, because they felt the school was understaffed. Since the school had only four staff members, the sudden resignations threatened school closure unless replacements could be found quickly.

If your school suddenly closes, you'll be out time, money—and a school for your child. As a result, you may have to register your child in whatever public school will take him or her, and that school might be far inferior to a school you could have found had you more time and were enrolling your child at a better time of year.

Another possibility is to homeschool your child. That takes much less time to start up than a private or charter school. You need to register with your state and comply with its regulations. Find out what, if any, help might be provided by the state, your local school district, and individual teachers. You may get useful advice on what to teach and how to teach. Your children may also be permitted to participate in some school classes, clubs, and teams. In addition, there are lots of web sites designed to help with homeschooling, some of which are listed in the appendix.

To homeschool your child, you or someone in your family must spend an enormous amount of time preparing to teach your child—learning how to teach and acquiring books and other materials—as well as actually teaching. Playing two roles—that of parent and teacher—can be difficult, but may also be very rewarding. Still, consider supplementing your children's education instead of taking on the entire teaching job.

PREPARING FOR COLLEGE MATH

Whatever school you end up choosing, if your child is at all gifted in math, he or she faces a new set of challenges toward the end of high school.

This is the time when parents tend to let go, especially if a child is far more advanced in a subject than a parent ever was. But you can still guide your teenager's progress in math and science even if you can no longer help him or her with homework. Indeed, your guidance can be especially important if your child aims to pursue advanced math in college. Here's what you need to know.

College math generally starts with calculus. Preparing for calculus requires mastering precalculus and all of the preceding math courses. For many, it also means taking high school calculus, which can serve as a preview to the college course. Bright math students with very good high school calculus teachers often can place out of a semester or year of college calculus with a score of 4 or 5 (on a scale of 1 to 5) on the more advanced (BC) version of the AP calculus test. But check with each college about their policy on credit for AP tests, and on the score needed to qualify for math beyond first-year calculus. College math departments often administer their own math placement tests too.

Your child may want to take courses beyond calculus if advanced math might be useful for his or her future career. Usually, the next course after calculus is multivariate calculus and then either linear algebra or differential equations. If your child finishes calculus in eleventh grade or earlier, he or she could enroll in one of these more advanced classes at a local college.

If your child wants to be a mathematician, suggest taking or auditing (taking without credit) a "pure math" college course to get a preview of the subject. At elite colleges, pure math courses—with names such as Analysis, Topology, or Abstract Algebra—can be tough even for highly skilled math students. Indeed, many such students drop out of math at elite schools because the courses are much more difficult than they expect. So if your child might take a pure math course at an elite college, he or she would benefit greatly from a gentle introduction to such a course at a less competitive university.

If your child is not accelerated in math, suggest taking or auditing a college course during the summer. Or hire a tutor to give your child a private minicourse in analysis, topology or abstract algebra. Alternatively, your child could delay taking a pure math course in college until after he or she has had a chance to audit one of these classes during freshman year.

When your child audits a course, he or she should complete at least some of the homework and tests to get as much out of the course as possible. Ask the instructor if he or she will grade these for a fee or hire someone else who will. Or perhaps there is another student in the course who is doing well and whose graded homework your child could borrow for comparison. Browse college bookstores for helpful books. Select those with complete solutions to all nontrivial problems.

When your child takes a pure math course for credit, he or she should seek out the best teacher by asking older math majors for recommendations. He or she can also ask specific questions indicating desirable teaching techniques:

- Which teachers provide examples of all proofs to be discussed in class in advance, so students can prepare for the class discussion?

- Which teachers group the steps of a proof into understandable, logical parts for easy digestion?

- Which teachers discuss general principles of theorem-proving that form the basis of the parts and the step-by-step proof of each part?

- Which pure-math teachers present good examples of mathematical systems in which a theorem is true and untrue?

If and when your child encounters difficulty in any math course, help should be sought immediately. Tell your child to write down specific questions to ask the teacher during office hours and keep visiting a teacher as long as problems persist. Find a tutor if necessary. Any delay in getting help will only make passing the class even harder. Sometimes a course is just too hard, and your child may have to switch to a different one.

PREPARING FOR COLLEGE PHYSICS

Another difficult course for which advance preparation is useful is college-level general physics, with or without calculus. General physics usually includes much more material than almost anybody can learn in a year, a problem some teachers attempt to solve by cutting back the amount they teach. A better solution would be for middle or elementary schools to offer serious physics instruction for interested students. This, however, is unlikely to happen anytime soon. So the next best thing is preview.

A year or more in advance, buy a good noncalculus college physics text with answers to at least half the problems and, if possible, additional books with solutions to lots of problems. Have your child read the text and do the problems with answers, and perhaps solve mechanics problems in a separate physics problem book. Like learning math, learning physics requires solving lots of problems. Unless your child is a budding physics genius, hire a good tutor to teach your child basic mechanics and maybe a little electricity and magnetism before the first term. That way, your child will appreciate the beauty of physics instead of being mired in confusion and despair.

Chapter 4

Supplementary Instruction

S upplementing the math education your child gets in school can be critical to helping your child succeed in math. Such instruction can help
your child master the math in his or her current grade, catch up to
grade-level, enrich his or her knowledge of math, or jump ahead one or
more grades in math.

Of course, one way to augment your child's math education is to teach
your child the necessary math yourself. Part 2 of this book provides how-to
advice for parents who wish to do at least some of this. But if you don't have
the time or expertise to teach your child all the math he or she needs to
learn, secure supplementary math instruction—such as tutoring, educa-

tional summer camps, and distance-learning courses. This chapter will tell you how to do this, and the appendix provides more specific information on how to acquire the specific types of materials discussed under each heading.

MATH BOOKS

Math textbooks and workbooks are essential materials for anyone teaching your child math. They are also often needed to evaluate a tutor, and as a reference for understanding how best to use supplementary math resources. Other kinds of math books are valuable materials for enrichment activities.

Math texts and workbooks can sometimes be obtained from local bookstores, but more reliably from on-line bookstores, or directly from the publisher. Your child's school or teacher is another good source of books and information about books. If you are looking to accelerate your child and need books for a more advanced grade, your school may have extra copies of books for those grades. You may also be able to buy used books from the parents of older children.

If you cannot afford to buy the books you need, be aware that schools and teachers regularly dispose of books they no longer need—including texts replaced by newer editions, worn texts, or books a publisher sent for evaluation. From teachers, you may also be able to obtain partially used workbooks from students who left the school early. And you might be able to borrow a book that is not in use. Ask assistant principals and heads of math departments for other sources of texts and workbooks. Math books can be borrowed from libraries, but you might have difficulty renewing a book for as long as you need it.

Browse bookstores and libraries for math enrichment books, including biographies of mathematicians and scientists, or books on the history of math and science. In addition, order books of math contest problems and solutions.

TUTORING

Home tutoring is often the crux of any strategy for helping your child master the math at grade-level and, if necessary, in previous grades. Tutoring can also be extremely useful for giving your child a preview of the next year's math, for providing the education needed for acceleration, and for general math enrichment. Whatever the objective, being taught by a good tutor is probably the fastest way for students of all levels to learn.

If your child is behind in math or is having trouble with the math in his or her grade, a skilled tutor can often trace the problem to deficiencies in math knowledge and remedy this problem by providing appropriate instruction and practice problems. If your child is no more than one grade behind in math, the right tutor should be able to help your child catch up in math and master the math in his or her current grade.

If no one in your family has time or expertise to tutor your child in math, the best option is to hire an expert tutor. Pay as much as you can afford. You don't want to lose a tutor you like, and the tutor deserves it. If you have a limited budget, consider hiring a student tutor, even one as young as your child. Young students are not likely to be expert tutors, but some of them are very good.

How do you find a good tutor? Ask for recommendations from your child's teachers, your friends, and even math department heads and math teachers in nearby schools. Call a college or high school math department to find out how to locate a student tutor or possibly a teacher. The secretary might put up an ad on their bulletin board for you, or you could go there and do that yourself. Look at postings on boards around the local college campus and in the campus newspaper for tutors advertising their services. Also look to any nearby tutoring agencies and cram schools. Look up *Tutoring* in the Yellow Pages. Consult newspaper classified ads. Place your own classified ad.

No matter whom you hire, evaluate him or her regularly, starting a week or two after hiring. There are a few straightforward ways of doing this. One is to ask your child: "How easy is it to understand the tutor?" and "Are you learning a lot of math?" If you are aware of the math your child needs to learn now, observe portions of the tutoring session and judge its quality by your standards. For instance, I would not choose a tutor who taught basic addition facts by having your child manipulate objects. That's a useful tactic for teaching the meaning of addition, but nearly useless for learning addition facts. The flash-card method works better, but not as well as enriching the connections in the mind with memory devices such as rhymes and songs or, best of all, more general and important relations between numbers.

But unless you are an experienced math teacher, don't be too quick to criticize the tutor's method. What counts most is how much your child learns and how fast he or she learns. The best tack is to test your child's knowledge when the tutor is absent.

A simple way to do this is to ask your child questions and pose problems you devise. You can also obtain tests on the topics the tutor is teaching and administer the appropriate test after the tutor finishes each topic. Tests for various math topics can be obtained from teachers, school-district math specialists, textbooks, or supplementary testing materials sold by textbook publishers. Do not use a test from the text the tutor is teaching from, since you don't want the tutor to prepare your child for the specific questions on the test.

After a couple of months of tutoring, talk to your child's math teacher to find out whether your child's homework and test grades have improved over that period. If your child isn't making good progress, find a different tutor. Tutor quality varies enormously. Keep switching tutors until you find one you and your child like a lot.

If you can't pay a tutor, ask teachers at your child's school if they would help your child in math before or after school, at lunchtime, or at another available time. Does the school have a math resource room staffed by a teacher to help children in math? Is there an after-school or summer school program for helping children catch up in school? Watch for announcements of free math tutoring at your school or local community centers. A math teacher at my children's middle school sent a flyer home stating that she was available for 45 minutes every day before school to help any student with math. Some very dedicated teachers go far beyond the call of duty to help children.

If no adult teaching help is available, find out whether the school has a student tutoring program in math. Ask your child if he or she knows a skilled math student who might help him or her for free. My children spent hundreds of hours tutoring their friends for free over the phone and in person. If your child needs extensive free help, consider bartering services—that is, doing something for the tutor or the tutor's family in exchange for help in math.

Whatever kind of tutoring you get for your child, you can improve the efficacy of the tutor by gathering resources and information for him or her. If your child needs help with math in his or her current grade or in previous grades, ask your child's current and previous teachers for a detailed (ideally written) list of the math concepts, facts, and types of problems your child still needs to master. In addition, keep the math worksheets your child brings home and the math workbooks brought home at the end of the year. Your child's wrong answers can help a tutor reveal your child's math deficiencies.

School workbooks are also useful as a source of practice problems for the tutoring session, as students typically don't come close to completing all the problems in them. Similarly, the tutor can help your child correct mistakes on worksheets from school and use those as a starting point to discuss misunderstandings.

Supply any tutor who is not a professional teacher with math texts and new workbooks that cover any math your child has not mastered, including those from prior grades if necessary. Your tutor is unlikely to be able to generate a set of homework problems that are as good as the ones textbooks provide. In any case, it is a waste of the tutor's time (and your money) for the tutor to do so. You may use your child's math books from previous years, if you still have them. If not, see the previous section for tips on acquiring math books at little or no cost.

TUTORING SCHOOLS

An alternative to a tutor is after-school or weekend classes at tutoring schools. A lot of the business for tutoring schools comes from students preparing for aptitude tests like the SAT, the GRE, various achievement tests, or admissions tests for local high schools. However, these schools often also provide supplementary instruction in school subjects at various grade-levels. Before enrolling your child, consult the school about the subjects and levels of their courses to be sure there is a class at your child's level or aimed at the part of the math curriculum your child needs. Local tutoring schools also exist in many cities, often listed under *Tutoring* in the Yellow Pages. (In addition, see this book's appendix for sources of information.)

SUMMER CAMPS AND COURSES

Each summer, educational schools and camps nationwide offer thousands of courses to children. Some of them can help enrich your child's math education or accelerate your child in math by teaching him or her the math in an upcoming grade. Some organizations run talent search "contests"—essentially, math and verbal ability tests—to identify academically gifted students from second grade through high school. Students who score well on these tests qualify for both academic summer programs and year-round distance-learning courses at places such as the Center for Talented Youth (CTY) at The Johns Hopkins University, the Talent Identification Program at Duke University, and the Center for Talent Development (CTD) at Northwestern University.

Other academic summer camps do not limit who may attend, so you should be able to find a camp that will help your child learn math, no matter what his or her skill level. Many such camps also offer other subjects that can benefit your child. In addition, many colleges and universities offer summer instruction in math or math research programs for talented high school students.

DISTANCE LEARNING

Distance learning, in which instruction is delivered to you on paper, computer disks, CD-ROM's, or via the Internet, is another good option. Distance learning is the modern incarnation of correspondence courses, now much enhanced by computers and the Internet. It often comes with access to tutorial help by mail, phone, or E-mail. Some distance education courses in math and other subjects are available to all students at costs middle class parents can afford.

There are also distance-learning courses specifically for academically gifted students. For instance, students who score in the upper 15 percent in math ability on an admissions test can take courses covering an entire K–12 math curriculum from the Education Program for Gifted Youth (EPGY) at Stanford University. For the upper 2 percent in ability, courses are offered by institutions such as the CTY, Duke's Talent Identification Program, and the CTD. These all appear to be very well designed math teaching programs.

Free distance-learning resources in every subject abound on the Internet. If you can't afford a home computer with Internet access, find out if your children can use a computer at their school or local public library. Math and other educational software may also be available for their use.

The main problem with free distance learning resources is that they are not organized into a comprehensive K–12 math curriculum. For instance, one site will provide flash card–type practice with basic addition, subtraction, multiplication, and division facts—information that spans grades 1 through 4 in the usual curriculum. Another site may provide practice with long addition, subtraction, multiplication, and division, which also spans grades 1 through 4. And still another site presents story problems spanning many grades. It's up to you as a parent to pull together parts from several different sites to construct the information taught in the curriculum for any one grade. You can often do this by using a textbook or workbook for the grade of math being learned as a guide.

One good use of free distance learning is to help your children master their current math topics, as revealed by their homework and the class work they bring home. In addition, some distance learning sites will answer specific questions that you or your child might have about a math topic or problem—and you can often scan an inventory of previous questions and answers.

EDUCATIONAL SOFTWARE

I bought many educational computer software products for my children, some of which were also fun enough that the kids played them without my prodding. I used the software as an auxiliary part of their home math education, for which textbooks, workbooks, math contest problems, and my own knowledge were the essential resources. Still, my children learned something from the software and it may have helped spur their interest in math.

Since I purchased these programs, new and improved math-learning software has been created. If you have a computer, such software can be an inexpensive way to help your child learn large parts of the K–12 math curriculum. To be sure of that, however, you'll need to carefully compare the content of the programs with what is covered in textbooks and workbooks for the parts of the curriculum your child needs to learn.

Don't rely solely on math learning software for accelerating your child in math, since the software might not cover all the math in the grades to be skipped. Still, software can play a supplementary role in your child's math training. The right software can also be a valuable enrichment tool for helping a child solve unusual problems or think about math concepts not covered in the curriculum.

COLLEGE COURSES

If your child finishes high school math early, you might want to enroll him or her in a math course at a nearby college. Your child might also take a summer college class to jump ahead a year in math or repeat a high school course for better mastery. If you can't afford tuition or a college does not permit part-time enrollment by high school students, professors will often accept a student into a class informally.

VOLUNTEERING IN SCHOOLS

Another excellent way to supplement your child's education is by volunteering at your child's school. There are many ways to help. You might, for instance, raise funds for the school or for particular classrooms or serve on school committees, which may weigh in on important educational issues. You might become a "class parent" who helps organize special class events and serves as an interface between the teacher and the other parents, shaping these events and making them possible. You could accompany the class on trips when an adult chaperone is needed, or do administrative work for the teacher, giving the teacher more time to prepare lessons.

If you wish, you can help teach. This can take many forms, some of which require a lot of initiative and others that largely involve taking instructions from a teacher. I began with the latter approach when my first child entered elementary school. I volunteered in her math class once a week, helping students who raised their hands solve a problem or understand something in their workbooks. Later I tutored children who needed remedial help, answered student questions in after-school review sessions for the New York State Regents Exams, and ran pull-out math enrichment classes for high ability students. In these classes, the teacher preapproved my general curriculum, but gave me considerable freedom in what and how I taught. At one point I enjoyed almost complete independence when I taught a weekly forty-minute math course to fifth and sixth graders for a year, and when I coached math teams.

Teaching in a child's school is often impractical for parents who cannot take time out from their jobs during the day or do not feel competent to teach. But if you can teach, you will enhance your child's education in several ways. First, your presence improves the student-teacher ratio. Second, you may be able to offer specialized instruction to students wanting to do advanced math or needing help with remedial math. Maybe you have math-related knowledge a teacher doesn't. Perhaps you are an engineer, electrician, banker, or physicist and want to show how math is important in your work. Or perhaps you just want to teach something you feel is missing in the curriculum. If you teach a special class, kids can enjoy a variety of teaching styles and topics. And your presence in the classroom provides social support for your child and for others to work hard to excel in math.

If you want to be a volunteer teacher, be aware that many teachers are reluctant to use parent teachers because amateur help can require more supervision than it's worth or because parents can be disruptive and interfere with a teacher's plans. And some teachers, especially new ones, are uncomfortable with any adult observing what they do in class. When I volunteered in New York City public schools, where teachers tend to be very cautious, I clearly laid out my qualifications and desire to be cooperative beforehand. I often sent a letter to my child's teacher volunteering to help, describing the ways I wished to help, outlining my previous experience, promising that my efforts would be supportive and not disruptive, and providing references from teachers who had used me as a volunteer before.

When I wanted to coach a student math team by myself, I took similar steps. I described my approach and experience—I had already been coaching for a year—to the school's director. I also outlined the space and other demands on the school that a math team would require, and provided references. As a result of this planning and straightforwardness—along with my record as a responsible, cooperative volunteer—I earned the trust of educators, and they let me coach without supervision.

Indeed, I always kept my promises to be cooperative, continually striving to do exactly what the teacher wanted and not trying to change anything about how the class was run. To do otherwise is disruptive. Volunteers are helpers. The teacher is in charge. As a parent, you can discuss anything you wish concerning your own child's education, but as a volunteer, don't suggest changes in the teacher's methods or approach unless the teacher specifically solicits your suggestions.

If you play by these rules, you can do a world of good for your child and for other children by volunteering, whether you are helping to teach, fund raise, chaperone a field trip or perform any other job for a teacher or administrator. No matter what services you provide, your effort will not only directly help the school and your child's class, but will also convey to your child and others that you think school is important.

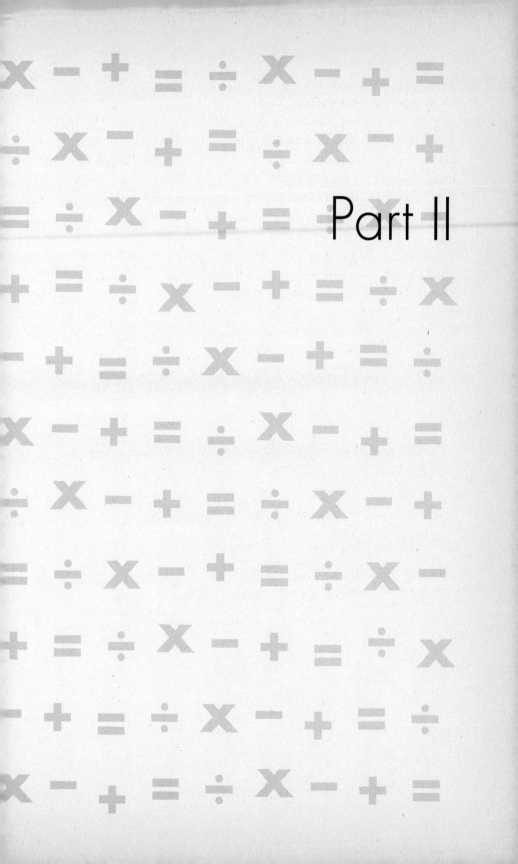

Part II

Chapter 5

Teaching Tips

Over the years, I have taught my children almost all the math in the school curriculum from kindergarten through precalculus. From such instruction, and their own studying, they were able to skip to higher grade-levels in math in school and win numerous math contests. You may have similar goals for your child. Or perhaps you want to help your child master grade-level math, or enrich your child's appreciation of math through problem solving, reading, or other activities. Whatever your goals, if you want to accomplish some of them by teaching your child math yourself, read on.

Part 2 is designed for parents who want to teach math to their children. It is geared toward home schooling as a supplement to, not a replacement for, regular schooling, though virtually all the advice applies to full-time homeschooling. One exception: Full-time homeschooling requires much more time than I suggest on these pages. This chapter provides general, practical teaching guidelines regarding the time required to achieve different goals, scheduling, and learning and motivation techniques. Its advice will also help you productively use the following chapters, which discuss how to teach specific math topics from addition facts to algebra.

SETTING GOALS AND ALLOTTING TIME

As you embark on a homeschooling program, first decide what you want to accomplish. The least time-consuming goal is increasing your child's interest in math without any particular endpoints in mind. For this, set aside about an hour per week, perhaps in two half-hour stints, for fun math-related activities you can do with your child. These might include solving math puzzles; playing computer, card, or board games that involve math; and reading nontechnical books about math or mathematicians. Monopoly, for example, will provide practice with, and an incentive to learn, arithmetic, which is needed to play more skillfully, though the game does not directly teach arithmetic facts and operations. Since your child will probably enjoy such activities, you won't have to force or nag, making your job easier and more pleasant.

Don't kid yourself, though. Your child won't learn a huge amount of math this way, because games and puzzles are not a very efficient way to learn math. So if you have goals for your child that require mastery of a significant amount of math, you will need to take the more structured approach, which requires more time. Say your child is doing reasonably well in math at school but needs supplementary instruction to fully master the school math curriculum and qualify for honors math. To accomplish this, your child will need to devote between one and three hours per week to learning math at home. This should be an organized effort, as discussed below, not a smattering of fun activities. If your goals for your child include acceleration, accolades in math contests, or participation in math-related research, your child will probably have to devote three to seven hours—and perhaps as much as ten hours—per week to supplementary math learning.

How much time will you spend teaching math to your child? For younger children who must be continually supervised and need immediate feedback on their work, your time is the sum of your child's time plus the time it takes you to prepare for the lessons. That will depend on how much math you know, how easily your child grasps math concepts, and your experience as a math teacher. When your child is sufficiently mature, you can do other things while he or she reads the text and solves problems. Just be available to answer questions.

Of course, any math learning activity a child chooses to do all on his or her own is a clear win no matter how inefficient, since such activities take up none of your time. Some kids will engage in math-related activities for reasons having little to do with math such as the lure of competition (in a game) or of spending time with family or friends. Watch for math games your child can and will play without you or a math TV program your child enjoys. In my experience, these are difficult to find, so if you find something your child likes, don't forget about it! A few children find serious math learning fun, but most of the time motivating a child to learn math is one of the challenges of homeschooling.

HOMESCHOOLING TIPS

How do you begin? First, as long as you have a decent math background, don't fret about your teaching qualifications. Teaching math to your children is easier than teaching math to a class because your class size is much smaller. Even if you have several children, you usually must teach them separately, so you will be teaching one-on-one—the most favorable teaching situation for learning. In this environment you'll be able to quickly diagnose your child's misunderstandings, proceed at a pace tailored precisely to your child's rate of learning, and keep your child's attention much more easily than can a teacher with a big class. However, creating an ideal learning environment for your child will not happen automatically. To make the process as efficient, valuable and pleasant as possible, heed the following tips for organizing and running your homeschooling sessions.

Assign a Set Time for Math

Set a specific time each day or week for your child to do math, and determine the length of each math-learning session ahead of time. That way, you won't waste time haggling about such things with your child. When there is a conflict with the scheduled math session, try to recognize this in advance and set up an alternative time with your child. Your child should be required to keep these math "appointments" unless there is a serious conflict or a problem like sickness. Don't let your child out of a lesson because he or she doesn't feel like doing math or wants to do something else. If you treat the sessions seriously, your child will know that it's no use trying to get out of it.

Prepare Each Lesson

Before sitting down with your child, prepare your lesson. That means first gathering textbooks, workbooks, and teacher's guides for the grades you're going to teach your child. *Math Coach*, of course, is also a very useful resource, but you will also need math texts if you want to systematically cover any significant portion of the school's math curriculum. In addition, you may need objects for a young child to manipulate; math project materials for an older child; problems from math contests; computer math-learning software; math games; and perhaps useful math-learning web sites.

Once you've got everything you need, read the appropriate sections of books in advance of each lesson to be sure you understand them. Then develop a plan for teaching the information—outlining (at least, in your mind) the main facts, concepts, and problem-solving techniques your child must learn in that unit and how you will teach them. Will you use activities with objects or number lines? What kinds of questions might best test your child's understanding? Which problems will you ask your child to solve? In planning your lesson, keep the following four math-teaching principles in mind.

Keep Concepts in Order

In math, the order in which concepts are learned is extremely important, because each concept builds upon ones learned before. For instance, children must learn to count by ones before they learn basic addition facts. And those facts must be known before learning to add integers with more than one digit. If a child fails to understand a concept, he or she will fail to understand every other concept built upon it. Thus, teach concepts in the order prescribed in textbooks and in the following teaching chapters.

Indeed, if your child has difficulty understanding something you are teaching, that may be because your child has not completely learned—or has forgotten—an earlier concept. Test this possibility by asking your child questions pertaining to some of that prerequisite knowledge. This kind of difficulty is frequent in math, and is far less frequent in nonmathematical subjects such as history or literature, in which understanding new facts depends far less on knowing other facts first.

Assign Lots of Problems

In each lesson, have your child solve lots of problems of different types instead of deeply analyzing a small number of problems. However, the amount of feedback you give your child on an individual problem should vary, depending on the difficulty of the problem and whether your child used the best method to find the solution.

Teach Facts by "Relational Chunking"

Many methods of memorizing arithmetic facts don't work well because the facts are so similar to each other. For example, the brain will associate the number 4 with many different facts, including the sum "4" in $4 + 0 = 4$, the sum "5" in the problem $4 + 1 = 5$, and the sum "12" in $4 + 8 = 12$, and so on. This creates interference or cognitive static in the brain that slows the learning of addition facts if they are simply memorized. But such interference can be drastically reduced using a special technique that enables a child's brain to relate the numbers to be added in more meaningful ways. The technique, called "relational chunking," uses relations between the numbers to be added to further distinguish sums, such as "the numbers to be added are the same" for the facts $0 + 0, 1 + 1, 2 + 2, \ldots, 8 + 8$, and $9 + 9$.

Once a child learns these like-number facts, the child can learn rules that relate new sums to the already-learned facts and make the new sums easier to learn. Not only that, but the mathematical relationships a child learns using relational chunking—such as the idea that the sum $5 + 3$ is the same as $4 + 4$ because 5 is one more than 4 and 3 is one less—will enrich your child's understanding of math. So learn the methods outlined in the next chapter, which are rooted in principles gleaned from cognitive science. They will enable your child to learn faster, learn more, and remember what he or she has learned far better than by simple memorization.

Make It Abstract

No matter your child's age, help him or her develop abstract mathematical concepts. As explained in chapter 2, a concept becomes more abstract, and more useful, the more knowledge that surrounds it. One way to make a math concept abstract is to associate it with a variety of concrete experiences—counting objects, traveling a distance, measuring weight, and so on. Another way is to associate it with different numerical relationships. Don't skimp on activities in the following chapters designed to make a child's number concepts as abstract as possible.

Make the Learning Interactive

To keep your child focused on what you are teaching, make the session interactive by asking your child lots of questions in addition to having your child read the text and listen to your explanations. Encourage your child to ask questions about things he or she doesn't understand. Psychologists have learned that people who ask and answer questions remember facts longer and learn more than people who only absorb information by reading or listening.

Teach How to Ask and Answer Questions

Teach your child that answering certain questions requires first answering one or more related questions. For instance, if your child isn't making progress answering a question or solving a problem, pose easier questions that you think may help your child get the answer.

You can also teach the skill of asking questions by having your child devise math problems for others to solve. Your child will need to solve these problems to be sure they can be solved and to determine the correct solutions. Through this kind of training, your child will begin to understand that math problems describe a world he or she can explore and learn about.

When Your Child Is Stuck, Give Hints

Instead of explaining an entire solution to a problem your child hasn't been able to solve, give your child a hint to help the child figure out the solution on his or her own. Though hinting at the solution takes more time than simply providing it, hints let your child play an active role in the problem solving, and that's the only way you can be sure your child is learning. The more your child figures out for himself or herself, the more he or she will learn and remember.

If Your Approach Isn't Working, Try a New Tack

Giving hints worked well with all of the students I've taught except for two of my children, who were annoyed by this method. It took me a while to abandon this technique with them, but eventually I adopted another way to provide the solution when they resisted hints. My new approach: Let them try to correct an incorrect solution without hints. When the child didn't succeed, I would then explain the entire solution. It's not as good a method as hints, but if a child won't tolerate hints, try this. Be open to a variety of approaches and use what seems to work best with a child. Each child is unique, so be flexible.

In some cases, especially with contest problems, there are several ways to solve a problem, and the best method is one a child is unlikely to think of on his or her own, even with lots of hints and discussion. To save time in such cases, don't wait long for a child to figure out the answer before providing it.

Review Ideas Periodically

Review is critical to learning. People do not remember most pieces of knowledge they've been exposed to just once. To be sure, they remember the knowledge for a little while, but then the idea fades with time until it is reinforced by being used or discussed again.

That reinforcement—review—can have a dramatic impact on how long your child remembers a fact. Let's say that the first time you teach your child something, he or she learns it well enough to remember the fact for just 1 minute. If a review succeeds in making the child's memory of that fact twice as strong, your child will remember the fact 100 times longer, or an hour and 40 minutes. Doubling the strength of that memory again will increase the length of child's memory to 10,000 minutes (about seven days) and further doublings will create a 700-day memory, and then a lifetime memory.

Many separate study sessions or "learning trials"—perhaps five, ten or more—are typically needed before a child knows a math fact, concept, or procedure well enough to remember it forever. In mathematics, review of concepts often occurs naturally during the course of instruction, since progress in math depends on a solid understanding (and stable memory) of previous ideas. However, it's important to recognize this, and to patiently review old ideas during each learning session when necessary. Don't become frustrated when your child forgets something. Forgetting and review is part of the learning process.

Perhaps more importantly, recognize that review must occur over many separate study sessions. You cannot accomplish the same thing by going over and over a concept in a single session, and you should not attempt to do so. For one thing, it's boring. Once students have learned a concept or solved a problem, they want to go on to something new. If you make them go over and over the same old stuff, they'll yawn and stop paying attention. And then no more learning occurs.

In addition, while learning increases with study time, it follows the law of diminishing returns: As a student continues to study something, he or she will learn it better and better, but at an ever-decreasing rate. Thus, the longer one dwells on a topic, the less efficient learning becomes.

So after teaching one topic or idea for a while, take a break or move on to something new, and review the first topic another time. This, in effect, spaces out the learning of the material into separate sessions. This is more interesting and efficient than cramming the learning of one idea into one long studying binge.

Although the child forgets between the study sessions, what remains is consolidated, or put into a form such that it will be forgotten at a slower rate. In addition, the mind is "fresher" for previously learned material after a break from it and quickly learns back what has been forgotten. This is probably because resting the brain area doing the learning enables that area to replenish certain molecules needed to form long-term memories. Trying to solidify such memories when the brain hasn't had time to replenish these molecules is thus more or less a waste of time.

Indeed, it is possible that kids' boredom with a belabored topic serves an evolutionary purpose—to discourage a type of learning and review process that is inefficient. So take your child's boredom as a sign to move on, but don't forget to revisit the topic later.

Arrange for Testing

If possible, arrange to have your child take an objective, ideally standardized, math test to demonstrate the child's mastery of an area of math. The prospect of a test will motivate your child to study math at home, since the child will want to get a good score. In addition, high scores on some tests may help persuade educators at the child's school or at another school that the child is ready for an advanced math class.

For elementary and middle school kids, try to arrange with a math teacher to give your child an exam for any grade-level your child has mastered and may be able to skip. In New York, high schools and some middle schools test students on the first three years of integrated math, which cover geometry and two years of algebra. These tests are known as Regents Exams. If your child wants to skip one or more years of math at school, ask the head of the school's math department whether there is a similar test your child could take to demonstrate mastery of the math required to make the jump.

At many sites in the U.S., you can register your child (for a fee) to take the SAT 2 math achievement tests as well as two AP calculus exams—tests administered by the College Board and prepared by the Educational Testing Service. A high score on SAT 2 Math 2C (covering math through precalculus), for example, might help your child skip into calculus. The AP calculus tests are used for college placement.

Provide Plenty of Free Time

Don't spend so much time teaching your child math that it drives out other important childhood experiences, such as being with friends, playing sports, participating in family activities, or talking with you. This applies to all educational activities your child is required to do at home. Thus, if you decide to supplement your child's school instruction in another important school subject, it should generally replace—not add to—the time spent learning math.

I've abided by this rule when instructing my children in subjects like reading, grammar, writing, science and social science. If the instruction was fun for a child, as reading some books can be, I felt comfortable adding it to whatever math I was teaching that child. But if the new homeschooling was hard work, I taught the child less math to compensate.

With rare exceptions, my children spent no more than an hour a day engaging in educational activities directed by me. Over several years a lot can be accomplished in an hour a day. For limited periods of time, of a year or so, it's okay to raise this to as much as ten hours per week to meet a specific goal, such as skipping a year of math in school or catching up with classmates. But childhood is fleeting, and neither you nor your child will be happy if you require your child to spend an inordinate amount of time studying academic subjects to the exclusion of other parts of a child's life.

COPING WITH COMPLAINTS

Even if you give your child lots of free time and abide by the hour-a-day limit, your child is likely to complain about any structured homeschooling in math. Your child may say it's unfair because none of his or her friends have to do extra schoolwork at home, which may be true. If your child voices such arguments, explain why you want your child to learn some math at home: The effort will lead to big accomplishments now and in the future, such as better scores on school math tests or on national math contests (if that's relevant). It will also enormously improve your child's chances of getting into the college he or she wants to attend, and of being successful in college and thereafter. Tailor your discussion to your child's personal goals as much as possible. Explain that such achievements won't come without hard work.

Accept that moderate amounts of complaining are usually unavoidable in our culture. And remind *yourself* of the rewards of this endeavor for your child, which will be worth the unpleasantness. If you and your child stick with it, your child will gain a priceless feeling of accomplishment and a big boost in self-confidence in math that is likely to endure for some time.

However, be alert to complaints that go beyond whining and indicate a hatred for math, or negative feelings toward you for teaching the math. If you think your child is developing such a hate reaction, figure out what's wrong—maybe your teaching style is grating on the child or you are giving your child hurtful feedback—and make amends as soon as possible. One possible cause of your child's negativity is hostile, degrading remarks, such as "Don't be stupid," "You're an idiot," or, "You're not trying." Never degrade your child. Be firm, but also reward good performance and attempts to learn, even if your child is making mistakes. Indeed, be especially kind and loving—not punitive—when your child makes mistakes; he or she feels bad enough already.

If you can't control your frustration and be a patient, encouraging, and loving parent-teacher, turn the job over to someone else or take a break from it to improve the situation. If you take a break, make sure it is long enough—perhaps several months—to repair your relationship with your child and to fully formulate your new approach to teaching. If you decide to employ a different tutor for your child, instruction can begin right away.

PUSHING YOUR CHILDREN

What about nagging your child to work or study? Is that also a bad thing? Many people view having to push a child to work as a sign of a parent's failure, because parents ought to be able to motivate their children in better ways. I labored under this misconception for years until I read an article by the wise humorist Erma Bombeck, who said it was a parent's duty to nag. I can't tell you what a wave of relief I felt when I read that. I'd been feeling guilty for years whenever I nagged my kids to study, which was fairly often. Now I was liberated, free to nag ad libitum and without guilt, indeed with pride in the performance of a necessary, but unpleasant, parental duty.

Why? If a parent wants a child to excel in math or any other difficult subject, the parent has to motivate the child to spend lots of time learning the subject. You can do this in part by explaining the benefits of studying, citing rewards like good grades. But in most cases, such discussions alone won't induce a young child to devote the effort needed to meet the goals you have in mind. In the best of circumstances, it generally takes at least 15 years for a child to develop the self-motivation required to pursue ambitious goals without adult intervention. In the meantime, you will probably have to continually push the child to work to achieve important goals. Indeed, as Bombeck said, it is your duty to do so.

That said, many types of pushing are bad for children, so it's important to do the job right. Make sure to tailor your goals to your child's abilities and interests, not to what is important or prestigious to you. And have realistic expectations. Knowing what's realistic is not easy, but do your best, erring somewhat on the high side and adjusting your expectations if necessary. Discuss your goals with your child so the child has input and learns how to set goals. Tell your child it's okay to reach for the stars sometimes, since no one can know one's full potential—but also to set clearly achievable goals, and to be happy about meeting those whether or not the more ambitious goals are ever met.

Reward effort and achievement. Praise your child's accomplishments at every opportunity. Do not criticize your child when he or she has failed after making a strong effort. But do reprimand the child if he or she has not made, or is not making, a strong effort.

Coach your child to handle failure. If your child is upset by wrong answers, say that everyone makes mistakes and that success comes to those who learn from their mistakes—and not to those who try to forget their errors or avoid challenges because they fear failure. When your child fails to reach an important goal, teach the child that only accomplishments, not failures, count when measuring success in life. Success is measured like points in a basketball game. Misses don't count in determining who wins. So it's best to take a lot of shots—that is, to keep setting goals, shooting for more points no matter how many times you miss the basket. In short: "If at first you don't succeed, try, try again." It's one of the important aphorisms my mother and father taught me.

Be a good model for your child. Point out your own mistakes, and show your child what you learned from each one. Reach for the stars yourself, but set realistic goals too. And set a good example when life kicks *you* in the teeth.

Can your child achieve absolutely anything if he or she works hard enough? That's an exaggeration. As Clint Eastwood said in the movie *Magnum Force:* "A man's got to know his limitations." But with the right attitude, striving to succeed within one's limits need set no limit on happiness. Everyone can carve out a niche in life where he or she will meet success. That will happen for your child if you push the child wisely and with compassion.

GUIDE TO THE FOLLOWING CHAPTERS

Now, let's turn to the specific task at hand: Teaching your child math. The following teaching chapters will help you speed your child's learning of essential math topics from arithmetic to algebra. They can help your child master grade-level material, catch up in math, preview difficult math to come, or get ahead. To accomplish any of these goals, however, you'll also need grade-level textbooks and workbooks. You may replace parts of these grade-level books with *Math Coach* lessons, but *Math Coach* does not replace a textbook. Why? Textbooks and workbooks supply many homework problems that your child will need to solve to fully master critical facts, concepts and problem-solving methods. *Math Coach* includes many valuable activities, explanations, and problems for illustration purposes but not ample practice problems.

Second, *Math Coach* is not designed to cover the entire math curriculum for any particular grade or grades. It focuses on some of the most central and broadly useful facets of the math curriculum, and those for which I have new techniques for speeding a child's learning. For example, the next chapter on basic addition, subtraction, multiplication, and division facts, covers a central part of the early elementary math curriculum. But this chapter does not teach a number of important pieces of knowledge taught in the early grades, such as telling time; sorting; identifying patterns, shapes, and geometric solids; measuring distances, volumes, masses, areas, and perimeters; making change for a dollar; and various graphing skills. In addition, this chapter focuses on the basic single-digit facts, and does not teach how to do arithmetic with larger numbers.

Similarly, the chapter on fractions emphasizes traditional fractions, and does not include decimals, percents, scientific notation, or rounding. The algebra chapter focuses on what I consider the essence of basic algebra. However, it omits some algebra concepts like the quadratic formula as well as radicals, equations involving absolute value, and properties of real numbers. Integrated math topics such as logic, geometry, statistics, probability, and clock arithmetic are likewise beyond the scope of this book.

Each of chapters 6 through 9 is organized into larger sections, which in turn are divided into lessons. Each lesson is designed to offer an amount of material that most children could cover in a day's learning session. However, some children might be able, and want, to cover more than one lesson in a day. At the same time, most children will need to be taught each lesson more than once, given the necessity of review for establishing long-term memories.

In general, please teach these lessons in order, interspersing them with textbook problems and lessons as directed. One exception: If you would like to teach your child some rudimentary fraction concepts, such as the concept of one half, before your child masters all the arithmetic facts, that's okay. Just take a break from the arithmetic chapter at some point and do the first few lessons of the fractions chapter. This could provide a useful preview of fractions. However, it is also fine to wait to teach everything about fractions until after your child has mastered all of basic arithmetic. Now, let's get started.

Chapter 6

Basic Arithmetic

One lazy summer afternoon years ago, I was driving my two young children, ages five and seven, home from a family trip when they asked: "Daddy, what do you think is the hardest times fact to learn?" They opined it was **7 x 8 = 56**. So I tried to think of a way to make this fact easy to learn. I realized that **56 = 7 x 8** is the sequence 5678 when the symbols are removed. I then realized that the same thing is true for **12 = 3 x 4**.

I was pleased to have so quickly invented this memory trick, or mnemonic, but I was more pleased when my children shot back, "Does that always work?" I told them it didn't, that it was just a trick that happened to work in these two cases.

However, after that, I got to thinking about more principled ways to learn the basic addition and multiplication facts, so that a child would not only master the facts more quickly, but also learn some general relations between numbers that "always worked," that is, general principles about integers.

One of the reasons math is so difficult for children is not the number of facts to be learned, but that many of those facts are very similar to one another. To see this, let's first look at what your child has to learn. It's all in a table with the numbers 0 to 10, the numbers to be added or multiplied, on each side. Where the numbers intersect in the table are their sums or products. In such a table, there are just **11 x 11 = 121** facts. This isn't much. Every day, a child learns far more than 121 facts of this size about other life events well enough to correctly answer a question about them the next day. To remember most facts longer than a day requires just repeating them maybe a day, a week, a month, and a year later. It doesn't require the ten to thirty minutes of daily studying over many weeks that children need to learn 121 addition or multiplication facts. What's the difficulty here?

It's the similarity between the facts. That is, the fact **3 + 5 = 8** is not so different from **3 + 6 = 9**. They both contain 3's; they both contain +'s, and they both contain single-digit numbers. In other words, each number 0 through 10, in different pairs and with one of two different operation symbols (**+** or **x**), is associated with many different answers. No one answer sticks out in the mind.

Thus, to a child beginning to learn such facts, the facts overlap in the brain, creating a blur that makes it easy to confuse them and difficult to remember any single answer. In cognitive psychology, this "blur" is called associative interference, which occurs when one idea, A, is linked in the mind to two or more other ideas. It's like static on the radio, which often occurs when other stations or electrical impulses interfere with a radio station's music or speech. When the child sees **3 + 5 = _____**, all the facts involving 3 and 5 get activated in the mind, and the wrong answers create interference for the right answer.

Indeed, such interference is probably the main reason why *all* mathematics is harder to learn than other subjects. In every area of math, unlike nonmathematical subjects, a relatively small number of basic concepts are used to express a large number of facts or more advanced concepts. This situation creates interference because each basic concept activates many other facts or concepts, which in turn interfere with one another.

The human mind possesses a way around this problem, namely, to create a new idea that binds together a set of constituent ideas or facts into "chunks"—making them hang together in logical ways, like notes in a song. Students who are very skilled at math may often do this without explicit instruction, but all students can benefit from instruction that helps them do this.

Using my training in learning and memory, I decided to find a way to help children create chunks in math—to glue mathematical facts together in a manner that creates a kind of mathematical melody that is much easier to remember than a sequence of disconnected notes. The key is forming as many connections between the ideas and facts as possible.

Forming such connections using my method involves promoting an understanding of the relationships between numbers and arithmetic operations, such as addition and subtraction. Understanding these relationships, in turn, reduces the amount of material children have to learn by rote, and highlights the distinctive qualities of different math concepts, making them easier to remember.

The method is divided into two main parts. The first builds on the simple ritual of counting, forward then backward, to introduce addition, subtraction, and the concept of negative numbers. The concepts are fortified by illustrating their use in the real world in more than one way, making them more abstract and more useful.

The second part involves "rules" that serve as memory aids and that tend to bind simple addition facts together in the brain. The simplest is how to add 0 to a number. There are other simple rules for adding 1, 2, 9, and 10. After that, only a few more basic rules, if learned in the proper order, enable children to determine answers for all the basic addition facts except for six. These six facts can then either be memorized or learned using rules.

Learning such rules enhances a child's general understanding of mathematics and speeds the learning of basic arithmetic facts by getting around the interference problem. Even so, learning to use these rules is not the final goal in learning these basic math facts. The goal is a direct association in the brain from the cues in the problem, for instance, **6 + 4**, to the answer, 10—the same goal as learning by rote repetition. This goal is, however, achieved much faster by learning rules.

Now, let's get started. You'll begin with some basic concepts that form a foundation for your child's learning of addition and subtraction.

1.1 Counting with Objects

I'll assume your child has learned the sequence of number names from 1 to at least 20. Although people generally refer to calling out those number names as "counting," that is just a first step toward learning to count. Here's how to teach your child to apply counting to objects and other aspects of the world:

First, gather a set of objects—perhaps pennies or toy cars or blocks—and place them in a bin, bowl or just a spot on the floor. Next, ask your child to pick up each object and put it in a different bin or place while saying its number, starting with 1. Make sure the child actually picks up and moves each object rather than just touching it and advancing the count. In the latter case, it's hard to keep track of what objects have been counted.

After your child has moved the last object, ask him or her: "How many objects are there?" Your child should learn to give the last number counted. Repeat the above using different numbers of objects. Also, switch the type of object counted, so your child is sure to understand that numbers can be used to refer to many types of objects. This variety in concrete experience is part of learning the abstract concept of number.

Now, teach your child to count starting with 0. Before the child has moved the first object, explain that there are 0 objects in the target bin. Ask him or her to say "zero" just before the first object has been moved and then "one" after the first object has been moved.

Next, if your child doesn't know them already, teach him or her the symbols that stand for each number name from 0 to 20. Write these symbols on a piece of paper (or use ones printed in books or that come with puzzles) and point to them while saying their names. Then test your child by pointing to different symbols at random and asking your child to name them.

1.2 Recognizing Coins and Tallying

Teach your child to recognize pennies, nickels, dimes and quarters. Explain that a penny is worth 1 cent, a nickel is worth 5 cents, a dime is worth 10 cents, and a quarter is worth 25 cents. Ask your child to write down the values of each coin as you present them to him or her.

You can now teach your child to tally coins. Ask your child to put all the nickels in one pile, dimes in another, quarters in another and pennies in another. Ask the child to count the number of each kind of coin by making a mark (a check mark or short vertical line will do) on a piece of paper when each coin is moved. Keep the tallies for each type of coin separate: The marks for the pennies should be in one place on the paper, those for the nickels in another place, and so on. In the end, ask your child to count up the marks to determine how many of each kind of coin there are. He or she should write the number down on the paper next to each group of markings.

You can teach your child to tally other kinds of things too, such as different fruits—oranges, apples, and bananas—or different writing utensils—pens, pencils, and erasers.

1.3 Counting and Distance

The final counting exercises focus on moving counting to a new context—distance. Teach your child to measure distance by counting the number of equal "steps" from one end of a line. Here's how.

Draw a number line on a piece of paper that has 0 at the start followed by 1, 2, 3, . . . up to 20, with each number as a label for 1 of 21 equally spaced tick marks. Ask your child to count "steps" along the line starting with 1 first, and then—pointing to the initial "0" mark—starting with 0. Stop your child's count at various points along the line and ask him or her how many steps he or she has gone. Explain that this number of steps measures the distance between the stopping point and the left end of the line (where your child started to count). If your child has any problem with left and right, point to the 0 mark when you say the left end of the line.

Tell your child that when you are counting steps, it's easier to start with 1 than with 0, but that it is important to have a name for the distance of each tick mark from the left end, and that includes the 0 distance point.

Draw another number line but this time extend the line to the left of 0, and create tick marks with labels –1, –2, –3, etc. Simply explain to your child that these are negative numbers and that the – sign indicates that fact, and that these numbers exist to the left of 0. Ask your child to count negative numbers starting with "zero," and proceeding to "negative one," "negative two," and so on. Don't go into depth here (as we will continue the discussion of negative numbers below), and don't worry if your child seems perplexed. Your goal here is simply to introduce your child to negative numbers, which will help him or her feel much more comfortable with them later.

1.4 Ranking Numbers

Next, be sure your child understands the order of the numbers he or she has been counting in terms of which numbers are "bigger," "greater," or "more than," and "smaller," or "less than" which other numbers. Ask your child questions such as: "Which number is greater, seven or three?" "Is seven more than three?" "Which number is smaller, four or eight?" "Is eight less than four?" Ask these types of questions using various numbers to be sure your child understands these concepts. If your child needs help, illustrate the numbers on a number line or by creating piles of different numbers of objects that your child can see. Your child will then be able to better visualize the rankings of these numbers.

1.5 Place Value

Now teach your child the concept of place value, limited here to the ones place and the tens place. Here's how. Tell your child that 9 means 9 ones, 8 means 8 ones, . . . , 2 means 2 ones, 1 means 1 one, 0 means 0 ones, which means "no ones." Test your child's understanding by asking, "What is the same as zero ones?" Your child should answer, "No ones," or, "Nothing." Test in both directions: "What does three mean?" (Answer: 3 ones.) "What number means five ones?" (Answer: 5.) Ask your child to point to the correct symbol and pronounce its name.

Explain that 10 means one 10 and nothing else, that 11 means one 10 and a 1, 12 means one 10 and a 2, and so on, up to 20, which means two 10's and nothing else. Then ask your child, "What does a ten mean?" It means ten ones. Make 2 little square boxes next to each other and point to the tens box and say, "This is the tens place." Then point to the ones box and say, "This is the ones place." Test your child by pointing to a box and asking what place it is. Ask your child to reply with the complete phrase, "tens place" or "ones place." Write numbers from 0 to 20 in the boxes, one at a time, and explain the numbers in terms of the places. For example, tell your child that 10 means 1 ten and 0 ones, which is 10 ones, 7 means 0 tens and 7 ones, or just 7 ones, 13 means 1 ten and 3 ones (or 13 ones), 20 means 2

Tick Marks vs. Steps

There is an interesting subtlety about number lines you might want to teach your child if he or she can handle it: One always needs to draw one more tick mark than the number of steps on the line. Here's how to help your child understand this:

Make a number line that goes from 0 to 1, with just 2 tick marks. Ask your child how long the line is. The answer is "One step long." Then ask your child, "How many tick marks did I use to create this line that is one step long?" Your child should answer "two tick marks," because you need 1 at each end to mark the boundaries of the step. Now tell your child: "So, you need one more tick mark than the number of steps."

Now draw a line that goes from 0 to 2 and has 3 tick marks and ask again: "How long is this line?" Then: "How many tick marks did I use to create this line that is two steps long?" Keep increasing the length of the line perhaps up to 8 and asking the same question each time. Now, without drawing a line with tick marks, ask your child, "How many tick marks are needed to draw a line with ten steps?" "How about thirteen steps?" Your child should answer 11 and 14. Test your child with various numbers of steps, and she or he should respond with the number of tick marks (boundary markers) that is 1 greater than the number of steps.

---

tens and 0 ones, or 20 ones. Now write a number, such as 16, in the boxes and ask "What does this mean?" Also ask, "How do you write zero tens and three ones?" Now fade out the boxes in 2 steps. First, change from 2 boxes to 2 adjacent underlines. Then eliminate the underlines and write the numbers in the normal way. Repeat the above tests using both of these formats.

1.6 Adding 1 and 0

Now it's time to introduce your child to addition, by teaching him or her to add 1 to any number, N, for instance $0 + 1 = 1$ or $7 + 1 = 8$. Learning to add 1 to any number, the $N + 1$ facts, requires some additional training after learning to count by ones, because, with counting, children rely on the entire sequence leading up to the next number rather than just the preceding number.

Here's how to teach your child how to add 1 to numbers from 0 to 19. First, count a few numbers out loud, say to 5, and ask your child which number comes next. Your child will say 6. Now explain that this "next number" is the answer you get when you add 1 to the previous number, in this case 5.

Now ask your child: "What is one plus five?" Your child may not know the first time, so you may have to answer "six" for him or her. But keep asking your child different "1+" questions until your child gets used to the process.

You can also teach "1+" facts using objects. Place a group of objects—pennies, beads, or toys—in front of your child and ask him or her to count them (by moving them to a new location, not just by touching them). Write down the number counted. Now ask your child to physically place 1 additional object in the group. Next, tell your child to count the total number of objects including the new object. Write this new number down. Ask your child to compare the numbers and ask him or her why they are different. The answer: The bigger number includes 1 additional object. Explain that this is the same as "adding one" to the first number.

Next, draw a number line and show your child that adding 1 in this context means counting 1 step to the right on the line. Ask your child to add 1 to 5 using this line. (Your child should begin at the 5 tick mark and move 1 to the right, landing on the 6 tick mark.) Write the symbols for this process on a piece of paper, in this case $5 + 1 = 6$. Repeat the activity with other numbers, writing down each time $6 + 1 = 7$, $7 + 1 = 8$, $9 + 1 = 10$, and so on.

At this point it is easy to teach them what it means to add 0 to a number—you simply get back the original number! And you stay at the same place on the number line, without moving at all—or taking 0 steps. Write down the equations for various examples of adding 0, for instance, $0 + 1 = 1$, $0 + 2 = 2$, and $0 + 28 = 28$.

1.7 Commutative Rule: Order Doesn't Matter

Right away, with these first addition facts, introduce your child to the commutative rule for addition. This rule says it doesn't matter in which order you add 2 numbers. Either way, the answer is the same. Thus, $5 + 6 = 6 + 5 = 11$ and $4 + 3 = 3 + 4 = 7$. Most relevant to what your child knows so far is that $7 + 1 = 1 + 7 = 8$, and so on for all the +1 facts.

Give your child practice adding 1 to numbers in either order. So after your child knows $N + 1$ for all N from 0 to 11, ask what $1 + N$ is for each value of N from 0 to 11. If your child does not immediately respond correctly, provide practice with $1 + N$ and $N + 1$, mixing up the order, until the child has mastered the concept.

And continue practicing the commutative rule—which can be generally stated as $N + M = M + N$—with all new addition facts your child learns. Note for future reference that this rule applies to addition and multiplication, but not for subtraction and division.

1.8 Counting Backward and Subtracting 1

Next, teach your child to count backward by ones from 20 to 0. Because of the "rocket countdown" business, this is usually fun for children. Now ask your child to start with the number 20 and count backward just 1 unit, to the number 19. Explain that this is the same as subtracting 1 from 20 or "taking away" 1 from 20. Repeat this activity starting with other numbers, such as 15, 11, 3, asking the child to count backward by 1 unit. Each time, ask your child: "So what is fifteen take away one?" or "What is eleven minus one?" Then write down an equation showing the question and the answer separated by an equals sign. For example, $15 - 1 = 14$, $11 - 1 = 10$, and $3 - 1 = 2$. Practice this with various numbers until your child gets it. This introduces the concept of subtraction as an inverse operation to addition—going backward in counting as opposed to going forward.

1.9 Negative Numbers: Developing the Concept

Teach your child to relate the negative or minus (–) sign to counting backward from 0. Understanding negative numbers is a big hurdle for older children learning algebra, when these numbers are typically introduced, largely because the kids have for years thought of the minus sign only as an operation. Discussing negative numbers early on—as early as preschool, kindergarten or first grade—makes it much easier for children to handle them later. Here's a good way to continue your discussion of negative numbers, touched on above.

As before, draw a number line that shows negative as well as positive numbers. Ask your child what number comes before 0. He or she should answer "negative one." Now ask: "What do you get when you take one away from zero?" The answer should be the same. Repeat this line of questioning for other numbers until your child gets it.

Explain to your child that for all the negative numbers, –1, –2, –3, etcetera, the minus or negative sign shows that the number is to the left of 0 (or the opposite direction from the positive numbers), and that the number itself indicates how far it is from 0. If you think your child can handle it, you could now explain that –1 means the same thing as **0 – 1**, just as 1 (or +1) means the same thing as **0 + 1**. If your child is confused, don't worry. You can continue this discussion later.

An excellent way to enhance your child's understanding of negative numbers is to make up real-world stories that use them. For now, don't present any story *problems*; your goal is to simply illustrate negative numbers with real-world events that can be thought of as less than 0. For instance, suggest that if a person has neither money nor debt, he or she could be said to have 0 money. But if a person owes somebody money, that person could be said to have negative money. In addition, negative numbers are used to describe cold temperatures. Explain to your child that if it is very cold outside, the temperature drops below 0 to a temperature measured in negative degrees. You might think of other examples too.

I often try to make negative numbers fun with a little rhyme I made up based on the Dr. Seuss book *On Beyond Zebra*, which introduces fictitious letters that come after the letter Z. My version, called "On Beyond Zero," introduces real negative numbers that, of course, come before 0.

On Beyond Zero
Said Reginald Richard von Bostrom von Blount,
my very young friend who is learning to count,
"The nine is for nine pool balls in a diamond,
the eight is the eight ball—don't get behind him,
4's a quadruple, 3 is a trio, 2 is a couple, and 1 is a single.

"Though zero is for nothing, I know the amount,"
said Reginald Richard von Bostrom von Blount.
"So now I know everything anyone knows,
from highest to lowest,
from the infinite to the close,
because zero's as far as the whole numbers go."

Then he almost fell flat on his face on the floor, when I picked up the chalk and wrote 1 number more,
a number he never had dreamed of before. And I said:
"You can stop if you want with the zero,
because most people stop with the zero, but not me-o.

"In the places I've gone, there are things that I've sought
that I never could count, if I stopped with the nought.
I'm telling you this cause you're one of Jeanette's [or your child's] friends:
Negative numbers start where the whole numbers end.

"They start with the number negative one (–1);
it's the number I use when I owe you one."
At negative two, there's double the debt.
Maybe, just maybe I shouldn't have bet!
Unless you can guess what comes after that . . .

Of course, you may go on with the poem, beyond –2.

Section 2:
ADDITION

2.1 Counting by 2's, Adding 2

After counting by 1's, first forward, then backward, it's natural for children to learn to count by 2's. Usually, kids enjoy this. First, demonstrate what it means to count forward by 2's starting with 2—i.e. 2, 4, 6, 8, 10, 12, . . . 20—and then ask your child to repeat the same number sequence. After that, ask your child to count by 2's starting with 0. Next, show your child how to count by twos starting with 1: 1, 3, 5, 7, 9, . . . 19. (These latter two activities are rarely done, but are very important.)

Once your child has mastered counting forward by 2's, teach the child to add 2 to numbers from 0 to 18, or higher if you wish. These are the **N + 2** facts. They include **0 + 2 = 2, 4 + 2 = 6** and **1 + 2 = 3, 5 + 2 = 7**. Here's how to teach them:

First, count by 2's out loud, say to 6, and ask your child which number comes next. Your child will say "eight." Now explain that this "next number" is the answer you get when you add 2 to the previous number, in this case, 6. Now ask your child: "What is two plus six?" Your child may not know the first time, so you may have to answer "eight" for him or her. But keep asking your child different "2+" questions until your child gets used to the process.

An Excursion to Infinity

When my son Peter reached this point in his knowledge of arithmetic, I told him that "the numbers never end." We discussed infinity a lot, because Peter was fascinated with infinity. I encouraged his interest by telling him that lots of advanced math is concerned with infinities, that there are different sets of numbers (integers versus reals, for example) that are both infinitely large, but one infinity is bigger than the other. Of course, he did not understand this very well, but he found it interesting—more interesting than addition facts.

If your child is like Peter and is interested in the concept of infinity, you can chat about it early on in a low-key way, without expecting your child to really understand it. You can even illustrate the idea with a number line. Draw a number line and ask your child to make that line longer and longer. Now ask: "Do think there is a limit to how long you could make the line?" Your child will probably answer no, which is correct. (This answer assumes the line does not curve around in a circle, in which case there would be a limit to its length, but most children do not think of that possibility.)

This kind of exercise is useful if your child finds it fun, because such "cool" ideas may help him or her enjoy math. In addition, such early introductions provide a beneficial preview of mathematics to come that can speed later learning.

Continue teaching "2+" facts using objects. Assemble a group of objects—pennies, beads, or toys—and ask your child to count them. Write down the number counted. Ask your child to physically place 2 additional objects in the group, and then to count the total number of objects including the 2 new ones. Write this new number down. Ask your child to compare the numbers and ask him or her why they are different. The answer: The bigger number includes 2 additional objects. Explain that this is the same as "adding two" to the first number.

Draw a number line and show your child that adding 2 in this context means counting 2 steps to the right on the line. Ask your child to add 2 to 5 using this line. (Your child should begin at the 5 tick mark and move 2 steps to the right, landing on the 7 tick mark.) Write down the symbols for this process on a piece of paper, in this case **5 + 2 = 7**. Repeat the activity with other numbers, writing down each time **6 + 2 = 8, 7 + 2 = 9, 9 + 2 = 11**, and so on.

Then switch the order of the numbers to be added, so that the 2 comes first, for example: **2 + 6 = 8** or **2 + 11 = 13**, and ask your child to add 2 in these problems. Note that the answer is the same as when the 2 comes second in the problem. These are the **2 + N** facts. Make sure your child can mentally convert **2 + N** into **N + 2** and get the correct sum.

2.2 Even and Odd Numbers

Introduce the concept of even numbers by creating pairs from groups of objects. Again, find maybe 10 or 20 coins, blocks, or toys but place them in clusters of different sizes, some with an even number of objects and others with an odd number of objects. Then ask your child to group pairs of objects together from each cluster. Explain that even sets of objects are those where all the objects can be paired up, with no unpaired object remaining. Odd sets have an odd unpaired object remaining. Now ask your child which clusters have an odd number of objects and which have an even number. Finally, ask your child to count the number of objects in each cluster and then to say again whether that number is "even" or "odd."

Next write down all the numbers your child said were "even" in one column on a piece of paper, and the numbers your child said were "odd" in another column. Show this to your child. If the table isn't complete, add the missing numbers, and explain to your child that

- 2, 4, 6, etcetera are even numbers

- 1, 3, 5, etcetera are odd numbers

- Odd and even numbers alternate

- 0 must be an even number because of the alternation rule

- Counting by 2's starting with 0 or 2 generates only even numbers

- Counting by 2's starting with 1 generates only odd numbers

- Adding 2 to an even number gives you an even number

- Adding 2 to an odd number gives you an odd number

2.3 Addition Expanded: Other Numbers

To be sure your child understands the concept of addition, repeat the object and number-line exercises in lesson 2.1, but vary the amount to be added. For instance, to learn the meaning of **6 + 4**, have your child put 6 objects in a group on a table or floor and then add 4 to the group. Ask your child to count the total number of objects in the group now by moving them 1 at a time to a new place on the table or floor.

Go to the number line. Have your child start at 0 and count 6 steps to the right, ending up at the number 6. Then your child should move 4 steps to the right from 6, ending up at 10. Write the problem down on paper as well as saying it out loud. Repeat these kinds of exercises until your child gets the general idea—but do not use these exercises to teach the bulk of addition facts.

2.4 Adding 10 and 9

To teach your child to add 10 to all the numbers from 1 to 10, simply present examples of these problems both verbally and on paper and then test your child on them. Teach that **10 + 1 = 11, 10 + 2 = 12, 10 + 3 = 13 . . . 10 + 10 = 20**. Then teach **1 + 10, 2 + 10, 3 + 10, . . . 10 + 10**. Kids usually find these facts easy to learn.

Next, teach your child to add 9 to a number, the **9 + N** and **N + 9** facts, up to a sum of 19. This is easy once the child knows the **10 + N** facts, because all he or she has to do is think of adding 10 to the number, and then think of the number that comes before that sum or is 1 less than it. Explain this to your child and give him or her practice with adding 9 to various numbers both verbally and on paper. For each fact, ask: "What would be the answer if you were adding ten?" And then: "What is one less than that?" That will be the correct answer.

2.5 Adding Like Numbers

How many times have you a heard a 5-year-old say, "How much is two plus two?" or "How much is three plus three?" Or "Four plus four equals eight" or "Five plus five equals ten." For some reason, kids seem to glob on to adding like numbers. Young kids rarely recite facts such as **5 + 2 = 7** or **3 + 4 = 7**. It is almost as if kids believe that when they have learned to add all the like numbers—**0 + 0, 1 + 1, 2 + 2, 3 + 3, 4 + 4, 5 + 5, 6 + 6, 7 + 7, 8 + 8, 9 + 9**, and **10 + 10**—they will have learned something fundamental about the basic addition.

Amazingly, there is a lot of truth to this, because knowing these facts can easily lead to deriving many others using simple rules, as we shall see

---

Limitations of "Real-world" Demonstrations

Object and number line activities are an excellent way of teaching children the *concept* of addition. However, they are not a good way of teaching a child a large number of addition facts. Manipulating objects inserts a long delay while the child is counting, say, 4 pennies, then 3 pennies and finally 7 pennies, to come up with the answer for 4 + 3 = 7. During this delay, the link in the mind between the numbers being added and the sum gets weaker.

To efficiently learn addition facts, a child must get the answer quickly. That is encouraged by presenting problems and answers in verbal and written form, and by teaching a child simple, quick mathematical tricks as I show below. It's okay if your child has to think a bit to determine an answer, but it's important not to continually insert a long delay during the learning process. That will only impede learning.

---

below. But first, teach your child these like-number addition facts: **0 + 0 = 0, 1 + 1 = 2, . . . 10 + 10 = 20.** Some of these are repeats of facts they already know, but that just makes this learning more rewarding. Simply present the problems and answers verbally and in writing, and then give your child lots of written and oral practice problems. For example, ask: "What is five plus five?" and write: **5 + 5 = _____** . If your child is having problems, you can reinforce these facts with some practice with objects or number lines. But at this point, such activities begin to get cumbersome and tedious for many children, and are often unnecessary.

2.6 Adding Numbers That Are 2 Apart

Once your child has memorized the 11 like-number facts, 2 simple rules can provide answers to 10 more addition facts that have not yet been learned. One of them is noting that it is possible to create an equal sum from each of the like-number facts by adding 1 to one of the addends and subtracting 1 from the other. Take **5 + 5 = 10.** One less than 5 is 4, and 1 more than 5 is 6. So, teach your child to notice that **4 + 6** would also equal 10, and of course, the reverse: **6 + 4 = 10.** You can use this rule, which can be denoted as $N + N = (N - 1) + (N + 1)$, for each of the $N + N$ facts to teach your child 5 addition facts (10, if you include the equivalent reversed-order problems) he or she has not learned. They are:

$$2 + 2 = 1 + 3 = 4$$
$$4 + 4 = 3 + 5 = 8$$
$$5 + 5 = 4 + 6 = 10$$
$$6 + 6 = 5 + 7 = 12$$
$$7 + 7 = 6 + 8 = 14$$

Your child has already learned that $0 + 2 = 2$; $2 + 4 = 6$; $7 + 9 = 16$; $8 + 10 = 18$ and $9 + 11 = 20$. But go over these facts again, to reinforce your child's knowledge, and to show it is possible to get correct answers to these problems using this method too.

The second rule that uses the **N + N** facts is that adding 1 to either addend produces a sum that is 1 greater than the sum **N + N**. This idea can be represented as **N + (N + 1) = (N + N) + 1**. But in teaching this, use specific examples, not the letter N. For example, note that **6 + 7 = 6 + 6 + 1** (or one more than **6 + 6**) **= 12 + 1 = 13**. Demonstrate this for:

$$1 + 2 = 1 + 1 + 1 = 3$$
$$2 + 3 = 2 + 2 + 1 = 5$$
$$3 + 4 = 3 + 3 + 1 = 7$$

And so on, for every number up to 10. This yields 4 new addition facts, since your child already knows **0 + 1, 1 + 2, 2 + 3, 8 + 9**, and **9 + 10** from previous exercises. Again, though, it doesn't hurt to help your child relearn them using this method. Together, knowing the **N + N** facts and the 2 rules that use them teaches your child 15 more addition facts.

How many total addition facts has your child learned? He or she knows 11 "**N + 1**" facts, 10 "**N + 0**" facts, 9 new "**N + 2**" facts, 8 "**10 + N**" facts, 7 "**9 + N**" facts, and then the 15 we just learned from **N + N** and its associated rules. That makes a total of 60 facts, leaving only 6 basic addition facts left to learn.

2.7 The Final Addition Facts

The last unlearned facts are **6 + 3 = 9, 7 + 3 = 10, 7 + 4 = 11, 8 + 3 = 11, 8 + 4 = 12**, and **8 + 5 = 13**. You could just teach your child to memorize these, but I prefer using a more sophisticated method, because this method builds upon previous knowledge and helps children learn more about the workings of mathematics. Here's what I do.

First, I teach a child to count by 4's. 0, 4, 8, 12, 16, 20. Using that knowledge, the child readily learns **8 + 4 = 12** because counting by 4 from 8 reaches 12 as the next number. Then, I ask the child how he or she might derive **7 + 4** from the previous fact. If I get a blank stare, I say suggest that they notice what is the same and what is different about the problems. They should notice that the 4 is the same, but the 7 is 1 less than the 8. Thus, the sum **7 + 4** should be 1 less than **8 + 4**. I use the same procedure to teach **8 + 5**. The child should be encouraged to discover that the 8's are the same and the 5 is 1 more than the 4 in "**8 + 4**." Thus, **8 + 5** would be 1 more than **8 + 4**.

Now, teaching a child to count by 3's: 0, 3, 6, 9, and so on, will help him or her figure out the sum **6 + 3 = 9**. Then **7 + 3** is just 1 more than **6 + 3**.

If your child is good at math and has a very solid understanding of all the other addition facts, you can try yet another scheme, which has more steps but is interesting for any child who is ready for it. If your child is not extremely familiar with the other addition facts, however, don't try this. There will be too many mental steps involved and your child will lose track of the steps, since they are not well learned.

If you'd like to try, here's what to do: Tell your child to subtract 1 from 1 number and add 1 to the other number to get an equivalent problem that your child already knows. For **6 + 3**, your child would generate the problem **5 + 4**. If your child has already learned **5 + 4** so well that the answer comes automatically, this is an effective way to get the correct answer for **6 + 3** with only 1 intermediate step. Because this step is automatic for your child, with practice, your child will soon learn **6 + 3 = 9** as simply a fact on its own.

For the other 5 facts, your child can use the same trick. For instance:

$$7 + 3 = 6 + 4 = 10$$
$$7 + 4 = 6 + 5 = 11$$
$$8 + 3 = 9 + 2 = 11$$
$$8 + 4 = 9 + 3 = 12$$
$$8 + 5 = 9 + 4 = 13 \text{ or } 8 + 5 = 7 + 6 = 13$$

Notice how useful it has been for your child to know just a little bit of subtraction—how to subtract 1 from a number—in learning addition facts.

Lastly, be sure your child understands the equivalent sums to each of these 6 facts, using the commutative rule. For instance, your child should

Facts of N

Some people may notice I have not suggested that parents teach their child addition facts using the popular "facts of N approach." In this strategy, children systematically learn the different pairs of numbers that add up to the same larger number. For example, they would learn all the pairs of numbers that add up 10, or that add up to 11.

This approach seems logical, but it isn't optimal for learning addition. The problem is that the facts in each group (facts of 10, 11, and so on) are only similar in that they have the same sum or answer. This helps a child very little when he or she is presented with the problem: 8 + 3 = _____ . "To which group does this belong?" a child wonders. "Is it a fact of 9? 10? 11?" The question provides no clue. Only the answer reminds the child of how he or she learned the fact and, of course, the answer isn't given!

In subtraction, by contrast, the cue is in the question, because the largest number—which is what defines each group in the "facts of N" approach—is always part of

know both that **6 + 3 = 9** and that **3 + 6 = 9**, and so on for **3 + 7 = 10, 4 + 7 = 11, 3 + 8 = 11, 4 + 8 = 12**, and **5 + 8 = 13**.

Section 3:
SUBTRACTION

3.1 Subtracting 1 Revisited

To deepen your child's understanding of subtraction beyond the rocket countdown idea, give the child practice subtracting 1 by moving objects. To understand the meaning of **4 – 1**, for example, have your child put 4 objects in a group on a table or floor and then remove one of those and put it in another spot, called the "take-away" region. Then ask your child to count the number of objects remaining in the initial group by moving them one at a time to a third place on the table or floor.

Extend this concept to distance by drawing a number line on a piece of paper with tick marks labeled with the numbers 0 to 10. Have your child start at 0 and count 4 steps to the right, ending up on the number 4, of course. Then have your child move 1 step to the left from 4, ending up at 3.

the problem. For example, knowing the facts of 10 is great for solving 10-7. The 10 in the problem reminds a child to recall his or her facts of 10. Then the child finds the one that involves 7 as an addend, and supplies the other addend as the answer. Thus, I recommend waiting to teach the "facts of *N*" until your child has mastered addition facts and is ready to go on to subtraction.

What about using flash cards, rhymes, and songs to teach your child math? Nothing really wrong with them, but they are slower than the "relational mnemonic method" advocated in this chapter, because of the cognitive static problem explained earlier. Rhymes and songs work much better than flash cards, but they don't really deepen your child's appreciation of math, since the rhymes themselves are verbal not mathematical. So I recommend using memory aids that involve relevant arithmetic relations, because these produce a more complete understanding of arithmetic.

Now let's continue using such relational memory aids to teach your child subtraction beyond subtracting 1, which we discussed above.

Repeat these exercises with different starting numbers, to represent problems such as **5 – 1** and **10 – 1**.

3.2 Countdown by 2's, Subtracting 2

To teach your child to subtract 2 from any number from 2 to 20, teach a variation of the rocket countdown: the rocket countdown-by-2's, or counting backward by 2's. First teach this starting at the number 10 by counting out loud. When that's mastered, start at 20. Then, teach your child the same trick starting at 11, then 19.

Now start the rocket countdown from 10, ending at 6. Ask your child which number comes next. Your child should say "four." Explain that this "next number" is the answer you get when you subtract 2 from the previous number, in this case, 6. Now ask your child: "What is six minus two?" Your child may not know the first time, so you may have to answer "four" for him or her. But keep asking your child different "–2" questions until your child gets used to the process. For each problem, ask your child to think of the next number in the rocket countdown-by-2's.

Continue teaching minus-2 facts using objects. Collect a group of objects and ask your child to count them. Write down the number counted. Now ask your child to physically take away 2 objects from the group. Next tell your child to count the number of objects now without those 2 objects. Write this new number down. Ask your child why the 2 numbers are different. The answer: The smaller number is 2 objects less. Explain that this is the same as "subtracting two" from the first number.

Have your child collect various numbers of pennies or toys and take 2 of those pennies or toys away from the original set. Write down the problems represented by this exercise, such as **7 – 2 = 5** and **10 – 2 = 8**.

Next draw a number line and show your child that subtracting 2 in this context means counting 2 steps to the left on the line. Ask your child to solve **7 – 2 = 5** using this line. Your child should begin at the 7 tick mark and move 2 steps to the left, landing on the 5 tick mark. Write down the symbols for this process on a piece of paper, in this case **7 – 2 = 5**. Repeat the activity with other numbers, writing down the proper equations each time.

3.3 Subtracting Other Numbers

Vary the amount to be subtracted. For instance, to learn the meaning of **10 – 4**, have your child put 10 objects in a group on a table or floor and then remove 4 of those and put them in another spot, the take-away region. Then ask your child to count the number of objects remaining in the initial group by moving them one at a time to a third place on the table or floor.

Go to the number line. Have your child start at 0 and count 10 steps to the right, ending up at the number 10. Then your child should move 4 steps to the left from 10, ending up at 6.

Repeat these kinds of exercises until your child seems to fully understand the concept of subtraction. For each example problem, be sure to write it down on paper in addition to saying it out loud.

3.4 Subtraction and Negative Numbers, Part 1

Now, bring up negative numbers again, this time going a little beyond the basics outlined above. Here you will demonstrate negative answers to subtraction problems and compare subtraction with negative numbers.

Extend your number line to the left of 0 and mark off negative numbers to –20. Explain to your child that –20 is the same as **0 – 20**. This is easy to accept: Since 0 is "nothing," the 0 might as well not be there at all in this context. But if your child has any doubt, ask the child to subtract 20 from 0 by marching 20 steps to the left from 0. Repeat this process for other numbers. Explain, for example, that **0 − 5** is the same as −5, that **0 − 13** is the same as −13, and so on.

Using this number line, ask your child to solve the problem **3 − 7 =** ＿＿ by first moving 3 steps to the right from 0, landing at 3, and then 7 steps to the left from 3, to end up at −4. Repeat this exercise with lots of other subtraction problems that end up with negative numbers.

Also have your child solve **7 − 3 = 4** using the number line. Point out that the answer to this problem is the same as the answer to **3 − 7 = −4**, except that the negative sign is gone. Explain that this is true for other problems too. If you switch the order of the numbers in a subtraction problem such that the bigger number, instead of coming first, now comes second (and is the number being subtracted), the answer is the same except that it has a − sign in front of it. Provide many examples, writing down each problem on a piece of paper.

Now explain the concept of "absolute value." This is simply the value or amount of a number without any negative sign. It's also the distance from the 0 point on the number line, without indicating whether the direction is to the right or to the left. Thus, the absolute value of both 7 and −7 is 7. In symbols, this is written as $|7| = 7$ and $|-7| = 7$. Similarly, the absolute value of 13 equals the absolute value of −13, which equals 13, or $|13| = |-13| = 13$. More generally, $|N| = |-N| = N$, where N means any positive integer.

3.5 Subtraction and Negative Numbers, Part 2

Here's another fun way to help your child understand negative numbers. Get a set of cubes (or equivalent objects) in three colors, say red, white, and black. Tell your child that the white cube goes in the center, since it represents 0. The black cubes will go to the right of the white cube, since these represent positive numbers, with the number of cubes representing the value of the number. So 2 black cubes to the right of 0 represents 2, 5 black cubes represents 5 and so on. The red cubes are similarly used to represent negative numbers and belong to the left of the white cube.

Ask your child to solve various equations using these cubes. Start with, say, **7 − 4 = 3**. Your child should place 7 black cubes to the right of 0, then take 4 of them away, leaving 3 black cubes. Next, ask your child to solve exactly the same equation written this way: **−4 + 7 = 3**. The child should place 4 red cubes to the left of 0, and then place 7 black cubes to the right of 0. Removing 4 cubes from the left and the right sides (which cancel each other out) leaves 3 black cubes on the right.

This exercise shows your child that **7 − 4** and **−4 + 7** are just different ways of writing the same thing. Another way of writing **7 − 4** is **+7 − 4**. Show this to your child too, and note that the − in **7 − 4** can be thought of as either a subtraction operation or as combining "negative 4" with "positive 7." Provide other examples of subtraction problems that your child can represent using the blocks and write down the 2 equivalent equations in each case. Use both the "plus, minus" terminology and the "positive, negative" terminology frequently, pointing out that they mean the same thing.

Now, you can tell a story problem and let your child use the cubes to represent what you're saying. For example:

"Judy had no money, but today her mom gave her a weekly allowance of five dollars." Your child adds 5 black cubes to the right of the white cube.

"Judy went to the store to buy a game that cost seven dollars. The store owner said Judy could pay him five dollars now and owe him the remaining two dollars." Your child removes the 5 black cubes and puts 2 red cubes to the left of the white cube.

"Next week, Judy got her allowance . . ." Child adds 5 black cubes.

". . . and immediately went to the store to pay her debt." Child removes 2 red cubes and 2 black cubes.

There are 3 black cubes left. To prepare for the next story, tell your child that Judy spends these on a snack. Child removes the black cubes leaving just the white cube.

Now, in a variation of the above episode, tell your child:

"Judy liked the game so much that the next week, she decides to buy it as a birthday gift for a friend. After receiving her allowance, Judy talks her sister into loaning her the additional two dollars she needs." First, your child should add 5 black cubes to represent her allowance. Now tell your child to represent the additional money Judy got from her sister in black cubes. Your child adds 2 black cubes. However, since that money was not a gift, but a loan, it also must be recorded as a debt. Your child puts 2 red cubes on the left.

"Judy goes to the store and buys the game." Child removes 7 black cubes.

"Next week Judy gets her allowance again." Child adds 5 black cubes.

"Judy pays back her sister." Child removes 2 black and 2 red cubes.

In another episode, Judy might borrow money to set up a lemonade stand and repay it gradually, using the money she makes from selling lemonade. Say Judy borrows $10 to set up her lemonade stand. She makes $3 per day selling lemonade, but only pays back $1 of her debt each day because she needs the other $2 for new lemonade mix. Have your child keep track of the days, taking $1 off the debt each day, to figure out how many days it will take to pay off the debt.

Later, say that Judy's debt increases each week because the person she owes is charging her interest on the loan. Make this interest in whole-dollar amounts, say $1 a week, because your child does not know about fractions or percentages yet.

If you have other colors of blocks, you can have them denote 10 and –10, 100 and –100 for problems that involve larger numbers. Indeed, you could just increase the amounts for the problem above, to make them more realistic—say, a debt of $50, and $10 of daily revenues, with $5 going to pay back the debt. Do this only if your child seems ready. At some point, you could even switch from blocks to play money and your child could simply keep track of debts by writing them down. In this way, your child takes a small step toward learning to represent debt and negative numbers more abstractly.

3.6 Subtraction Facts

Once your child understands the concept of subtraction, teach him or her the basic subtraction facts. This is the point where we abandon toys, blocks and number lines and stick with numbers and written equations. The goal is to be able to quickly solve basic subtraction problems on paper without props.

As noted in our discussion of addition, teaching your child the pairs of numbers that add up to a single larger number—the "facts of N" approach—is an excellent way for your child to learn the basic subtraction facts. In this method, a child learns all the number pairs that add up to, say, 10, as a group.

First, show your child what the facts of 10 are by writing them down on a piece of paper like this:

$$5 + 5 = 10$$
$$6 + 4 = 10$$
$$7 + 3 = 10$$
$$8 + 2 = 10$$
$$9 + 1 = 10$$
$$10 + 0 = 10$$

Your child should already know these facts, but he or she will not have thought of them as a group before now. The child's mind will begin to associate or link together the sum 10 to a small set of number pairs that add up to that sum. Turn the paper over and ask your child to write down as many of the facts of ten as he or she can remember. Repeat this until the child can remember them all. Check that your child remembers that **6 + 4** is equivalent to **4 + 6** and similarly for the other facts of 10.

Once you've taught your child the facts of 10, write them down on a piece of paper in this form:

$$10 = 5 + 5$$
$$10 = 6 + 4$$
$$10 = 4 + 6$$
$$10 = 7 + 3$$
$$10 = 3 + 7$$

. . .

Now explain that all of these facts can be easily made into a subtraction problem, involving the big number (10). Give examples. If **10 = 3 + 7**, then **10 − 3 = 7**. Similarly, if **10 = 7 + 3**, then **10 − 7 = 3**. Ask your child to convert all these facts of 10 into subtraction problems.

Now, help your child solve a subtraction problem involving 10. Take **10 − 2 =** _____ . Explain to your child that the big number 10 means this involves facts of 10. This is the cue to scan through all the facts of 10 to find the one that involves a "2." Hmm. 2 plus what equals 10? Your child should think of 8. Walk your child through this process a couple of times with different examples. Then give your child subtraction problems involving the facts of 10, and let him or her try to solve them without help. Don't forget to mix up the order of the problems.

Next, teach your child another set of "facts of *N*," say, the facts of 9. These are: **4 + 5 = 9, 3 + 6 = 9, 2 + 7 = 9, 1 + 8 = 9**, and **9 + 0 = 9**.

Repeat the above activities that you did with the facts of 9. First write all the facts of 9 in the form:

9 = 3 + 6
9 = 6 + 3
9 = 2 + 7
9 = 7 + 2
. . .

Next have your child convert them all into subtraction problems and then give your child subtraction problems involving 9. This time, your child should catch on to each step more quickly.

Continue teaching your child the facts of *N* for the numbers 0 through 20. After the facts of 10 and 9, proceed to the facts 11, then 8, then 12, and so on. For each set of facts, repeat the activities above, skipping any steps your child doesn't need. After your child knows all the facts of *N*, test him or her with subtraction problems involving all of these facts in random order. Continue this practice until your child is very good at solving basic subtraction problems.

3.7 Introducing One Half—Numbers Only

In the following sidebar, and in the multiplication section, your child will need to know what it means to take half of a number. Teach this now. Gather a group of objects, say, 10, and write that number down on a piece of paper. Ask your child to divide that group into 2 groups of objects that are the same size. Explain that each of the smaller groups is one half of the larger group. Ask your child to count the number in each smaller group. He or she should count 5 objects. Write that number down and compare it to the total number of objects, or 10. State that the smaller number (5) is half of the larger number (10).

You might illustrate this using a number line, by dividing a line of a certain length in half and asking your child to count the lengths of the 2 halves that result. Or you could show your child the number that corresponds to the midpoint of a number line of a given length. That number is

Fun Facts About Facts of *N*

You can now teach your child some interesting rules about subtraction facts. First, teach your child how to generate all the facts of *N* from the middle fact, *H*, which is half of *N*. Write the first fact as $N = H + H$ using a numerical example. The next facts are generated by adding 1 to one of the addends and subtracting 1 from the other. (Algebraically, this is written as $N = (H + 1) + (H - 1)$, $N = (H + 2) + (H - 2)$, and so on.) So, for the facts of 10, ask your child, "What is half of ten?" The answer is 5.

So $10 = 5 + 5$, and $10 - 5 = 5$.

For the next fact, add 1 to one 5 and subtract 1 from the other 5 to get $10 = 6 + 4$. Therefore $10 - 6 = 4$ and $10 - 4 = 6$.

Now, repeat that process for the 6 and the 4 to get $10 = 7 + 3$. And of course, $10 - 7 = 3$ and $10 - 3 = 7$.

The next fact is $10 = 8 + 2$. Thus, $10 - 8 = 2$ and $10 - 2 = 8$.

Next is $10 = 9 + 1$ ($10 - 9 = 1$ and $10 - 1 = 9$) followed by $10 = 10 + 0$, (so $10 - 10 = 0$ and $10 - 0 = 10$).

half the number corresponding to the endpoint of the line. Repeat exercises with different numbers of objects and different line lengths until your child understands what it means to take half of a number. In each case, however, limit the numbers of objects and line lengths to even numbers. Your child does not yet know what it means to divide a single object or unit length in half.

Section 4:
MULTIPLICATION

4.1 Place Value

We introduced place value for numbers from 0 to 20 in teaching addition facts. Use the same methods to teach place value for numbers 0 to 100. This means adding the hundreds place, which you should explain is 10 tens or 100 ones. In addition to the verbal activities in the addition section, do activities in which you give your child various numbers of small items from 0 to 100, and have your child make as many groups of 10 as possible. Write that number in the tens place (unless there are 10 groups of 10, which

When the sum is odd, such as 11, teach your child to generate the middle fact by first finding the even number that comes before that sum, namely 10. Ask your child for the number that is half of that. The answer for 10 is 5. So 5 is one of the addends. Then ask your child to add 1 to that addend to generate the other addend. So $(5 + 1) + 5 = 11$ or $6 + 5 = 11$. Now your child can generate the other facts by adding 1 to one of the addends and subtracting 1 from the other addend, as above.

Another rule about these facts is that if the sum, N, is an even number (such as 0, 2, 4, 6, 8, 10, and so on), it has an odd number of facts. If you count facts such as $6 = 4 + 2$ as different from $6 = 2 + 4$, the total number of facts is equal to one more than the number, or $N + 1$. If you don't count equivalent facts separately, the number of facts is one more than half the number, or $\left(\frac{N}{2}\right) + 1$ or $H + 1$.

If N is an odd number, such as 9, it has an even number of facts. The number of facts is equal to either $N + 1$ or $\frac{(N+1)}{2}$ depending on whether or not you separately count each fact in which the addends are in a different order.

requires writing a 1 in the hundreds place and a 0 in the tens place). Then write the number of remaining single items in the ones place. If you wish, extend the concept of place value to the thousands place and ten thousands place, and even higher if your child seems interested. By third grade, many children will have been taught place value in school, so you may be able to skip through some of this lesson quickly.

4.2 Understanding Multiplication

As with addition and subtraction, the first step in teaching your child multiplication is to explain what multiplication means. Multiplying 2 numbers, M times N, means taking M sets of N things. For example, multiplying 2 times 3, written **2 x 3**, means taking 2 sets of 3 things. Explain this to your child using the following activity. First write the problem **2 x 3** on a piece of paper. Next, ask your child to create 2 separate groups of 3 objects on the table or floor. Then ask him or her to count all of these objects by moving them one by one to a separate place on the floor. Your child should end up with the number 6.

Now give your child a different problem, say, **4 x 5**. Write it down first, and then ask your child to create 4 groups, each of which contain 5 objects.

Then have your child count the objects one by one (by physically moving them, of course) to come up with the answer: 20. Keep repeating this exercise until your child seems to understand what to do, and can come up with the answer to any simple multiplication problem by collecting groups of objects.

You can also use the area of rectangles to illustrate the meaning of multiplication. For example, for **4 x 7**, have your child draw a 4-by-7 rectangle, draw interior parallel lines at the 1, 2, and 3 marks on one set of parallel sides and at the 1, 2, 3, 4, 5, and 6 marks on the other pair of parallel sides. Have your child note that this rectangle is made up of 4 groups of 7 boxes or 7 groups of 4 boxes, which total 28 boxes in all. Tell your child that 28 is the area covered by the rectangle. If the sides of the rectangle are equal, this is a special kind of rectangle called a square. The numbers that are areas of squares—1, 4, 9, 16, etc.—are called "square numbers." All squares are rectangles, but only some rectangles are squares. Test your child's knowledge of these facts.

4.3 Multiplication Is Commutative: $M \times N = N \times M$

Multiplication has a lot in common with addition. One of the similarities is that both multiplication and addition abide by the commutative rule. The commutative rule says it doesn't matter what order you multiply (or add) two numbers, the answer is the same. Thus, **2 x 3 = 3 x 2 = 6**, and **4 x 5 = 5 x 4 = 20**. More generally, **$M \times N = N \times M$**.

Let your child figure this out by experimenting with objects. Write down **2 x 3** and **3 x 2** on a piece of paper. First ask your child to collect 2 sets of 3 objects and then count the total, as he or she did above. Write down the answer (6). Next, have your child collect 3 sets of 2 objects, and once again count the total number of objects. It's 6, of course. Use other examples— say, **1 x 2 = 2 x 1, 4 x 5 = 5 x 4**—to show your child that this always works. Review the rectangle area example, where commutativity is very obvious.

4.4 Multiplying by 0, 1, and 2

First, teach your child the simple rules for multiplying by 0, 1, and 2. Here's what to do:

1. Explain that any number multiplied by 0 equals 0. For example, **0 x 3 = 0, 0 x 5 = 0, 0 x 105 = 0**. Test your child's ability to use this rule by asking him or her to solve various "times 0" problems on a piece

The Basic Multiplication Facts

Your child is now ready to learn the basic multiplication facts. The method I use to teach these is very similar to the one I used to teach addition facts. First, you will teach your child the simple rules for how to multiply by a single number or factor: 0, 1, 2, 9, 10, 5. Then, your child will memorize the multiplication facts where the factors are the same, for example, 3 x 3 = 9, 4 x 4 = 16, and so on. Next, you will teach your child rules for multiplying factors that are 1 apart or 2 apart, leaving just 5 basic multiplication facts to memorize or learn using simple rules.

of paper. This is such an easy rule that your child should catch on quickly.

2. Explain that any number times 1 is the number. For instance, **4 x 1 = 4** and **8 x 1 = 8**. Again, give your child a pencil-and-paper test to be sure he or she understands this simple rule, and that it applies to all the numbers.

3. Explain that any number times 2 equals the number added to itself. Thus,

1 x 2 = 1 + 1 = 2
2 x 2 = 2 + 2 = 4
2 x 3 = 3 + 3 = 6
2 x 4 = 4 + 4 = 8
2 x 5 = 5 + 5 = 10
2 x 6 = 6 + 6 = 12
. . .
2 x 10 = 10 + 10 = 20

Since your child has already learned to add like numbers such as **3 + 3, 4 + 4**, and **5 + 5**, learning the "2 times" facts shouldn't be difficult. Be sure your child can solve these facts up to **2 x 10**.

4.5 Counting by 10's and the 10 Times Facts

Next, teach your child to count by 10's to 100. The sequence goes 10, 20, 30, 40, 50, 60, 70, 80, 90, 100. Ask your child to write down these numbers as well as recite them out loud.

Now, teach your child how to multiply any number by 10 using this easy rule: Any number times 10 is that number with a 0 added to its right (in the "ones place"). Thus, **2 x 10 = 20, 3 x 10 = 30, 4 x 10 = 40, 5 x 10 = 50**, and so on up to **10 x 10 = 100**. Multiplying by 10 by adding this 0, in effect, promotes a number one place to the left, to the tens or hundreds place. Explain this to your child if you like.

4.6 Counting by 5's and the 5 Times Facts

Teach your child to count by 5's to 100, reciting 5, 10, 15, 20, and so on. Ask your child to write down these numbers as well as saying them out loud.

Now, teach your child to multiply any number by 5 using this rule: Any number times 5 equals half of that number times 10, or **$5 \times N = \left(\frac{1}{2}\right)(10 \times N)$**.

Teach   **2 x 5 = half of (2 x 10) = half of 20 = 10**
4 x 5 = half of (4 x 10) = half of 40 = 20
6 x 5 = half of (6 x 10) = half of 60 = 30
8 x 5 = half of (8 x 10) = half of 80 = 40
10 x 5 = half of (10 x 10) = half of 100 = 50.

Start with the even numbers—that is, multiplying 5 by an even number—because taking half of 40, 60, 80, and 100 is easy.

Next, help your child solve **3 x 5**. Using the above rule, **3 x 5** = half of **3 x 10** = half of 30. To divide 30 in half, point out that **30 = 20 + 10** and that half of 30 is half of 20 plus half of 10. Thus half of **30 = 10 + 5 = 15**.

Work through the problem **5 x 5**. By the above rule **5 x 5** equals half of **5 x 10** or half of 50. Since **50 = 40 + 10**, half of 50 = half of 40 plus half of 10. So half of **50 = 20 + 5 = 25**. Use this same procedure for **7 x 5** and **9 x 5**.

4.7 Multiplying by 9

Here is a great trick for teaching your child to multiply a number by 9. First take the number you are multiplying by 9—let's say 8—and subtract 1 from it. You get 7. This is the first part of the answer, the part that goes in the tens place. Now, subtract this number, 7, from 9. You get 2. This is the rest of the answer—the part that goes in the ones place. Thus **8 x 9 = 72**. Tell your child to note that the 7 and the 2 in the answer add up to 9.

Now, try this for another number, say 3. Write down the problem you are solving: **3 x 9**. Okay, first subtract 1 from 3. **3 − 1 = 2**. That is the tens place answer. Now subtract 2 from 9. **9 − 2 = 7**. So the answer to **3 x 9** is 27! Point out again that the 2 and the 7 in the answer add up to 9.

Repeat this procedure for all of the "9 times" facts: **1 x 9, 2 x 9, 3 x 9, 4 x 9, 5 x 9, 6 x 9, 7 x 9, 8 x 9, 9 x 9, 10 x 9**. In each case, the digits in the answer will add up to 9. The most general notation for this rule for multiplying **N x 9** is that the tens place of the product is **N − 1** and the ones place is 9 minus the number in the tens place. (This exact trick doesn't work for numbers higher than 10, so don't go beyond **10 x 9**. However, many of the bigger 9 times facts will have digits that add up to 9.)

4.8 Multiplying Like Numbers

Now teach your child to multiply a number times itself. As with the addition facts, children easily recognize the sameness of two numbers, or factors, being multiplied. It does not take long for them to memorize all the **N x N** facts: **3 x 3 = 9, 4 x 4 = 16, 5 x 5 = 25, 6 x 6 = 36, 7 x 7 = 49, 8 x 8 = 64, 9 x 9 = 81, 10 x 10 = 100**.

Point out that when multiplying two numbers that are the same, this is sometimes called "squaring" a number. So **3** squared **= 3 x 3 = 9**, **4** squared **= 4 x 4 = 16**, and so on.

At this point, spend several learning sessions testing your child's knowledge of the multiplication facts he or she has learned thus far. Provide a mixture of problems that involve multiplying by 0, 1, 2, 10, 9, 5, and like numbers. Don't tell your child which rule applies to each problem; see if he or she can figure it out. If not, provide hints. Give your child extra practice with any rules or facts he or she has forgotten. Once you are confident that your child has mastered these facts, proceed to lesson 4.9.

4.9 Multiplying Numbers That Are 1 Apart

Once your child knows how to multiply a number by itself, you can use a simple rule to teach him or her to multiply a number by a number that is 1 greater than it, such as **3 x 4, 4 x 5, 5 x 6, 6 x 7, 7 x 8**, and so on. Here's the rule: First multiply the number by itself. Then add the number.

For example:

$$3 \times 4 = 3 \times 3 + 3 = 9 + 3 = 12$$
$$4 \times 5 = 4 \times 4 + 4 = 16 + 4 = 20$$
$$5 \times 6 = 5 \times 5 + 5 = 25 + 5 = 30$$
$$6 \times 7 = 6 \times 6 + 6 = 36 + 6 = 42$$
$$7 \times 8 = 7 \times 7 + 7 = 49 + 7 = 56$$

If your child is not yet totally comfortable with addition, he or she may find this rule difficult to carry out. If so, here is an alternative way to learn to multiply numbers that are 1 apart. First of all, note that your child has already learned the facts **0 x 1, 1 x 2, 2 x 3, 4 x 5, 5 x 6, 8 x 9, and 9 x 10** using other rules. That leaves just **3 x 4, 6 x 7** and **7 x 8** left to learn. Note that **7 x 8** is the "hardest times fact" mentioned in the beginning of the chapter and for which I invented the silly memory trick or mnemonic, **56 = 7 x 8**, which is the sequence 5, 6, 7, 8 with the symbols removed. I also noted that, by luck, **12 = 3 x 4** is the sequence 1, 2, 3, 4 with the symbols removed. So this little trick covers 2 of the 3 remaining multiplication facts where the factors are 1 apart. This leaves only **6 x 7** to memorize or to learn by the rule explained above: **6 x 7 = 6 x 6 + 6 = 36 + 6 = 42**.

4.10 Multiplying Numbers That Are 2 Apart

Next, teach your child to multiply numbers that are two apart such as **2 x 4, 3 x 5, 4 x 6**, and so on. Explain how to do this using the following three simple steps:

1. Ask: What number lies in between the 2 numbers being multiplied? For **2 x 4**, the answer is 3.

2. Multiply that middle number times itself. **3 x 3 = 9**.

3. Subtract 1. **9 – 1 = 8**. That's the answer to **2 x 4**.

Here are other examples:

$$3 \times 5 = 4 \times 4 - 1 = 16 - 1 = 15$$
$$4 \times 6 = 5 \times 5 - 1 = 25 - 1 = 24$$
$$5 \times 7 = 6 \times 6 - 1 = 36 - 1 = 35$$
$$6 \times 8 = 7 \times 7 - 1 = 49 - 1 = 48$$
$$7 \times 9 = 8 \times 8 - 1 = 64 - 1 = 63$$

More generally, the rule for multiplying numbers that are two apart is to first square the number in the middle and then subtract 1, or **(N − 1) x (N + 1) = N x N − 1**. Give your child lots of paper and pencil practice with this rule. Eventually, he or she will simply know the answers, but this may take some time.

4.11 The Final Multiplication Facts

At this point there are only 5 times facts to learn: **6 x 3 = 18, 7 x 3 = 21, 7 x 4 = 28, 8 x 3 = 24, 8 x 4 = 32**. If your child knows how to count by threes—if not, you may want to teach him or her to do so now—he or she would easily learn three of the above five facts: **6 x 3 = 18, 7 x 3 = 21**, and **8 x 3 = 24**. Simply tell your child to count by 3's for 6 steps for the first problem: 3, 6, 9, 12, 15, **18**. For the second problem, your child would count by 3's for 7 steps: 3, 6, 9, 12, 15, 18, **21**. For the third problem, your child would count by 3's for 8 steps: 3, 6, 9, 12, 15, 18, 21, **24**.

Alternatively your child could learn these 3 facts by piggybacking knowledge of one of 2 other facts: **5 x 3 = 15** or **9 x 3 = 27**. To **5 x 3 = 15** your child would add 3's. Adding one 3 would yield an answer for **6 x 3**; adding two 3's would solve **7 x 3**, and adding three 3's would solve **8 x 3**. An equivalent method would be to teach your child to subtract 1, 2, or 3 sets of 3 from the answer of **9 x 3 = 27**.

Your child can simply memorize the last 2 facts—**7 x 4 = 28** and **8 x 4 = 32**—or could derive them using a rule that uses 2 known times facts. For **7 x 4**, tell your child to use the fact **7 x 2 = 14**. Because 4 is 2 times 2, **7 x 4 = 2** times **7 x 2**. So **7 x 4 = 2 x (7 x 2) = 2 x 14 = 28**. For **8 x 4**, your child should use the fact **8 x 8 = 64**. Since 4 is half of 8, **8 x 4** equals half of 64, which is 32.

These rules can also be used to figure out the other 3 facts in this set too, if you wish to use them. For example, **6 x 3 = 2 (3 x 3) = 2 x 9 = 18**. That is, since **3 x 3 = 9, 6 x 3** is 2 times 9 or 18. For **7 x 3**, your child would use knowledge of **7 x 6 = 42**. Since 3 is half of 6, **7 x 3** would be half of 42 or 21.

5.1 Dividing by 2 and 1

To teach your child the meaning of division, start with a simple problem, say, **4 ÷ 2**. Write the problem and tell your child that this means dividing four of something into 2 equal parts. To illustrate this, ask your child to collect 4 objects and then to divide those objects into 2 equal groups. Now ask your child to count the number in each group. The number in each group is 2, and that is the answer! Write down the problem you just solved on a piece of paper: **4 ÷ 2 = 2**. Point out that this is the same as dividing the number 4 in half, as you taught your child above.

Repeat this exercise with other even numbers of objects, asking your child to divide each group of objects into two parts. Each time, write down the problem as your child solves it. For example, **6 ÷ 2 = 3, 8 ÷ 2 = 4, 10 ÷ 2 = 5**.

Teach your child another way to think about dividing by 2. Give the child a number of objects, say 8, and ask him or her to make as many groups of 2 with those objects as possible. The problem is still the total number of objects—say 8—divided by 2, or **8 ÷ 2**. But the answer is the number of groups, rather than the number of objects in each group. Have your child divide various numbers by 2 using both methods to show that both yield the same answer.

Next, ask your child what it might mean to divide a group of objects by 1. If he or she doesn't know, explain that it means to divide the group into 1 part. What happens when you do that? You get back the whole group— or the same number you started with. Write down examples—**4 ÷ 1 = 4, 7 ÷ 1 = 7, 10 ÷ 1 = 10**—and illustrate this idea with objects if your child wants you to.

Also explain to your child that you can't divide 1 or more objects into 0 groups because there is no group for objects to be in. Tell your child that while he or she might think **0 ÷ 0 = 0** makes sense, mathematicians have found it's best to follow the general rule that "You can't divide by 0."

5.2 Dividing by Other Numbers

To expand your child's understanding of division, illustrate other problems with objects, such as **10 ÷ 5**. Tell your child to collect 10 objects and divide them into 5 equal groups. This may take more experimenting, but your child should eventually come up with 5 groups of 2. The number in each group is the answer: 2. Write down **10 ÷ 5 = 2**. Then tell your child to divide a number, such as 10, into groups of 5 objects and find the answer by counting the number of groups. Point out that the answer to the problem is 2 either way.

Repeat these exercises with other numbers, until your child seems to understand the concept of division. Each time, write down the problem your child solved. However, do not belabor this exercise after your child gets the general idea. Explain that this is not the way to do division problems, since with large numbers it becomes *very* cumbersome. It is just a way of understanding what we mean by division.

A better way to understand division for the sake of solving division problems is to relate division to multiplication. Explain that dividing one number by another, say **10 ÷ 5**, is the same as asking: What number when multiplied by 5 gives you 10? And write that question down mathematically as follows: **5 x ＿＿ = 10**. If your child knows the multiplication facts well, he or she should immediately know the answer: 2.

Write down other division questions, say, **12 ÷ 3, 16 ÷ 4, 18 ÷ 2, 3 ÷ 3**. Each time, ask your child the same question. For instance, what number when multiplied by 3 gives you 12? If it helps your child, have the child write this question mathematically as **3 x ＿＿ = 12**. Repeat this line of questioning for every problem you pose until your child can pose the question himself or herself.

Explain to your child that division is the inverse operation for multiplication just the way subtraction is the inverse operation for addition.

5.3 Basic Division Facts

As the previous section implies, your child should find learning basic division facts easy, as long as he or she has a solid grasp of the multiplication facts—that is, he or she can quickly and automatically recall all the basic multiplication facts without using rules. Indeed, you should not teach your child the basic division facts until he or she has completely mastered the multiplication facts. But once that has happened, your child should be able to answer any basic division fact without further learning.

All that is necessary is to explain the relationship between division and multiplication, as you did above, and then give your child pencil-and-paper practice with various division problems to be sure the simple relationship is mastered. You should provide problems that involve dividing various larger numbers by 1, 2, 3, 4, 5, 6, 7, 8, 9, and 10. At this point, stick to dividing a larger number by a smaller number. We will address the reverse, fractions, later.

Why should division be so easy? Once your child knows the basic multiplication facts by heart, the facts are stored in the brain's wiring as connections between various ideas, or "chunks." These ideas can be numbers like 1, 2, and 12; operations like multiplication; and relations such as equals. The ideas can also be various sizes. They can be a single number or sign or they can express relationships between numbers and operations.

For every multiplication fact your child knows by heart, such as **3 x 4 = 12**, there is wiring in the brain representing the whole fact: **3 x 4 = 12**, and the smaller ideas: **3**, **x**, **4**, **=**, **12**, and **3 x 4**. All of these facts that go together are wired together in the brain.

In division, your child makes use of the same brain connections. The cues in the problem are different—they are the product, say, 12, and one of the factors, say, 3—but these numbers are still connected to the number 4 as well as × and =. The task is to provide the other factor (4). Although × is not explicitly present in the problem, once your child learns that division is the inverse of multiplication, the ÷ cue will activate the multiplication "chunk"—and thus all the appropriate connections. So your child easily comes up with the answer (4).

Indeed, using these connections to solve a division problem is in some ways easier than using them to solve a multiplication problem. That's because knowing the product, which is the first number in a division problem, is more informative than knowing the factors in a multiplication problem. Each factor in the set of 121 basic multiplication facts is associated with 11 different products. By contrast, each product—except for 0—is associated with only 1 or 2 pairs of factors. Thus, knowing a product points to fewer possible answers.

If your child has not learned his or her multiplication facts well enough to solve division problems quickly and accurately, give the child more practice with these facts in conjunction with the corresponding division facts.

You *can* teach "counting by *N*'s" as a way of solving dividing by *N* problems, but this is a very slow way of solving division problems compared to the method I describe here.

MOVING ON

At this point, your child knows how to add, subtract, multiply, and divide single-digit numbers, but does not know how to perform these operations with most two-digit, three-digit, or multidigit numbers. Your child will need to know how to do arithmetic with bigger numbers to successfully complete the exercises in the following chapters, so please teach your child these procedures now, using a textbook to guide you if necessary. Start simply, with addition problems that don't involve carrying, and then teach your child to carry. Similarly, start with subtraction problems that don't involve borrowing before teaching borrowing. In teaching long multiplication and long division, begin with single-digit factors and divisors before moving to bigger numbers.

Chapter 7

Basic Story Problems

Take this problem: Jim had five marbles in his pocket, found two more on his way to school and put them in the same pocket. How many marbles does Jim have in his pocket now?

Of course, this requires solving the simple addition problem **5 + 2 = _____** . Your child can undoubtedly solve this problem written in this way. The difficulty is that the problem isn't written this way. So your child may have no idea that this is the arithmetic called for by this story about Jim and his marbles. To solve such a problem, your child must first translate the English words and sentences into the language of math by writing a mathematical equation he or she knows how to solve. And there's the rub.

Kids don't automatically know how to do this.

Unfortunately, many teachers don't teach them either. They leave students to figure out how to do this translation on their own and do not give explicit instruction on the translation process itself. Teachers that do instruct students on translating from English to math often do an incomplete job. Meanwhile, the translation step is extremely difficult to intuit—and indeed only the most able students succeed in figuring it out on their own, or with minimal help. The rest simply never learn to solve story problems.

This chapter will prevent this from happening to your child by eliminating the most important reason that kids have trouble with story problems: inability to translate from English to math. It explains how to do this translation for a variety of English words and mathematical symbols and provides sample problems focusing on just the translation step of story problems. After that, your child will apply his or her translation skills to story problems, which involve a combination of translation and computation.

Section 1:
THE LANGUAGE OF MATHEMATICS

1.1 The Nature of the Problem

Tell your child the following story: "Julie went to the market and spent forty-two dollars. The trip took her two hours. Julie's dad paid her back and gave her a dollar for every ten minutes she spent on her shopping trip."

Now ask: "How much money did Julie's dad give her?"

Your child will undoubtedly not know. Explain that this is a hard problem and you will help him or her solve it by first teaching the child to translate the words of the problem into mathematical symbols. That will create a math problem that the child can solve.

Although knowledge of English is helpful in understanding the mathematical meaning of each English word, phrase, and statement in a story problem, it is far from sufficient. The vocabulary and grammar of mathematics is different from that of English. Math uses a subset of the words in a spoken language like English, and gives those words more precise mathematical meanings. Mathematics also imposes a new grammar on English phrases and sentences. Introduce your child to mathematical grammar as you would English grammar—by explaining the parts of mathematical speech described below.

1.2 Nouns

First, teach your child to translate the English names for whole numbers into the symbolic names used in mathematics. In the above problem, ask your child how many numbers he or she can find mentioned in the problem. He or she should immediately find "forty-two," which he or she should translate as 42. But also coax the child to translate "a dollar" into 1, "two hours" into 2, and "ten minutes" into 10. Ask the child to write those numbers on a piece of paper.

Explain that other problems may require similar translations such as translating "zero" into 0, "seven" into 7, or "two hundred fifty-seven" as 257, though in most story problems, large numbers such as 257 are already written symbolically as "257," making translation unnecessary.

To solve the above problem, your child needs to know that a dollar is $1 is equal to 100¢ and that an hour is 60 minutes. If your child doesn't understand these concepts, take the time to explain them now.

This first level of translation involves what I call the nouns of the problem. Mathematically, these are known as "expressions," entities with numerical values. These values may be natural or whole numbers, integers, fractions, or real numbers. For now, we'll keep the discussion limited to whole numbers, since these are what your child knows. Give your child practice translating words representing simple expressions into their numerical entities.

For example, ask the child to translate each of these words into numbers by writing the numbers down on a piece of paper:

Fifty-six (56)

Two dollars ($2 or 200¢)

A dollar ($1 or 100¢)

Two hours (2 hours or 120 minutes)

Seven pounds (7)

Ten yards (10)

Give your child numerous other examples, involving hours, days, dollars, whole numbers of objects, distances, volumes, weights, and other quantities. Provide practice problems until your child finds all the exercises easy.

1.3 Basic Verbs

The next step is translating English phrases into more complex expressions. These combine the nouns, numbers in this case, with verbs. Mathematical verbs are known as arithmetic "operations," such as addition (+), subtraction (−), multiplication (×), or division (÷ or /). Tell your child that these basic operations go in between numbers, as in **23 + 46**, **18 − 5**, **91 × 6**, and **112 ÷ 7**. Give your child practice translation problems that involve 2 simple numbers. At first, just use words that obviously mean add, subtract, multiply, and divide. For instance, ask the child to write "seven plus six," "twenty-two minus eleven," "sixty-two times three," "twelve divided by four."

1.4 Translating Addition

Now introduce a greater vocabulary. Teach your child to recognize other key words and phrases that signal the basic operations of addition, subtraction, multiplication, and division. Start with addition.

Key words or phases that mean addition in story problems include: *sum, and, add, plus, total, in all, altogether,* and *more.* Write these down on a piece of paper for your child and ask the child to copy them.

Explain that a story problem could imply addition without using any of these key words. For example, if John has 14 marbles and *finds, wins, buys, receives* or *gets,* 6 marbles, addition is implied, especially if the problem then asks: How many marbles does John have *in all?*

Ask your child to translate this problem. He or she should write **14 + 6**. In our example problem, Julie's dad is giving her $42 and some money for her effort. Ask your child to translate this idea. He or she should come up with **42 + ＿＿**.

Make up additional translation problems using the above words. You

---

Algebra Nouns

There is another kind of noun your child will learn about in algebra. Unknown numerical quantities, or simply "unknowns." Unknowns are typically represented by letters; finding the numerical value of these letters often provides either the answer to the problem or a quantity useful in determining the answer. You may want to introduce the idea of these letters being a new kind of noun as a preview to algebraic story problems.

---

can get ideas from addition story problems in math books. Just take phrases from the problems and ask your child to translate them, always writing the translation on a piece of paper.

1.5 Translating Subtraction

Key words and phrases indicating subtraction include: *minus*, *subtract . . . from*, *take away*, *take away . . . from*, *difference*, *less*, and *more*. Subtraction may also be implied by a wide range of verbs such as *lose*, *drop*, *sell*, *give*, *transfer away from*, *leave*, *go away*, and so on. Write down all these subtraction words and ask your child to copy them. Next give your child translation problems involving subtraction such as:

Suzy had 5 pennies and lost 3 of them. Translation: **5 – 3**.

Meg has 27 marbles, which is 4 more than Phil has. How many marbles does Phil have? Translation: **27 – 4**.

There were 22 people at Sam's party. Five of them left. How many were still at the party? Translation: **22 – 5**.

1.6 Translating Multiplication

Key words and phrases indicating multiplication include: *times*, *multiply*, *for every*, *of* (as in two thirds of 15), *product*, *twice*, *thrice*, *doubled*, *tripled*, and so on. Tell your child that *twice* means 2 times some quantity, not just 2, that *thrice* means 3 times something, not just 3, and so on. Similarly, doubled means 2 times a quantity, tripled 3 times, and so on. Other types of things that come in common bundles such as a *dozen* (12), a *week* (7 days) can also imply multiplication if the answer is required in smaller units. For instance, "dozen" means to multiply by 12 when the answer requires finding the total number of objects. If one has to translate weeks into days, one must multiply by 7.

Write down each of these words and ask your child what they mean. He or she should write **x** or 2 **x** or 3 **x**, or whatever is appropriate.

Ask your child to translate:

"Sam has twice as many marbles as Jim. Jim has two marbles." Translation: **2 x 2**.

"Jim started out with ten butterflies in his box, but the number of insects had multiplied by four. How many butterflies were in Jim's box?" Translation: **10 x 4**.

"Melvin had three dozen eggs." Translation: **12 x 3**.

In our example problem, your child would need to recognize the words *for every* as suggesting the need to multiply a dollar or $1 by the number of 10-minute periods Julie spent at the market. Thus, the translation should be: $1 **x** (number of 10-minute periods). Simply explain this to your child. It is unlikely that he or she could figure this out.

1.7 Translating Division

Key words and phrases indicating division include: *divide, divided by, split, quotient, half, quarter, third, percent,* and *percentage*. Introduce your child to these words, but do not test the child on words that involve percentages and fractions until the child has been introduced to those concepts.

There are a lot of subtle indications of division too. Give your child numerous translation problems invoking the above words. For example,

"Sam's three friends split twelve pieces of candy evenly between them." Translation: **12 ÷ 3**.

"Ashley, Mary, Jose, and Flint found twenty dollars and wanted to fairly divide the loot between them." Translation **$20 ÷ 4**.

"Ginger opened a can of six sardines and wanted to create two equal portions for herself and her brother." Translation: **6 ÷ 2**.

In the example problem, explain to your child that he or she must determine how many 10-minute periods Julie spent at the market. To determine that, explain to your child that he or she has to divide Julie's time into 10-minute periods. Point out that Julie spent 2 hours at the market. Ask your child to write a mathematical expression to determine how many minutes that is. (Answer: **2 x 60 = 120** minutes.) Now ask: "How many 10-minute periods can that be divided into?" The answer is **120 ÷ 10** or 12 ten-minute periods.

1.8 Relations

Relations relate two expressions as equal or unequal in some way. By far the most common relations in K–12 math are =, <, >, ≤, ≥, and ≠, which are typically signaled in English by: *is or equals, less than, greater than, less than or equal to, greater than or equal to,* and *not equal to.*

Many children have trouble remembering which symbol, < or >, means less than and which means greater than. To help your child remember which is which, tell him or her this memory trick: The smaller pointy end points to the number that is smaller and the larger open end points to the number that is bigger. The signs are read from left to right. So if the pointy end is on the left, the number or expression on the left is *less than* that on the right, if the large open end is on the left, the number or expression on the left is *greater than* the one on the right.

Ask your child to write the relation for "equals." Then, tell him or her to write the relations, in turn, for "is," "greater than," "greater than or equals," "less than," and "less than or equals." Mix up the order of these terms to be sure your child can recognize them in any order. Go in the other direction also: Present each symbol and ask your child to translate it into English. Continue with this translation test until your child can rapidly and accurately translate between these phrases and symbols.

1.9 Statements

Statements are like sentences. They tie all the parts of speech together. A statement in ordinary arithmetic is a relation between two expressions. Statements may be equations or inequalities. Examples include:

$$5 + 2 = 7$$
$$6 < 5 + 2$$
$$a \times b = b \times a$$
$$a(b + c) = ab + ac$$
$$7 \leq 5 + 2$$
$$X < 0$$
$$X - 3 > 8.$$

To be sure your child understands what a statement is, ask him or her to make up any number of statements and write them down on a piece of paper. If your child writes down a numerical statement that is false, say,

Building Complex Statements

So far, you have taught your child about fairly simple expressions and statements. Explain that expressions, the nouns, can be more complicated. They are not always just a single number, like 21. They can also be sets of numbers such as 3 x 6 or even 54 – (3 x 6). Note that parentheses are sometimes used to indicate the order in which operations are to be performed in complex expressions. For example, 54 – (3 x 6) = 54 – 18 = 36. By contrast, (54 – 3) x 6 = 51 x 6 = 306. We explore this in more detail in chapter 9. For now, ask your child to generate complex expressions using numbers and various combinations of numbers.

If you wish, introduce your child to complex expressions that include unknowns, represented by letters, which he or she will encounter in algebra. For instance, 3x is an expression, as is the more complex (3x – 5) or the entire, more complicated 4 (3x – 5) + 6x.

Explain that the more complicated statement 4 (3x – 5) + 6x < 21 is composed of the relation, <, which holds between two expressions 4(3x – 5) + 6x and 21. Have your child make up more complicated expressions and statements using combinations of letters and numbers. For each expression, ask him or her which symbols are unknowns. (He or she should point to the letters in the statement or expression.)

5 + 3 < 7, explain that as with spoken sentences, mathematical statements can be false. However, tell your child to always assume that a statement in a math problem is true unless there is a strong reason to believe otherwise.

Section 2:
BASIC STORY PROBLEMS

2.1 Addition Story Problems

Give your child practice using the above parts of mathematical speech in simple story problems. Start with one involving addition like this one: "Jordan picked five apples. Pierre gave him two more. How many apples does Jordan have now?"

Ask your child to write down all the nouns, which are all the numbers in this problem. He or she should write:

5

2

Next, help your child include the verbs, or the operations. Since Pierre "gave" Jordan 2 apples, that means that 2 should be added to the amount that Jordan already had, which is 5. Ask your child to write an equation to represent that. Your child should write **2 + 5 = _____** . Ask your child to solve that equation to find the answer. Be sure the child frames the answer as both a number and in terms of apples.

One good way to help your child solve simple story problems is to "act them out," using objects or pictures as problem-solving aids. Take the problem "Jill has five butterflies in her insect collection. On Saturday, she catches four new ones. How many does she have now?" Your child can use beads for butterflies, putting 5 in a box to represent Jill's collection, then adding 4 more beads to the box, and finally counting the total. Or he or she could write 5 *B*'s in a box drawn on a piece of paper, then write 4 more *B*'s in the box, and, finally, count up all the *B*'s.

Make up more simple addition problems like this or glean examples from a textbook until your child can easily solve these problems.

2.2 Subtraction Story Problems

Mix in some problems that involve subtraction, like this one:

"Samantha found ten pennies and put them in her pockets. One pocket had a hole in it and four of the pennies dropped out. How many pennies did Samantha have left?"

Your child should first write the nouns:

10

4

Next, move to the verbs. "Found" indicates addition, so ask your child to write +10.

The words "dropped out" suggest that the pennies were lost, indicating subtraction. So ask your child to write – 4.

Tell your child to combine those 2 numbers into a statement:
10 – 4 = _____ .

You child should now solve this simple equation and answer the question the problem posed. Again, give your child practice with many types of simple subtraction problems.

2.3 Multiplication Story Problems

When your child is ready, demonstrate some simple story problems that involve multiplication such as: "Amy bought a dozen eggs at the store. Robert bought twice as many eggs as Amy did. How many eggs did Robert buy?"

First, your child should write the nouns. The only noun is in the first sentence: 1 dozen, or 12, for the number of eggs Amy bought. If your child writes 1 for the noun, ask your child to translate this into a number of eggs using the rule for a dozen explained above. He or she should write **1 x 12 = 12** eggs.

In finding the verbs, your child might note that the word *bought* in the first sentence suggests addition. This is fine. Encourage the child to represent that as +12. However, that piece of information does not really help us solve the problem. Help your child focus on the words *twice as many* and ask the child to translate those. He or she should say "two times something" and write **2 x ____**. What is that something? The number of eggs Amy bought—which we know to be 12.

Instruct your child to translate this. He or she should write: **2 x 12 = ____**. Your child should conclude that Robert bought 24 eggs.

2.4 Division Story Problems

Next, introduce a division story problem such as this: "Denise wanted to swim seven miles before her next race. She had two weeks until the race but she only wanted to swim every other day. How many miles does she have to swim per day, if she swims the same distance each time?"

The nouns:

7 miles
2 weeks, which your child should translate into 14 days

Hint that this is two division problems in one. First, ask your child to write an expression to determine the number of workouts she will swim in the 14 days. (If your child is stuck, hint that Denise swims only half of those days.) The correct expression is: **14 ÷ 2**. So Denise swims on 7 days.

Second, ask your child to write an expression showing how many miles Denise must swim *per* day. The answer is **7 ÷ 7 = _____** , or **7 (miles) ÷ 7 (days)**. Solving that expression yields 1 mile per day.

Move on to a story problem that involves a combination of addition and division. Here is one example: "Basil bought a box of forty donuts and wanted to split them evenly among himself and nine co-workers. How many donuts does each person get?"

Writing the nouns yields:

40
1 (for himself)
9

Adding the verbs, we start out with +40 donuts since "bought" indicates addition. Ask your child to translate the words "split evenly." He or she should write ÷. Now ask your child to translate "himself and nine co-workers." Since "and" indicates addition, your child should write: **9 + 1**.

Translating the entire story problem thus yields the statement:

+40 ÷ (9 + 1)

Remind your child that the parentheses indicate that 9 and 1 are added first, before doing the division. Explain that it's important to do the addition first in this problem to determine the number of people among whom the donuts must be divided.

Solving this problem yields **40 ÷ 10 = 4**. Each person gets 4 donuts.

Finally, ask your child to create a statement from our example problem in lesson 1.1. Here's the problem again: "Julie went to the market and spent forty-two dollars. The trip took her two hours. Julie's dad paid her back and gave her a dollar for every ten minutes she spent on her shopping trip. How much money did Julie's dad give her?"

In lesson 1.7, you determined that Julie's shopping trip took 12 ten-minute periods, so the correct equation is:

$$\$42 + \$1 \times 12 = \$ \text{ Julie's dad gave her}$$
$$= \$42 + \$12$$
$$= \$54$$

Julie's dad gave her $54.

Give your child many more examples, culling them from workbooks and textbooks. When your child masters problems involving one operation, such as only division or only multiplication, move on to problems with several parts and that involve combinations of operations. The more different problems your child solves, the better he or she will become at solving story problems.

Story problems are complex. But if you are aware of all the skills your child needs to solve these problems and help your child learn them, your child will master this difficult aspect of mathematics.

Chapter 8

Fractions

Even preschoolers can be introduced to the concept of fractions, which can be illustrated as simply as splitting a cookie into two equal parts and noting that the cookie has been broken into halves. Using the problems and activities in this chapter, your child's idea of a fraction will grow to include halves of other things, and to encompass a variety of fractions, their written representations, and their relationships to other mathematical ideas such as division. Your child will also become good at manipulating fractions and using them to solve problems.

As with basic arithmetic concepts, fractions are best taught initially through concrete examples, but soon more abstract representations of, and rules for, understanding and manipulating fractions should replace such examples. In some cases, there are no good ways of illustrating a new aspect or use of fractions using worldly objects or pictures; in these cases, I emphasize abstract explanations where necessary.

You can start this chapter with a child as young as 4, but not before the child knows how to count whole numbers and objects from 0 to 10, can write these numbers, and understands the 0–10 number line. Going beyond the most basic activities in this chapter requires that your child know the basic arithmetic facts and be proficient in adding, subtracting, multiplying, and dividing larger numbers by hand, with a calculator, or ideally both.

Section 1:
PROPER FRACTIONS

1.1 One half

Proper fractions are fractions with values less than 1. The simplest example is one half, so begin by illustrating that idea using an object, such as a cookie. Here's what to do.

Give your child a whole cookie, describing it as a "whole cookie." Next, give the child half of a cookie, describing it as a "half cookie." Do the same with a whole glass of milk and a half glass of milk. Repeat the exercise with various other objects and substances—say, pieces of paper, bowls of soup (full versus half full), pencils (short versus twice as long). Using a variety of examples will help your child understand that half of something is an abstract concept, not tied to any particular object or substance.

The exact phrases you use are also very important for developing your child's abstract understanding of fractions. If your child is young, *half* and *whole* are probably new words and somewhat new concepts, though your child has probably already learned something about parts and wholes from exploring the world. Be sure to start simply, using *half* and *whole* as adjectives for a cookie, cracker, or glass of milk. "Whole cookie" versus "half cookie" is not much different from "large cookie" versus "small cookie," and the physical difference is obvious to small children.

Once your child gets that idea, slip in the slightly more complex terms "one half" and "one whole." Without saying you are doing so, replace the phrase "half cookie," with "one half of a cookie." Repeat that phrase with other objects such as "one half of a glass of milk," "one half of a piece of paper," and so on. You might have to use these terms with various objects over several days before your child gets used to the language and links it with the correct idea.

1.2 Dividing in Half

When your child is ready, change the activity by breaking the cookie in half in front of the child. Explain that you are dividing the cookie into 2 parts, each the same size, and giving the child 1 of the halves. Go on to say that each of the 2 parts is called "one half," meaning 1 of 2 equal parts of a whole cookie. You can create similar fractions with a glass of milk: Start with a whole glass of milk and pour half of it into another identical glass. Again, demonstrate this idea with many different objects and substances. You are subtly showing your child how wholes and halves relate.

You are also demonstrating the procedure for getting a half, namely, dividing the whole into 2 parts of the same size and taking 1 of the 2 parts. Use this terminology next, explaining that breaking a cookie in half is the same as "dividing the whole into two parts of the same size." Use this phrasing while dividing various things in half.

Note that you can't make the 2 parts exactly the same, but that one half is what each part would be if you could divide the cookie into 2 parts of exactly the same size. Discuss all the hair-splitting distinctions that interest your child—which half has more chocolate chips or nuts, which half is thicker or weighs more. By explaining that dividing something in half is difficult in real life, you are helping the child learn that one half is an abstract concept, not tied to any particular act of division into parts. Indeed, you might invite your child to try to break a cookie in half. No matter how imprecisely he or she succeeds in creating 2 equal halves say that you can always *pretend* the 2 parts are exactly the same size and thus "one half" of a whole cookie.

Now mention that when 2 things are the same in some way, people often say they are "equal." Then repeat the idea that dividing in halves is the same as dividing the whole into 2 equal parts. Each part is one half. Notice that you are teaching the concepts of division and equality at the same time you are teaching the meaning of a half. To really know what a half is, your child needs to understand all of these concepts. It makes you appreciate how many different ideas your child has to learn!

Dividing, in particular, is the single most essential concept in understanding a fraction. When explaining a fraction, emphasize that you got the fraction by first *dividing* a whole into parts. This physical meaning of division will later tie fractions to the mathematical concept of dividing.

1.3 One Third, One Fourth, One Fifth

Next, move from one half to other examples of the simplest set of proper fractions: Those resulting from dividing a single whole into 1 or more parts. Aside from $\frac{1}{2}$, such fractions include $\frac{1}{3}$, $\frac{1}{4}$, and $\frac{1}{5}$.

Talk to your child about dividing 1 whole into 3, 4, 5, or more equal parts, and then taking 1 of those parts. Use cookies, pieces of paper, drawings of circular "pies" on pieces of paper, and sticks you can break. For each object or drawing, show your child how to divide it into 2 equal parts, 3 equal parts, 4 equal parts, and 5 equal parts. Then give your child one of the parts, have the child give one part to you, or ask the child to color the part in on a piece of paper (in the case of the pie drawing). Then ask: "This part is one of how many parts?" The child will answer 2, 3, 4, or 5, depending on the case. Then say, "Okay, so this is one third"—or one half, or one fourth, or one fifth—whichever it is. In this way, you begin to teach the child these terms.

Now introduce the notation for fractions. Explain that fractions are written as two numbers, one above the other, with a line between them. One half, for example, is written as $\frac{1}{2}$. One third looks like $\frac{1}{3}$. One fourth looks like $\frac{1}{4}$, and so on. Help your child draw these fractions and learn how to say them. Explain that $\frac{1}{4}$ means dividing 1 whole into 4 parts and taking 1 of the parts. Repeat this explanation for the other fractions of this simple type until your child understands. Test your child by giving little problems like: "Say I divided one whole into three parts and I take one of those parts. How would you write this as a fraction?" Keep asking these types of questions. It may take more than one learning session before your child masters this.

Explain more generally that the bottom number of the fraction tells you how many parts you divided the whole into. The top number tells you how many of these parts you are taking. You may mention that the top number is called the numerator of the fraction and the bottom number the denominator, but if your child doesn't pick up these terms, don't worry. You'll go over them later. Remember, you are asking your child to learn a lot of different things right now.

1.4 Other Proper Fractions

Point out that so far you've been content to take 1 part of the whole, no matter how many pieces you divided that whole into. But you could be greedier and take 2, 3, or more parts. For instance, you could divide a whole into 3 parts and take 2 of these. Ask your child how to write this as a fraction. (The answer is $\frac{2}{3}$.) Now say you are dividing a whole into 6 parts and taking 3 of those parts. Ask your child to write that fraction $\left(\frac{3}{6}\right)$. Ask similar questions until your child can answer them easily for any proper fraction.

1.5 Proper Fraction Stories

To help your child understand more about the use of fractions in the real world, pose story problems such as: "Mrs. Harris offered to give Billy an apple pie if he would rake her lawn. Billy got his friend Jim to rake one third of the lawn. What fraction of the pie should Jim get as fair pay for his work? What fraction should Billy get?"

First, tell your child to write down the fraction of the lawn Jim raked. This is the only noun specified in the problem. Your child should write $\frac{1}{3}$. Ask: "How many parts does that fraction say the lawn is divided into?" Your child should say 3. Ask: "If Jim took one of those parts, how many are left for Billy to rake?" Presumably, your child will say 2 and can then write the fraction $\frac{2}{3}$ to indicate what fraction of the lawn Billy raked.

Now ask your child to answer the questions. Since Jim raked $\frac{1}{3}$ of the lawn, he should get how much of the pie? Your child should say and write $\frac{1}{3}$. And since Billy raked $\frac{2}{3}$ of the lawn, Billy should get $\frac{2}{3}$ of the pie.

Make up similar stories to give your child additional practice. For instance: "Elaine's mom buys a jug of milk for her children every week at the supermarket. Elaine drinks one fourth of the jug every week. What fraction of the jug is left over after the Elaine has drunk her portion?"

Tell your child to write down the fraction of the milk Elaine drinks, $\frac{1}{4}$. Ask: "How many parts does this fraction mean the milk was divided into?" Your child should say 4. "Now, how many of those parts did Elaine take?" Your child should say 1. So how many of these parts are left over? Your child should say 3. Next, ask your child to write a fraction expressing the number of parts—out of 4—that were left over. Your child should write that $\frac{3}{4}$ of the jug is left over.

Continue providing examples of simple story problems involving different proper fractions until your child can do them on his or her own.

1.6 0 and 1 Fractions

Include "0" fractions and "1" fractions in some of your problems. For instance, "Billy asked both Frank and Jim to help him rake Mrs. Harris's lawn, and Jim did his third of the work, but Frank went to play baseball and didn't help at all, so Billy did his third and Frank's third. How much of the pie should Frank get?" Obviously, Frank should get nothing, which you encourage your child to write as $\frac{0}{3}$, meaning "0 thirds," and point out that $\frac{0}{3} = 0$. Do the same for other denominators. For instance, have 4 boys (or girls) divide up the task of raking a lawn or vacuuming a house with 1 of the kids running off and doing none of the work. In this way, your child will begin to understand that some fractions are equal to some whole numbers.

Now tell your child that neither Frank nor Jim help Billy rake the lawn. So Billy does all the work and receives $\frac{3}{3}$ of the pie, which is the same as 1 whole pie. Also, tell your child that $\frac{4}{4}$, $\frac{5}{5}$, $\frac{6}{6}$ and all other fractions in which the top and bottom numbers are the same, are equal to 1. Ask your child to write down some other fractions that are equal to 1.

1.7 The Fractional Number Line

To demonstrate that fractions are part of the number system, show your child a number line that includes both whole numbers and fractions. Place the fractions between the whole numbers, focusing on those between 0 and 1. (You will add fractions greater than 1 later when your child learns about those.) You can use a ruler that already has markings for halves, quarters, eighths, and sixteenths, or a metric ruler marked off in tenths. However, you should also draw your own rulers on pieces of paper that are marked off in thirds, fifths, and other fractional divisions. For instance, draw one number line with halves, thirds, fourths, and fifths marked on it. Such a ruler shows the relationship between a variety of different fractions. Make the unit length—the distance between 0 and 1—much longer than 1 inch, so you can write all the fractional values clearly below their tick marks.

1.8 A Second Look at Proper Fractions

So far, you have taught your child that fractions represent 1 whole divided into a number (D) of parts, with people taking a smaller number (N) of those parts. (Thus, $\frac{N}{D}$ means dividing a whole into D parts and taking N of those parts.) When your child has fully grasped that idea, give your child another way to look at proper fractions: These fractions can also represent the division of more than 1 whole into parts.

Start with a problem like this: "Mrs. Harris offers Billy, Jim, and Frank two blueberry pies for weeding her garden. This time, each of the three boys does an equal share of the work. Write a fraction to express how much pie each boy should get."

One way to solve the problem is to divide each pie into 3 equal parts, yielding 6 thirds. Dividing 6 thirds among 3 boys means each boy gets 2 of the thirds, which is written as the fraction $\frac{2}{3}$.

But there is another way to think about this problem, a way that will give your child a deeper understanding of fractions—and provide a 1-step way of solving problems like the above. Tell your child that the fraction $\frac{2}{3}$ can also be thought of as what you get when you divide 2 *wholes into 3 equal parts.* Remind your child that until now, you learned that a fraction such as $\frac{2}{3}$ was what you get when you divided *1 whole into 3 equal parts and take 2 of them.*

Expand this idea by providing more examples. Take the fraction $\frac{4}{5}$. Ask your child to provide both meanings for this fraction. The first: Divide 1 whole into 5 parts and take 4 of those parts. The second: Take 4 wholes and divide them into 5 parts. Repeat this exercise for other fractions until your child can easily state the 2 meanings without prompting.

Then pose more word problems in which 3 wholes are divided among 4 people, 2 wholes are divided among 5 people, 4 wholes are divided among 7 people, and any other examples you can imagine. In your problems, different numbers of people can divide up various numbers of pies, cans of soda, candy bars, or chores (lawns to mow or floors to vacuum). With each problem, state the two meanings of a fraction and make sure your child understands that both ways are correct and always stand for the same fraction in the real world. For instance, you'll get the same amount when dividing 4 pies equally among 7 people as when dividing 1 pie into 7 equal pieces and taking 4 of the pieces. You'll also get the same amount when dividing 5 lawns to mow among 8 people as when dividing 1 lawn into 8 equal pieces and taking 5 of those pieces to mow.

Once your child becomes good at solving such problems using both methods, state the general principle underlying all the examples. Use letters now to stand for the numbers in a fraction. Write the fraction $\frac{N}{D}$ on a piece of paper. Tell your child that this means both "what you get when you divide N wholes into D equal parts and what you get when you divide one whole into D equal parts and take N of them."

1.9 Numerators and Denominators

Now, use the $\frac{N}{D}$ notation to explain that the top number in a fraction is called the "numerator" and the bottom number is called the "denominator." Tell your child to remember which is which by reading $\frac{N}{D}$ from top to bottom as "North Dakota." So your child won't forget whether the order was top to bottom or vice versa, tell him or her to remember that North is on the top of almost all maps, and N for numerator is the top number in a fraction. The "North Dakota" mnemonic, or memory trick, along with North being the top of the map should almost guarantee that your child will never miss points on a test because he or she confuses the names for the top and bottom of fractions. Of course, it wouldn't hurt to discuss the mnemonic of the 2 parts of a fraction on different occasions. As discussed earlier, providing separate learning sessions is the way to make a memory last.

Section 2:
IMPROPER FRACTIONS

2.1 Defining Improper Fractions

Now it's time to extend fractions to represent quantities greater than 1. In these fractions, called improper fractions, the fraction's numerator is bigger than its denominator. First give your child examples of improper fractions, such as $\frac{9}{8}, \frac{8}{5}, \frac{13}{10}, \frac{6}{5}, \frac{3}{2}$, and so on. Emphasize that the top number is always bigger than the bottom number. Ask your child to make up more improper fractions and write them down. Next, test your child on the difference between proper and improper fractions by writing down different fractions of each type and asking him or her whether they are proper (less than 1) or improper (greater than 1).

2.2 Understanding Improper Fractions

Tell your child that Mrs. Harris has a big job, such as picking all the ripe cherries on several large cherry trees, and offers 5 cherry pies to Billy's club of 4 boys to pick all the ripe cherries. If all the boys work equally hard at picking cherries, how much pie should each boy get?

There are two good ways of solving this problem. Be sure your child understands both of them. First, ask your child to write down the nouns of the problem. They are 5 pies and 4 boys. Hint that if all the boys work equally hard, they should divide the pies equally between them. If so, ask your child to write a fraction describing how to divide 5 pies among 4 boys or into 4 equal parts. He or she should come up with the fraction $\frac{5}{4}$. So each boy gets $\frac{5}{4}$ of a pie. This method uses the meaning of a fraction your child learned in the previous section.

Be sure your child also practices the more concrete method of dividing 5 pies among 4 boys. In this way, each pie is first divided into 4 equal parts. Ask your child how many total parts that creates. Encourage your child to write **5 x 4 = 20** parts. Explain that those parts need to be divided among 4 boys. Ask your child to write an expression to determine how many parts each boy gets. Your child should write **20 ÷ 4 = 5** parts for each boy. Since each part is one-fourth of a pie, each boy gets 5 fourths of a pie. Ask your child to write that as a fraction. He or she should write $\frac{5}{4}$. So each boy gets $\frac{5}{4}$ of a pie.

Give your child other similar problems that involve improper fractions, gleaning examples from a textbook. In each case, be sure your child understands both ways of solving the problem. Provide practice until your child can solve the problems alone without difficulty.

2.3 Introduction to Adding Fractions

For your child to understand the next section, on mixed numbers, he or she needs to know the simple rule for adding fractions with the same denominator. Teach this now. The rule is: Add the top numbers just as you would add 2 whole numbers. This gives you the solution's numerator. The denominator of the fraction stays the same. Give your child a few examples, such as these: $\frac{3}{4} + \frac{1}{4} = \frac{4}{4}$, $\frac{1}{3} + \frac{1}{3} = \frac{2}{3}$, $\frac{5}{8} + \frac{7}{8} = \frac{12}{8}$. Then provide new problems for him or her to solve.

We will practice this again later, so your child need not demonstrate perfection in applying this rule, but he or she should demonstrate a fair understanding of it. I believe in this abstract approach. Students who have a concrete understanding of the meaning of addition and the meaning of fractions should have no trouble understanding what it means to add fractions.

2.4 Mixed Numbers

In the problem with the pies in lesson 2.2 above, it is also possible to give each boy a whole pie and then divide up the remaining pie into fourths. Draw 5 pies on a piece of paper. Write each boy's name (you can just write "Boy 1," "Boy 2," and so on) inside each of 4 pies, and show that 1 pie is left over. Ask your child to divide the remaining pie into 4 equal parts and give each boy 1 part. Since each part is one fourth of a pie, explain that each boy gets 1 whole pie plus $\frac{1}{4}$ pie. Write that as $1\frac{1}{4}$ (1 and one fourth). Explain that this is known as a "mixed number." It is called a mixed number because it is a mixture of a whole number and a fraction. Since we know that $1 = \frac{4}{4}$, and $\frac{4}{4} + \frac{1}{4} = \frac{5}{4}$, you see that $1\frac{1}{4} = \frac{5}{4}$. Explain this to your child.

Teach your child how to convert back and forth between other mixed numbers and improper fractions. First start with mixed numbers. Take $1\frac{1}{3}$. Ask your child to convert the 1 into thirds. He or she should write $\frac{3}{3}$. Then ask the child to add $\frac{3}{3}$ and $\frac{1}{3}$ to find the equivalent fraction. Your child should write: $\frac{3}{3} + \frac{1}{3} = \frac{4}{3}$. The equivalent improper fraction is $\frac{4}{3}$.

Ask your child to convert other mixed numbers into the equivalent improper fractions. For instance, your child might find the equivalent improper fractions for $1\frac{1}{2}$, $1\frac{3}{4}$, $2\frac{2}{3}$, 1, and $1\frac{5}{6}$. (Answers include: $\frac{3}{2}$, $\frac{7}{4}$, $\frac{8}{3}$ $\frac{4}{4}$ and $\frac{11}{6}$.) Take your child through the above process for each one until he or she gets the hang of it and can do it alone.

Next, teach your child to find the equivalent mixed numbers for improper fractions. Take the improper fraction $\frac{3}{2}$. To convert that to a mixed number, ask your child to break up those 3 halves into 2 halves and one half. He or she should write $\frac{2}{2} + \frac{1}{2}$. Since $\frac{2}{2} = 1$, $\frac{3}{2} = 1\frac{1}{2}$ or 1 and one half. Explain that the general rule is to split up an improper fraction into a whole number and a fraction.

Give your child additional practice with this idea. For instance, ask your child to determine the equivalent mixed numbers for $\frac{8}{7}$, $\frac{5}{3}$, $\frac{4}{2}$, $\frac{6}{4}$, and $\frac{5}{5}$. In the first case, your child would first split up $\frac{8}{7}$ into $\frac{7}{7} + \frac{1}{7}$. And since $\frac{7}{7} = 1$, the equivalent fraction is $1\frac{1}{7}$. (The other equivalent mixed numbers are $1\frac{2}{3}$, 2, $1\frac{2}{4}$, and 1.) You can give your child practice with bigger numbers too, if you like. Much of mathematics involves knowing how to translate from one equivalent expression to another, and the sooner your child gets used to this fact the better.

2.5 Mixed Numbers and Number Lines

To reinforce the equivalence of mixed numbers to various improper fractions, go back to the fractional number lines you made and add improper fractions and mixed numbers to them. Write mixed numbers below their equivalent improper fractions to give your child a visual image of the relationships. Extend this number line to 4 or thereabouts and make it clear that the line never ends.

In this way, your child begins to learn that fractions are a large set of numbers that includes the whole numbers, like 1, 2, 3, and so on. If your child has learned some arithmetic, tell your child that the arithmetic operations of addition, subtraction, multiplication, and division apply to fractions as well as to whole numbers, though the rules are more complex.

Section 3:
EQUIVALENT FRACTIONS

3.1 Understanding Equivalent Fractions

It's now time for your child to learn how to create and recognize other kinds of equivalent fractions. Explain that some proper fractions are equivalent to other proper fractions and that some improper fractions are equivalent to other improper fractions. These equivalent fractions are those that can be converted from one to another by multiplying or dividing a fraction's numerator and denominator by the same number.

For example, tell your child that $\frac{2}{4}$ is equivalent to $\frac{1}{2}$ and $\frac{1}{3}$ is equivalent to $\frac{3}{9}$. Similarly, $\frac{1}{4} = \frac{2}{8} = \frac{4}{16}$, and so on. In each case, ask your child what number the numerator and denominator of the simpler fraction (the one with the smaller numbers) had to be multiplied by to create the fraction with the larger numbers.

Next, justify this equivalency by finding a standard ruler marked in halves, quarters, eighths, and sixteenths. On the ruler, show your child that $\frac{1}{2}$ is the same length as $\frac{2}{4}$, as $\frac{4}{8}$, and as $\frac{8}{16}$. An elaboration of this idea is to represent fractions with different denominators on separate strips of paper (handmade rulers), each of which has exactly the same length between whole numbers. For example, mark off one strip in halves, another in thirds, yet another in fourths and others in sixths and twelfths. Place one strip next to another to show that $\frac{1}{6} = \frac{2}{12}$, $\frac{1}{4} = \frac{3}{12}$, $\frac{1}{3} = \frac{2}{6} = \frac{4}{12}$, $\frac{1}{2} = \frac{2}{4} = \frac{3}{6} = \frac{6}{12}$, $1\frac{1}{6} = \frac{7}{6} = \frac{14}{12} = 1\frac{2}{12}$, $1\frac{1}{4} = \frac{5}{4} = \frac{15}{12} = 1\frac{3}{12}$, and so on.

3.2 Using Multiplication to Create Equivalent Fractions

Teach your child to generate equivalent fractions by multiplying the top and the bottom of the fraction by the same thing. Start with a simple fraction such as $\frac{1}{2}$. Ask: "What should we multiply the top and bottom of the fraction by?" Your child can choose any number. But let's say he or she chooses 3. Ask the child to multiply the top by 3. That yields 3. Next, tell the child to multiply the bottom of the fraction by 3. That yields 6. So the resulting equivalent fraction is $\frac{3}{6}$. To show your child that any factor will do, ask him or her to pick another factor, say, 2. The equivalent fraction is thus $\frac{2}{4}$. Then write: $\frac{1}{2} = \frac{3}{6} = \frac{2}{4}$. Next, ask your child: Which of these fractions is largest? The correct answer is none of them. They are all equivalent!

Now, introduce a new notation for generating equivalent fractions. Explain that multiplying the top and bottom by the same thing is the same as writing, say: $\frac{1}{2} \times \frac{2}{2} = \frac{1 \times 2}{2 \times 2} = \frac{2}{4}$.

Repeat all of the above steps with other simple fractions such as $\frac{1}{3}$, $\frac{1}{4}$, $\frac{3}{4}$, $\frac{5}{8}$. Ask your child to generate a number of equivalent fractions for each one by multiplying the top and bottom numbers by the same factor. And each time, guide your child through the new multiplication notation with a couple of examples until he or she can copy that notation without prompting. This is a preview to multiplying fractions.

3.3 Finding Common Factors

When your child gets the hang of that, teach the child to use division to generate equivalent fractions. To do that requires first finding the common factors of the fraction's numerator and denominator. Those factors are what both the numerator and denominator will be divided by to get an equivalent fraction with a smaller numerator and denominator. Explain that a common factor is a number that divides evenly into both numbers. For example, 2 is a common factor of 4 and 8, 3 is a common factor of 6 and 9.

Ask your child to find the common factors of pairs of numbers. For instance, ask: "What is a common factor of 2 and 4?" The best answer is 2. (Another answer is 1, but tell your child that dividing by 1 will not generate a new equivalent fraction, so he or she should focus on common factors other than 1.) Next ask your child to divide both 2 and 4 by this common factor. Your child should write: **2 ÷ 2 = 1** and **4 ÷ 2 = 2**. Now, write the fraction $\frac{2}{4}$ and ask your child to divide the top and bottom by the common factor of 2 and 4 and to write the resulting fraction after he or she has done so. Your child should come up with $\frac{1}{2}$.

Give your child a number other simple examples until he or she knows the procedure well and can use common factors and division to create equivalent fractions.

3.4 Reducing Fractions

Explain that using division to generate equivalent fractions is called "reducing fractions," because it reduces the size of the numerator and denominator. Repeatedly using division to create simpler equivalent fractions until one has created the simplest possible fraction—the one with the smallest possible numerator and denominator—is called "reducing a fraction to its simplest form." A fraction is in its simplest form when the numerator and denominator have no more common factors.

Tell your child one way to do this: First, divide a fraction's numerator or denominator by 2 until either number is odd. Next, divide the numerator and denominator by 3 until either number can no longer be divided by 3. Next, try 5. Continue testing all prime numbers smaller than or equal to the numbers in the fraction. A prime number is a whole number that can be evenly divided only by itself and 1. Prime numbers include 1, 2, 3, 5, 7, 11, 13, 17, 19, 23, 29, 31, 37, 41, and 43. If your child doesn't already know what a prime number is, explain the concept and ask him or her to generate a long list of them. Check the list for mistakes and explain any that are made.

Ask your child to use this technique to reduce the fraction $\frac{18}{48}$. Dividing the numerator and denominator by 2 yields $\frac{9}{24}$. At this point, ask your child: "Can we divide by 2 again?" The answer is no, because 9 does not divide evenly by 2. Ask your child to try 3. That works. Dividing both the numerator and denominator by 3 yields: $\frac{3}{8}$. Next, ask if it's possible to divide by 3 again. The answer is no, because 8 is not divisible by 3. Ask your child whether you should test any more numbers. The answer is no, because there are no other prime numbers to test that are smaller than or equal to *both* the numerator and denominator.

Give your child practice using this technique to reduce other fractions until he or she is comfortable with it.

Another way to reduce fractions is by first breaking down the numerator and denominator into their factors and canceling out common ones. In the above problem, for instance, this method would yield: $\frac{18}{48} = \frac{6 \times 3}{6 \times 8} = \frac{3}{8}$. Please give your child practice factoring various numerators and denominators and canceling out common factors. If your child's initial factoring doesn't show a common factor, instruct your child to factor the numerator and denominator down to their prime factors. In the above example, that wasn't necessary, but it would work as follows: $\frac{18}{48} = \frac{2 \times 3 \times 3}{2 \times 3 \times 8} = \frac{3}{8}$.

3.5 Explaining the Rules

Explain why multiplying or dividing a fraction's numerator and denominator by the same number yields an equivalent fraction. Write down the fraction $\frac{3}{4}$, and say: "If I multiply both the numerator and the denominator of this fraction by five, I get fifteen over twenty." Now write $\frac{15}{20}$. Show that this is equal to three 5's on top and four 5's on the bottom. Obviously the fraction is equivalent to $\frac{3}{4}$. This explanation works equally well for any factor. Provide other examples.

Another way to explain this is to use the notation you introduced in section 3.2. Show your child this again: $\frac{1}{2} \times \frac{2}{2} = \frac{1 \times 2}{2 \times 2} = \frac{2}{4}$. Now note that both $\frac{2}{2}$ and $\frac{3}{3}$ are equal to 1. And remind your child that multiplying any whole number by 1 gives you back the same number. The same is true for fractions. That is why multiplying a fraction by $\frac{2}{2}$ or $\frac{3}{3}$ doesn't change the fraction's value. If your child doesn't catch on to this explanation right away, don't worry about it.

3.6 Ratios and Proportions

Explain to your child the meaning of the word *ratio*, which is essentially the same as fraction. A ratio of 2 numbers, *a* and *b* (sometimes written as *a:b*) is equal to $\frac{a}{b}$ or ***a ÷ b***. Ask your child to write the ratio of 3 to 4 (answer $\frac{3}{4}$) of 5 to 6 (answer $\frac{5}{6}$) and of various other numbers.

Next explain that a "proportion" is an equality of two ratios. Provide examples of proportions such as $\frac{3}{2} = \frac{6}{4}$, $\frac{4}{5} = \frac{8}{10}$, $\frac{11}{12} = \frac{110}{120}$. Thus, proportions are like equivalent fractions. Test your child's understanding of proportions by writing down various fractions that are and are not proportional and asking your child to identify which ones are proportions. Provide examples of things that are commonly proportional to one another, such as photographic enlargements, whose sides are often proportional to the original photo. Scale models of buildings are also often proportional to the actual buildings. In each case, one multiplies each side or dimension of the smaller photograph or building by a common factor to create the larger object.

Section 4:

ADDING AND SUBTRACTING FRACTIONS

4.1 Adding Fractions with the Same Denominator

Review the rule for adding fractions with the same denominator, described above: Add the two numerators to get the solution's numerator; the denominator of the solution stays the same. Next, give your child additional practice adding two fractions with the same denominator. When necessary, have your child reduce the answer to its simplest form, the equivalent fraction with the smallest possible denominator.

When your child is good at this, explain how to add mixed numbers with the same denominator. The rule is: Add the two whole numbers; add the 2 fractions; then combine the two sums. Start with these easy problems: $1\frac{1}{3} + 2\frac{1}{3} = 3\frac{2}{3}$ and $2\frac{1}{4} + 3\frac{2}{4} = 5\frac{3}{4}$. When your child gets the hang of it, slip in problems for which your child must convert the fractional portion of the answer to a mixed number. For instance: $1\frac{7}{8} + 1\frac{5}{8} = 2\frac{12}{8}$. Ask your child to convert $\frac{12}{8}$ to $1\frac{4}{8}$, which is equivalent to $1\frac{1}{2}$. Then $1\frac{1}{2}$ should be added to 2 to get $3\frac{1}{2}$ as the final answer.

4.2 Subtracting Fractions with the Same Denominator

Explain the rule for subtracting fractions with the same denominator: Subtract the numerator of the second fraction from the numerator of the first fraction. The result is the numerator of the solution. The common denominator of the two fractions is also the denominator of the solution. Start simply with problems such as $\frac{3}{4} - \frac{1}{4} = \frac{2}{4} = \frac{1}{2}$ and $\frac{7}{9} - \frac{5}{9} = \frac{2}{9}$. Make up as many of these relatively easy subtraction problems as it takes for your child to get the hang of solving them.

Move on to subtracting mixed numbers with the same denominator. The rule: Subtract the second whole number from the first one and then subtract the second fraction from the first. Provide a few examples such as $8\frac{5}{8} - 7\frac{1}{8} = 1\frac{4}{8}$ and $9\frac{3}{4} - 7\frac{2}{4} = 2\frac{1}{4}$. Test your child with problems until he or she gets the hang of it.

Next, provide more difficult problems involving mixed numbers, such as $7\frac{1}{8} - 4\frac{5}{8}$, in which one of the mixed numbers $(7\frac{1}{8})$ must be converted to a mixed number with an improper fraction $(7\frac{1}{8} = 6\frac{9}{8})$ before the fractional parts are subtracted. Explain that doing this conversion requires taking 1 away from the whole number in the mixed number and adding it to the fractional part of that number. First ask your child to take 1 away from the whole number, which should be easy, $(7 - 1 = 6)$. To add 1 to the fraction, suggest that your child first convert 1 into a fraction with the same denominator as the fraction in the mixed number. In the case of $\frac{1}{8}$, that fraction would be $\frac{8}{8}$. Adding $\frac{8}{8}$ to $\frac{1}{8}$ yields $\frac{9}{8}$. So the correct conversion is $6\frac{9}{8}$.

Ask your child to substitute $6\frac{9}{8}$ for $7\frac{1}{8}$ in the above subtraction problem. He or she should write $6\frac{9}{8} - 4\frac{5}{8} = 2\frac{4}{8} = 2\frac{1}{2}$. Give your child other problems of this type until he or she can do them on his or her own. In each case, make sure your child reduces the answer to its simplest form.

4.3 Adding Fractions with Different Denominators

When your child has mastered adding and subtracting fractions and mixed numbers with the same denominator—and this may take many separate learning sessions—teach your child to add and subtract fractions with different denominators. This step requires that your child have completely mastered all the previous rules of fractions including those governing conversions, finding equivalent fractions, reducing fractions, and adding and subtracting fractions with like denominators. So if your child is shaky on any of this, review the concepts and rules he or she has not mastered before moving on.

First, explain that the above rules apply with 1 additional first step: Convert 1 or both fractions to equivalent fractions such that both have the same denominator. Then add or subtract the fractions as before. Provide examples, starting with addition. Take $\frac{1}{4} + \frac{1}{2}$. In this case, since 2 is a multiple of 4, the second fraction can be converted to fourths by multiplying the top and bottom of the fraction by 2 to get $\frac{2}{4}$. Now it's easy to add $\frac{1}{4} + \frac{2}{4} = \frac{3}{4}$.

A harder problem is $\frac{3}{8} + \frac{1}{20}$. Here, ask your child to think of a number that is divisible by both 8 and 20. The answer: 40. That is the least common denominator. In this case, both fractions must be converted to equivalent fractions with the denominator of 40. Pointing to the first fraction, ask your child: "What must the top and bottom of this fraction be multiplied by to get a forty in the denominator?" Your child should say 5. The fraction becomes $\frac{15}{40}$. Now point to the other fraction and ask: "What must the top and bottom of this fraction be multiplied by to get forty on the bottom?" The answer is 2. Multiplying by 2 yields $\frac{2}{40}$. Now the problem can be easily solved: $\frac{15}{40} + \frac{2}{40} = \frac{17}{40}$.

Next, explain to your child that a common denominator of two fractions can always be found by multiplying the denominators of the two fractions. In some cases, it will be the least common denominator; in other cases it will not, and the resulting fraction will need to be reduced.

Take $\frac{2}{5} + \frac{3}{4}$. In this case, the least common denominator can be found by multiplying the denominators of the two fractions: **5 x 4 = 20**. To make 20 the denominator, multiply the top and bottom of the first fraction by 4 to get the equivalent fraction $\frac{8}{20}$ and the top and bottom of the second fraction by 5 to get $\frac{15}{20}$. So you get $\frac{8}{20} + \frac{15}{20} = \frac{23}{20}$.

Now take the problem $\frac{1}{8} + 1\frac{1}{12}$. First, your child should convert both fractions to the same form, which means converting the mixed number into an improper fraction. That should yield $\frac{1}{8} + \frac{13}{12}$. Ask your child to find the least common denominator for 8 and 12. If he or she has trouble, just say the answer: 24. Instruct your child to rewrite the problem using this denominator. He or she should write $\frac{3}{24} + \frac{26}{24} = \frac{29}{24}$.

Now explain that another common denominator can be found by multiplying the two denominators—8 and 12—together to get 96. Using that denominator, the problem becomes $\frac{12}{96} + \frac{104}{96} = \frac{116}{96} = \frac{29}{24}$. Be sure your child understands that this method works too, but that it might require an additional step to reduce the fraction to its simplest form. Give your child lots of practice with these types of problems.

4.4 Subtracting Fractions with Different Denominators

Once your child gets the hang of the conversion step, subtracting fractions with different denominators should be easy. Explain that the idea is first to find a common denominator for the two fractions, convert them both to equivalent fractions with that denominator, and then subtract the numerator of the second fraction from the numerator of the first.

For example: $\frac{11}{12} - \frac{3}{5} = \frac{55}{60} - \frac{36}{60} = \frac{19}{60}$. Walk your child through any difficult conversions as you did above. Give your child lots of practice.

4.5 Adding and Subtracting Mixed Numbers with Different Denominators

Lastly, provide some problems in which your child must add or subtract mixed numbers and that require finding a common denominator for the fractional part of the mixed number. Here, the only difference is that the whole numbers must also be added or subtracted. In some cases, the mixed number is best converted to an improper fraction. In other cases, an improper fraction must be converted into a mixed number.

Section 5:
MULTIPLYING FRACTIONS

5.1 The Basic Rule

Multiplying and dividing fractions is much simpler than adding and subtracting them. As with adding and subtracting fractions, the best way to teach your child to multiply and divide fractions is to lay out the rules for doing so and illustrate their use with examples.

Describe these two steps for multiplying fractions. First, multiply the numerators of the two fractions to get the numerator of the product. Second, multiply the denominators of the two fractions to get the denominator of the product. That's it! Provide an example such as $\frac{3}{8} \times \frac{5}{3}$. Show your child that you will multiply the numerators: **3 x 5 = 15**. That's the numerator of the answer. Second, multiply the denominators: **8 x 3 = 24**. That's the denominator of the answer. So the answer is $\frac{15}{24}$. Now, your child can simplify the answer to get $\frac{5}{8}$.

Provide 2 or 3 additional examples, and then ask your child to solve several problems on his or her own. You might use: $\frac{1}{2} \times \frac{1}{4} = \left(\frac{1}{8}\right)$; $\frac{4}{9} \times \frac{1}{3} = \left(\frac{4}{27}\right)$, $\frac{4}{5} \times \frac{1}{8} = \left(\frac{4}{40} = \frac{1}{10}\right)$; $\frac{5}{7} \times 1\frac{1}{10} = \frac{5}{7} \times \frac{11}{10} = \left(\frac{55}{70} = \frac{11}{14}\right)$. But it really doesn't matter. Pick any fractions you wish. In each case, be sure your child reduces the answer to its simplest form.

5.2 Understanding the Rule

If you wish, generalize the rule using letters to stand for any whole number, as $\frac{M}{K} \times \frac{N}{D} = \frac{M \times N}{K \times D}$. This will help prepare your child for algebra, in which letters are used to denote numbers. If your child has difficulty understanding this algebraic notation, though, don't push it. It's not necessary to understand algebraic notation to multiply fractions.

Use specific examples of the rule to give your child a more intuitive understanding of it. First, explain the meaning of multiplying a fraction by the number 1. Clearly, $1 \times \frac{N}{D} = \frac{N}{D} \times 1 = \frac{N}{D}$, since multiplying by 1 doesn't change anything. In explaining this to your child, substitute numbers for the letters N and D, and provide a few examples so your child understands that the rule is not specific to any particular fraction, but applies to all fractions. Now since $1 = \frac{1}{1}$, apply the rule for multiplying fractions to the fractional form of 1 to show you get the same result: $1 \times \frac{N}{D} = \frac{1}{1} \times \frac{N}{D} = \frac{1 \times N}{1 \times D} = \frac{N}{D}$. Again, substitute a variety of specific numbers for N and D here.

Though your child learned earlier that $\frac{N}{D}$ means to divide something into D parts and take N of them, explain to your child that there is an equivalent meaning of $\frac{N}{D}$. It also means dividing 1 by D to get $\frac{1}{D}$ and then multiplying by N to get $\frac{N}{D}$. Use specific numbers here instead of letters. Any numbers will do.

5.3 Multiplying a Fraction by a Whole Number

Next, teach your child to multiply a fraction by any whole number. Explain that the procedure is the same as multiplying two fractions, *after* transforming the whole number into a fraction by using 1 as its denominator. For instance, $6 \times \frac{2}{3} = \frac{6}{1} \times \frac{2}{3} = \frac{6 \times 2}{1 \times 3} = \frac{12}{3} = 4$. Run through several more specific examples and then test your child with a few problems to be sure he or she understands how to do this. Any problems will do, but examples include $\frac{3}{4} \times 8$, $\frac{2}{7} \times 7$, $\frac{1}{3} \times 10$. (Answers are 6, 2, $\frac{10}{3}$.) If you wish, show your child the general statement governing this process using letters to stand for specific numbers: $M \times \frac{N}{D} = \frac{M}{1} \times \frac{N}{D} = \frac{M \times N}{1 \times D} = \frac{MN}{D}$.

5.4 The Meaning of Of

Define the meaning of *of* in expressions such as $\frac{2}{3}$ *of* some whole number. The word *of* after a fraction and before another number always means "times" or "multiplication." I say to my students over and over again, "of" means "times." So ask your child, "What is two thirds of three?" Answer: $\frac{2}{3}$ x 3 = 2. What is $\frac{2}{3}$ of 6? Answer: $\frac{2}{3}$ x 6 = 4. Pose several questions of this nature to your child.

When your child has mastered that, ask your child, "What is one half of two thirds?" If he or she looks puzzled, remind the child that *of* means "times." He or she should be able to translate that question into $\frac{1}{2}$ x $\frac{2}{3}$ to obtain the answer $\frac{2}{6}$ or $\frac{1}{3}$. If not, translate the question into the problem and then ask another question about taking one half of a fraction, such as "What is one half of one eighth?" Repeat this type of question (providing help when your child needs it), until your child gets the hang of it.

Next, ask your child questions about taking one third of various fractions such as "What is one third of one quarter?" Answer $\frac{1}{3}$ x $\frac{1}{4}$ = $\frac{1}{12}$. Repeat the procedure above if your child doesn't catch on right away. Next, ask your child to multiply fractions without a 1 in the numerator by asking, for example, "What is three quarters of five eighths?"

Section 6:
DIVIDING FRACTIONS

6.1 The Basic Rule

After your child masters multiplying fractions, move on to division. Start by stating this simple abstract rule for dividing two fractions: First, switch the numerator and denominator of the second, or "divisor" fraction. That is, flip it over. Second, multiply the two resulting fractions. Provide an example, such as $\frac{1}{2}$ ÷ $\frac{5}{6}$. Flipping the second fraction yields $\frac{6}{5}$. So $\frac{1}{2}$ ÷ $\frac{5}{6}$ = $\frac{1}{2}$ x $\frac{6}{5}$ = $\frac{6}{10}$ = $\frac{3}{5}$. Emphasize to your child that it is important to flip just one of the fractions and that the one to be flipped must always be the second fraction. Flipping the wrong fraction will yield the wrong answer.

Now give your child a division problem and ask him or her to follow the same steps. You may use any two fractions, but here are a few examples. (I'm including answers, but just give your child the problems and provide help only if he or she has trouble.)

When Multiplying Creates Smaller Numbers

Tell your child to notice that multiplying a number by a fraction that is less than 1 creates a number that is *smaller* than the original number. If this is confusing to your child, draw a circle on a piece of paper and call it 1 pie. Now say, what if we take a quarter of the pie? How would we write that mathematically? Your child should write $1 \times \frac{1}{4}$. Now ask your child to divide the pie into quarters and to color in 1 of the quarters, or $\frac{1}{4}$ of the pie. Note that this quarter is what you get when you multiply 1 by $\frac{1}{4}$ and that this is less than 1.

Ask what happens if you take one quarter of $\frac{1}{2}$. Ask your child to both write this mathematically $\left(\frac{1}{4} \times \frac{1}{2} = \frac{1}{8}\right)$ and draw it on a piece of paper by coloring in one quarter of just half of the pie. This should help your child see why multiplying a number—1 in the first example and $\frac{1}{2}$ in the second example—by a fraction less than 1 creates a number smaller than the original number—$\frac{1}{4}$ and $\frac{1}{8}$ and respectively.

$$\frac{5}{4} \div \frac{2}{3} = \frac{5}{4} \times \frac{3}{2} = \frac{15}{8}$$

$$\frac{7}{8} \div \frac{1}{4} = \frac{7}{8} \times \frac{4}{1} = \frac{28}{8} = \frac{7}{2}$$

$$\frac{2}{5} \div 1\frac{1}{12} = \frac{2}{5} \div \frac{13}{12} = \frac{2}{5} \times \frac{12}{13} = \frac{24}{65}$$

Give your child lots of practice dividing fractions until he or she is good at it and then state the general rule for division of fractions as follows:

$$\frac{M}{K} \div \frac{N}{D} = \frac{M}{K} \times \frac{D}{N} = \frac{M \times D}{K \times N} = \frac{MD}{KN}$$

Explain the equation above to your child, but if he or she has trouble understanding the algebraic notation, don't worry about it. The most important thing is to make sure your child knows how to divide fractions using numbers.

6.2 Making Sense of the Rule

Compared to simply teaching the rule for dividing two fractions, explaining *why* this rule works is very difficult. However, you may attempt to do this if your child is extremely bright. If not, skim this section, but do not use it with your child.

To make the rule for dividing two fractions seem plausible to your child, first show that dividing by 1 gives the expected answer. For example, $\frac{1}{2} \div 1 = \frac{1}{2} \div \frac{1}{1} = \frac{1}{2} \times 1 = \frac{1}{2}$. Provide a few other examples for good measure, and then state the general rule:

$$\frac{M}{K} \div 1 = \frac{M}{K} \div \frac{1}{1} = \frac{M \times 1}{K \times 1} = \frac{M}{K}$$

Second, show that dividing a fraction by any whole number also follows the rule. For instance, dividing $\frac{6}{7}$ by 3 means dividing the 6 parts specified into 3 groups. Each group thus contains 2 parts. The answer is $\frac{2}{7}$.

Note here that when you divide a fraction by a whole number (3 in this case), you divide the numerator by that number, which is the same as putting the number (3) as another factor in the denominator. Think of the denominator of a fraction as containing all the numbers to divide the numerator by. You may, if you wish, state this mathematically, walking through the expression with your child:

$$\frac{M}{K} \div W = \frac{M}{K} \div \frac{W}{1} = \frac{M}{K} \times \frac{1}{W} = \frac{M \times 1}{K \times W} = \frac{M}{KW}$$

Third, demonstrate that dividing a fraction by a reciprocal of a whole number Z, namely $\frac{1}{Z}$, also follows the rule. What does it mean to divide a fraction by $\frac{1}{Z}$? It means to find out how many parts of size $\frac{1}{Z}$ are in the fraction. Dividing $\frac{2}{3}$ by $\frac{1}{9}$ means dividing $\frac{2}{3}$ into parts of size $\frac{1}{9}$ and finding how many parts there are. Since $\frac{2}{3}$ is the same as $\frac{6}{9}$, there are 6 parts. That's the same answer obtained by flipping over $\frac{1}{9}$ and multiplying by 9: $\frac{2}{3} \times \frac{9}{1} = \frac{18}{3} =$ **6.** So when you divide a fraction by $\frac{1}{Z}$, it is the same as putting Z as another factor in the numerator of the fraction, or flipping over $\frac{1}{Z}$ to multiply by Z, as the rule states.

Now state the formula for dividing fractions for this special case:

$$\frac{M}{K} \div \frac{1}{Z} = \frac{MZ}{K}$$

You can also show that dividing $\frac{M}{K}$ by $\frac{N}{D}$ is equivalent to first dividing $\frac{M}{K}$ by N and then dividing the result by $\frac{1}{D}$, which is the same as dividing $\frac{M}{K}$ by N and multiplying the result by D. I won't go through the proof, but it should seem plausible to your child. Once that's accepted, the rule for division is established.

Abstract Learning and Fractions

While abstract explanations of fractions are often helpful and interesting to children, they are not necessary for multiplying and dividing fractions. For almost all children, following the simple abstract rules for such operations is the best course. The best way to justify the rules for multiplying and dividing fractions is to say mathematicians devised these rules because they work to make everything come out correctly. There is no good way of explaining the meaning of multiplying and dividing fractions using objects or other concrete representations. Indeed, I believe attempting such explanations will only confuse your child, so I do not discuss them.

Abstract, mathematical principles like the rules for multiplying fractions are not necessarily harder for people to understand than concrete, real world examples. The capacity for abstract thinking is what sets human intelligence above that of other animal species. To make numerical abstractions apply to the world, people first relate numbers to objects and operations to actions. But having done that, people should immerse themselves in the abstractions themselves without continually translating them into the "real" world.

It's like learning a second language. Once a person becomes fluent, he or she need not translate every word of the new language into the native one, since each word and phrase in the new language has taken on a meaning of its own. Indeed, it would be slow and cumbersome to do so. Similarly, after learning the language of math, it's most efficient—and easier—just to use the language, mastering it through continued use.

The above explanation, as with others in this book, is an attempt to help your child gain an intuitive sense of a problem-solving rule. It is not a mathematical proof, which is different for reasons beyond the scope of this book.

Section 7:
FRACTION STORY PROBLEMS

Translating between *English* and mathematics is important for solving story problems involving fractions. Though you already introduced your child to simple story problems involving fractions, give your child formal training in translating additional nouns and verbs that appear in these problems.

7.1 Nouns

Your child has already seen the most basic fraction nouns, those like one fourth, translated as $\frac{1}{4}$, and three fifths $\left(\frac{3}{5}\right)$. Even so, test your child to be sure he or she can easily translate the English forms of various fractions into mathematical symbols. Be sure your child can similarly translate a quarter and a half into fractions.

Other problems require students to translate the English names of percents or percentages. For instance, 27 percent is 27% or .27, which is equivalent to $\frac{27}{100}$. Fortunately, decimals and numbers expressed in scientific notation, such as .347 and 5.0034 x 10^{-3}, are virtually always expressed in mathematical form in story problems.

We have not explained percentages, decimals, or scientific notation in this chapter. Please use a textbook to ensure that your child understands these concepts, how to convert from one to another, and translate between fractions and decimals. Then test your child to be sure he or she can easily translate words such as 15 percent as 15% and .15.

Move on to monetary fractions. For instance, teach your child that a quarter is $.25 or 25¢, a dime is $.10 or 10¢, a nickel is $.05 or 5¢, and a penny is $.01 or 1¢.

Give your child mixed practice translating various words representing fractional expressions into numerical entities. For example, ask the child to translate each of these words into numbers by writing the numbers down on a piece of paper:

Two thirds $\left(\frac{2}{3}\right)$
Seventy-eight percent (78% or .78)
A dime (10¢ or $.10)

7.2 Verbs

Fraction story problems share the same verbs for addition and subtraction with whole-number story problems. However, test your child's ability to apply these words to fraction story problems by providing translation problems such as:

"Emily ate half a pie plus a third of a pie." Translation: $\frac{1}{2} + \frac{1}{3}$.

"Carlos bought a pound of coffee, but gave a third of the pound to his friend." Translation: $1 - \frac{1}{3}$.

If your child translated *of* as times in these problems, that's fine. But the number to be multiplied in each case is 1, so that doesn't change anything. In this example, a third of a pie is just $1 \times \frac{1}{3} = \frac{1}{3}$. In the second problem, a pound of coffee just means 1×1 pound $= 1$ pound and a third of 1 pound is just $1 \times \frac{1}{3} = \frac{1}{3}$.

There are verbs for multiplication and division that are somewhat more prevalent in fraction problems and that it would behoove your child to practice now. First, as we described above, *of* means times, and that word is frequently used in story problems involving fractions as well as in the number problems discussed above. Test your child's ability to translate phrases such as:

"Renee gave one eighth of her collection of twelve dolls to her younger sister." Translation $12 \times \frac{1}{8}$.

"Bob ate a quarter of the eight pies." Translation: $8 \times \frac{1}{4}$.

The words and phrases indicating division are commonly used in story problems involving fractions. They include *divide, divided by, split* (especially with *evenly*), *quotient, half, quarter, third, percent,* and *percentage*. Give your child numerous translation problems invoking the above words. For example,

"Kim's mother divided two pies among five girls." Translation: $\frac{2}{5}$.

"Francine received a ten-percent discount off a price of fifty dollars. How much did she save?" Translation: $.10 \times 50$ or $50 \div 10$.

7.3 Combinations of Operations

Some phrases in fraction problems imply a combination of operations, or verbs, instead of single ones. For instance, percentage increases involve both multiplication and addition. In general, to increase a quantity by a certain percentage means to multiply the quantity by the fraction implied by the percentage and then add the result to the original quantity. For example, the phrase "increased by thirty-five percent" means to multiply a number by .35 and then add the result to the number. In effect, this multiplies the number by 1.35, which is a superior way to represent this mathematically, but often more difficult for kids to grasp.

Still, explain both correct translations to your child and then test his or her understanding with problems such as:

"Three dollars increased by twenty percent." Translation: **(3 x .20) + 3**; or **3 x 1.20**.

"Five hundred butterflies increased by forty-two percent." Translation: **(500 x .42) + 500**; or **500 x 1.42**.

"A thirty-percent increase in a $30,000 salary." Translation: The increase itself is **30,000 x .3**. But the new salary would be **$30,000 + 30,000 x .3**. Explain the difference to your child.

Similarly, "increased by a factor of N" or "grew by a factor of N" means to multiply an amount by N and then add that to the amount. In effect, this multiplies an amount by **$N + 1$**. Now, give your child practice with this phrase, which is a difficult one for kids to grasp. For example:

"Stuart's collection of one hundred pennies increased by a factor of four." Translation: **(4 x 100) + 100**.

"Sandra's income of $25,000 grew by a factor of 1.5." Translation: **(25,000 x 1.5) + 25,000**.

By contrast, "multiplied by a factor of N" means just to multiply an amount by N. Give your child a few examples of this type of translation problem. For instance:

"The dish of 130 germs multiplied by a factor of three." Translation: **130 x 3**.

The town's population of 5,014 multiplied by a factor of ten. Translation: **5,014 x 10**.

Now, give your child a mixture of examples of the latter two types of problems so he or she learns to recognize the difference between them, which is subtle in English—but very important mathematically.

7.4 Fraction Story Problems

Walk your child through various story problems involving fractions, starting simply and moving on to more advanced problems. Here is one example of moderate difficulty: "Vilma spent a quarter of an hour getting dressed. Greg had to wait for her. In addition, Greg had to wait an eighth of an hour for the taxi to arrive. What fraction of an hour did Greg have to wait? What fraction of a day is that? How many minutes did Greg wait?"

In hours, Greg had to wait $\frac{1}{4} + \frac{1}{8} = \frac{2}{8} + \frac{1}{8} = \frac{3}{8}$, or three eighths of an hour. To translate that into a fraction of a day, your child must know there are 24 hours *per* day. That suggests you should divide by 24. Tell your child that if he or she is ever confused about whether to divide or multiply by a quantity in converting between minutes, hours, and days, he or she should think about whether the answer should be smaller or larger than the starting quantity. In particular, ask whether the fraction of the day should be smaller or larger than the fraction of an hour. Since a day is longer than an hour, the fraction should be smaller. That confirms that dividing by 24 is the right idea. So Greg waited

$$\frac{3}{8} \div 24 = \frac{3}{8} \times \frac{1}{24} = \frac{3}{192} = \frac{1}{64} \text{ day.}$$

To translate hours into minutes, your child must know that there are 60 minutes per hour. In this case, the answer should be larger, so you multiply by 60. Greg waited

$$60 \times \frac{3}{8} = \frac{180}{8} = \frac{90}{4} = \frac{45}{2} = 22\frac{1}{2} \text{ minutes.}$$

Be sure to give your child lots of practice solving story problems involving fractions. Glean examples from a textbook.

7.5 Decimal and Percent Story Problems

Walk through problems involving decimals and percents with your child. Here are two examples. If your child struggles with them, start simpler, using examples from a textbook or workbook.

1. "Joshua was given three dollars and fifty cents for his allowance. Then he found a five-dollar bill on his way to school. Since he was hungry, he spent half of his money on a snack. Later that day, Joshua dropped a quarter down a drain pipe. How much money did Joshua have left?"

Ask your child to write down all the nouns, which are all the numbers in this problem. He or she should write:

3.5

5

$\frac{1}{2}$

.25.

Unit Conversions

Another way to help your child convert between various units is to write down the units for each number and determine which operation makes them cancel out properly. Say your child needs to convert one eighth of a day into hours. He or she might write $\frac{1}{8}$ *day* and $24 \frac{hours}{day}$. To end up with an answer in hours, the child can see that multiplication would work, because when the 2 fractions are multiplied, the *days* cancel out, leaving *hours*. Write this down like this: $\frac{1}{8}$ *day* x $24 \frac{hours}{day}$ and put a slash through each *day* to show that *hours* are left. Of course, the answer to this problem is 3 hours.

Now say your child wanted to convert $\frac{1}{8}$ *hours* into days using $24 \frac{hours}{day}$. In this case, he or she could see that dividing by 24 is the only way to get the *days* in the numerator and get the *hours* to cancel out. Explain this to your child, using $\frac{1}{8}$ *hour* ÷ $24 \frac{hours}{day} = \frac{1}{8}$ *hour* x $\frac{1}{24} \frac{day}{hour}$ and putting a slash through each *hour* to leave *day*. This procedure is like the one for reducing fractions by canceling common factors. In this case the answer is $\frac{1}{8 \times 24}$ *day* $= \frac{1}{192}$ *day*.

Construct an explanation similar to the one above using minutes and hours. You might extend this discussion to other units that may be converted to one another, such as inches, feet, yards, and miles. Practice conversions between U.S. units and metric equivalents—inches and centimeters, yards and meters, miles and kilometers. And, of course, there are many other conversions you can teach your child, such as those involving different units of mass, volume, and area.

Next, help your child include the verbs, or the operations. Joshua was "given" $3.50, which means he starts with that positive number. He "found" $5, which means that the first two numbers should be added. So, Joshua started with **3.5 + 5** dollars.

Since *of* always means times, ask your child to write down the amount Joshua spent. The answer should be $\frac{1}{2}$ **x (his money)**. Given the above translation, that should be $\frac{1}{2}$ **x (3.5 + 5)**.

Now ask your child what operation "spent" suggests. He or she should say subtraction or minus. Tell him or her to write down the minus sign in front of the above expression. So he or she should write $-\frac{1}{2}$ **x (3.5 + 5)**.

Move on to the final sentence, asking your child to translate that. The word "dropped" suggests lost and subtraction. So the translation should be −.25.

Next, tell your child to combine the 3 expressions into a statement. The correct statement is: $3.5 + 5 - \frac{1}{2} \times (3.5 + 5) - .25 = $ **money Joshua had left**. Solving that equation to answer the question yields $8.5 - \frac{1}{2} \times 8.5 - .25 = 8.5 - 4.25 - .25 = 4.25 - .25 = 4$. So Joshua has $4 left.

2. "Jeremiah bought six hundred shares of stock. Each share cost twelve dollars and twenty cents. When the price of the stock increased by ten percent, Jeremiah sold all of his shares. How much money did Jeremiah make in this transaction?"

First, write down the nouns:

600
$12.20
10% or .10

Next, translate the first two sentences to determine how much money Jeremiah paid for his stock. The answer is **600 x 12.20 = $7,320**.

To translate the second sentence and determine the new price of the stock, your child must use the rule taught in lesson 7.3. The new price of the stock is **$12.20 + $12.20 x .10 = $13.42**.

To determine how much money Jeremiah made, explain that you need to subtract the amount Jeremiah paid for his stock from the amount Jeremiah received in the sale of his stock. You already determined how much Jeremiah paid for his stock, but you haven't yet determined how much money he received in the sale. Ask your child if he or she knows how to do that. The answer is to multiply the new price of the stock, which you determined above, by the number of shares. Or **600 x $13.42 = $8,052**. So, how much money did Jeremiah make? The answer is **$8,052 − $7,320 = $732**.

Supply numerous other examples of story problems involving fractions, decimals, and percents. Walk through any difficult parts of each problem with your child, but also test your child on his or her ability to solve steps or complete problems alone. Your child will probably need numerous practice sessions spread over many days or weeks to become good at solving the most difficult problems.

Chapter 9

Algebra

In algebra, students are expected to revisit many of the topics in the previous seven or eight years of math instruction, this time using letters—as unknowns or variables—in mathematical expressions and equations. Algebra also includes many new topics. This is a huge amount of material, 2 to 4 times as much as your child was asked to learn in any previous year. No wonder many American children find learning algebra so much more difficult than learning arithmetic!

You can ease the burden using the tips in this chapter. As discussed earlier, one of the best things you can do is introduce your child to algebraic concepts such as unknowns before they encounter them as part of their formal algebra training. Another is to teach them about negative numbers early instead of waiting until algebra, when they are encountering lots of new ideas.

For the purposes of this book, I'll assume your child is on the threshold of learning algebra without any previous introduction to it. I cannot possibly tell you how to teach your child first-year algebra in a single chapter. What I can do is identify key concepts within algebra that are commonly neglected or difficult for children, and so stand to benefit from my teaching methods. I will also cover some algebra fundamentals to put my methods in context. But please use this chapter along with a good first-year algebra text such as *Integrated Mathematics Course 1*, which is listed in the appendix.

Before attempting to teach your child algebra, be sure your child knows the basic arithmetic facts, how to manipulate decimals, percentages, and fractions, and how to convert between fractions, mixed numbers, decimals, and percentages. Your child should also know how to translate words and phrases in nonalgebraic story problems into mathematical expressions and how to draw and interpret graphs—for example, the number of peaches picked as a function of hours worked.

After covering negative numbers, this chapter will guide you and your child through the language of algebra, grouping its strange-looking equations into parts of mathematical "speech." Putting mathematical concepts into one of a few categories that relate to each other in simple ways can make learning algebra easier and more meaningful to your child.

Section 1:
INTRODUCTION TO ALGEBRA STORY PROBLEMS

First, show your child the fun part of algebra, the part that lifts it above grubby arithmetic like a shining star in the heavens: Its ability to turn the quantities and relations in a story problem into math that can be solved for the unknowns. This is the Holy Grail of precalculus mathematics, and you get to hand it to your child. Tell your child that the most exciting use of algebra is to solve story problems using simple rules for translating from English to mathematics. Though your child must practice these rules by solving many story problems, show your child the magic of this mathematical tool now.

Find a couple of story problems that do not involve multiplying or dividing negative numbers. Here is a good one to begin with. "Joan is three times as old as her sister. Joan is twenty-seven. How old is her sister?" Though your child can probably solve this problem without algebra, show him or her how to solve it with algebra, since algebra's tools will ultimately prove useful in solving more complex problems.

First, ask your child "What is the unknown number we wish to find?" The answer is: The sister's age. Let s be the age of the sister. This is the most basic step in algebra, letting a letter stand for an unknown number. It is usually best to use the first letter of the name of the unknown, in this case, s for the sister's age, because that helps you remember what the unknown stands for. Even so, know that the general convention is to use x for the unknown, so you will see x representing many unknowns in textbooks and in equations later in this chapter. The next step is to write an equation involving s and numbers that will allow you to figure out the numerical value of s, the unknown.

Tell your child to look in the story problem for the word *is*. In story problems, *is* almost always means = in mathematical language. Ask your child to circle all the "is" words. He or she should find *is* in all three sentences. Ask your child: "What is the translation for *is* in mathematics?" He or she should say "equals." Translate the last sentence, a question, as "$s =$ ___ ." Write this down and explain that it means that when you figure out the age of the sister, you will get a mathematical statement of the form, "$s =$ some number." This statement simply says what you are supposed to find— the numerical value of the unknown s.

Now, bring your child's attention to the sentence, "Joan is twenty-seven." While this is clearly useful information, this sentence, by itself, won't allow you to figure out the sister's age. However, to show that every sentence in this problem containing *is* can be translated into mathematics, say, "Let j be Joan's age." Then translate the sentence as $j = 27$.

So it must be the remaining sentence you will primarily use to solve the problem. That sentence reads: "Joan is three times as old as her sister." So write $j = 3s$, where the expression "$3s$" means "3 times s." In algebra, if no operation symbol appears between a number and an unknown, the number and the unknown are to be multiplied. From the second sentence, you know that $j = 27$. So following one of the rules of algebra that "equals may be substituted for equals in any expression," substitute 27 for j in the equation $j = 3s$, to get $27 = 3s$. This can be solved using another rule of algebra that dividing both sides of an equation by the same nonzero quantity gives you another true equation. Ask your child what you should divide both sides of the equation by to get an equation of the form "s = some number." The answer is to divide both sides by 3 to get $s = 9$, which means that Joan's sister is 9 years old.

Now your child might think that algebra is an overly complicated way of solving story problems like this one, which can be solved using mental arithmetic. That may be true. But the power of algebra is that it can be used to solve much more complex story problems that would be difficult or impossible to solve without it. Take this problem: "In four years, Joan will be six times as old as her sister will be in a year. Two years from now, Joan will be seven times as old as her sister is now. How old is her sister?"

This is a difficult problem to solve in your head. But it's not hard using algebra. The first step is to represent unknowns with letters. So first ask your child: "What are the unknowns?" The answer is Joan's age and her sister's age. Ask your child how these might be represented mathematically. The answer should be "Let j be Joan's age. Let s be the sister's age."

Now ask your child to try to translate each sentence in the problem, starting from the last one, which is simplest. If necessary, hint that *is* or *will be* translates as "=." Also, tell your child to represent the various mathematical parts, or expressions, before writing the full equations. These parts are

Joan's age in 4 years $(j + 4)$

Joan's age in 2 years or equivalently, "two years from now," $(j + 2)$

The sister's age in a year $(s + 1)$

Six times as old as the sister is in a year $(6 (s + 1))$

Seven times as old as the sister $(7s)$.

So with perhaps a few more hints and leading questions from you, your child should provide the following translation.

$s = \underline{\quad\quad}$?   (This is the last sentence, representing the problem's solution.)

$j + 2 = 7s$ (This is the second sentence.)

$j + 4 = 6 (s + 1)$ (This is the first sentence.)

Simplify these equations as much as possible. The first 2 are simple already, but the third one could be simpler. So ask your child to do this. Multiplying 6 by $(s + 1)$, $j + 4 = 6 (s + 1)$ can be changed to $j + 4 = 6s + 6$. Subtracting 4 from both sides of the equation then yields: $j = 6s + 2$. Next, you want to create 1 equation from 2. This is done by substituting for j. Since $j = 6s + 2$, tell your child to go ahead and use $6s + 2$ instead of j in the second equation. This yields the equation: $6s + 2 + 2 = 7s$. Now you can subtract $6s$ from both sides to get $2 + 2 = s$. So $4 = s$ or $s = 4$. The sister is 4 years old.

Help your child substitute the value of the unknown, s, into one of the equations written from the story problem to determine the value of the second unknown, j. Using the second sentence, you get $j + 2 = 28$, or $j = 26$. Now, tell your child to check the values of j and s by substituting both of them into the third equation to be sure the 2 sides of the equation are equal. They should be; if they aren't, a mistake was made in solving (or checking) the equations. In this case, your child should get $26 + 4 = 6 (4 + 1)$ or $30 = 6 \times 5$. So the values are correct.

Tell your child to always perform such a substitution check except on tests when there isn't time. (When there is just 1 unknown, your child will only have to substitute 1 value into 1 equation.) This kind of check catches calculation errors, but not translation errors, those made in translating the words of a story problem into equations. To check for both, your child can substitute the values found for the unknowns into the words of the story problem to check for inconsistencies. If your child finds this difficult or makes many errors doing it, tell him or her to just use the calculation check.

If your child knows no algebra, you will probably have to supply some, many, or all of the steps in the above problem. The goal of this introduction to algebra is not to teach algebraic methods, but to show your child that the purpose of algebra is to solve difficult real-world problems. That will motivate your child to learn algebraic simplification methods that are boring to many students. Point out this aspect of algebra throughout your teaching of the subject, and use an algebra textbook that peppers instruction of algebraic simplification methods with story problems that employ those methods.

2.1 The Concept

The computational side of algebra typically begins with negative numbers, and how to add, subtract, multiply, and divide these numbers. If you started this book when your child was young and just learning arithmetic, and followed the advice in earlier chapters, your child may already be familiar with the concept of negative numbers and how to add them. If so, he or she will only need to learn to subtract, multiply, and divide these numbers. Review what your child already knows about negative numbers, but your child should catch on to both the old and new ideas quickly.

However, if your child has been taught only the operations on positive numbers, algebra's introduction of negative numbers can be quite challenging. Changing one's concept of number is confusing to many children. Adults often forget how difficult negative numbers can be.

Your child must learn to distinguish between the negative sign on a number and subtraction, as well as between a positive sign and addition. Explain that addition and subtraction are binary operations, meaning they operate on 2 numbers or "inputs," and provide 1 solution or "output." The positive and negative signs, by contrast, operate only on a single number—the input—and the positive or negative number itself is the output. Invoking the language of math, explain that numbers with signs are simple "expressions," or nouns, while addition and subtraction are "operations," or verbs.

To explain the meaning of signed numbers, draw a number line using tick marks representing the numbers –20 through +20. Then show your child, for example, that +5 means 5 steps to the right of wherever you're starting from. If you start at 0, you end up at +5. If you start at +6, you end up +11. Ask your child to represent different positive numbers on the line.

Now explain that a negative sign denotes movement to the left, or a change in direction from the positive, default direction. For instance, –5 means 5 steps to the left of 0. Note that this is the same as subtracting 5 from 0. Next ask your child to start at +6, and then go –5, meaning walk 5 steps to the left of 6. He or she should end up at +1. This is the same as subtracting 5 from 6. Explain to your child that negative numbers and subtraction are very similar in this context. However, negative numbers can exist by themselves, as entities, whereas subtraction is an action done on two numbers together. Explain that the negative sign on a number alone implies moving to the left from 0. Thus –5 means 5 steps to the left of 0.

2.2 Adding Negative Numbers

Now, have your child start at +6 on the number line and move 5 units to the left again. Explain that this means that you are combining, or adding, +6 and –5. Tell your child that this is the same as writing **(+6) + (–5)**.

To reduce the number of + signs, tell your child that a number by itself, such as 6, is interpreted as a positive number, in this case as +6. Thus, the above problem can be written as **6 + (–5)**. To further reduce the number of + signs, explain that adding a negative number is the same as subtracting a positive number. Both mean moving left along a number line. Thus, the expression reduces to **6 – 5**. This equals 1, as you saw on the number line.

Ask your child to solve several similar problems. For instance: **7 + (–2), 15 + (–23), 1 + (–10)**, and so on. Start with small numbers and then move on to large 2- and 3-digit numbers. Be sure your child writes down the intermediate step in each case. For example, **7 + (–2) = 7 – 2 = 5**. (The answers to the other problems are –8 and –9.)

2.3 Subtracting Negative Numbers

Now here comes a principle many kids find difficult: Subtracting a negative number is the same as adding a positive number. For instance, **6 – (–5) = 6 + 5 = 11**. Perhaps the easiest way to make this seem correct to your child is to redefine the subtraction operation as changing the sign of the number being subtracted. It is also equivalent to changing direction on the number line. Since a negative number would prompt you to go left, subtracting a negative number would mean moving right, or adding.

Again, ask your child to solve a number of example problems until he or she gets the hang of it. You can choose any problems you wish, but examples include: **1 – (–1) = 1 + 1 = 2, 13 – (–10) = 13 + 10 = 23, 4 – (–18) = 4 + 18 = 22**. Again, give your child practice subtracting both small and large negative numbers. Finally, give your child some problems with a leading negative term, such as **–7 – (–12) = –7 + 12 = 5**. If this confuses your child, illustrate the problem on the number line.

2.4 Multiplying and Dividing Negative Numbers

Next, teach your child the rules for multiplying and dividing negative numbers. Point out that he or she already knows that multiplying or dividing two positive numbers yields a positive number for an answer. But what if one number or the other is negative? Explain that multiplying or dividing a negative number and a positive number (no matter which comes first) always yields a negative number for an answer.

Give your child multiplication and division problems using negative numbers such as **2 x (–3)**, **(–11) x 4**, **4 ÷ (–2)**, **(–12) ÷ 4**. (The answers are –6, –44, –2, –3.) Continue to provide such problems until your child masters the concept.

Most kids will accept the idea that multiplying a negative number and a positive number yields the same answer no matter which number comes first, since multiplication is commutative. However, some have trouble with the same rule when applied to division, since division is not commutative. If this confuses your child, invoke the principle that dividing by a number N is the same as multiplying by $\frac{1}{N}$. In this way, a division problem can be made into an equivalent multiplication problem, making it clear why the same rule applies to division too.

Next, explain what to do when both numbers are negative. In this case, tell your child that multiplying or dividing two negative numbers always yields a positive product or quotient. To help clarify this, repeat the rule that the negative sign means changing directions on the number line. So if the first negative sign means a change in direction from positive to negative, then the second negative sign means changing direction again, back to positive. Test your child with problems such as **–2 x (–6)**, **(–5) x (–4)**, **(–10) ÷ (–2)**, **(–12) ÷ –3**. (The answers are 12, 20, 5, 4.) Move on to problems with larger numbers such as **(–20) x (–16)**, **(–52) x (–41)**, **(–100) ÷ (–20)**, **(–180) ÷ (–18)**. When your child gets the hang of this, mix up multiplication and division problems containing one or two negative numbers to be sure your child can apply the appropriate rule in each case. Finally, give your child a large number of problems involving addition, subtraction, multiplication, and division of negative numbers, mixing up the order of the various types of problems.

Section 3:
THE LANGUAGE OF ALGEBRA

3.1 Algebraic Nouns

Now it's time to revisit the various mathematical parts of speech in the context of algebraic equations. This will help your child relate such equations to English and to other equations already encountered.

Remind your child that nouns, or expressions, have so far been numbers of various kinds—whole numbers, fractions, percents, and the like. In algebra, explain that these nouns also include letters, which often stand for unknown quantities, or simply "unknowns." Tell your child that the goal is very often to solve for these unknowns—that is, to solve an equation such that the solution reveals the numerical value of the unknown. Sometimes, letters in algebraic equations are not unknowns, but "variables," which do not have one or several possible values, but an infinite number of possible values. Later, you will more fully explain the differences between unknowns and variables. For now, just say that algebra's letter nouns may be either unknowns or variables.

3.2 Algebraic Verbs

Algebraic equations also contain action verbs. These include arithmetic operations such as $+$, $-$, $\times$, and $\div$ or $/$. In algebra, your child will learn other operations as well, such as exponentials—squares, cubes, and the like—and roots—square roots, cube roots, and so on. This chapter does not cover these, but be sure your child learns about them from a textbook. Indeed, please teach your child these concepts now. In doing so, explain that in contrast to binary operations like addition and subtraction, which act on two numbers, exponentials and roots—in which a number is raised to the nth power or the nth root of a number is taken—are unary and operate on only one number.

In algebra your child will also learn about simple functions, which represent another kind of unary verb discussed later in this chapter.

3.3. Algebraic Statements

Explain that algebraic equations and inequalities also contain relations such as =, ≠, <, ≤, >, ≥, and that the equations or inequalities are algebra's sentences or "statements." A relation with two expressions on either side of it is a statement. If both expressions are numbers, explain that the statement is either true or false, and that's all there is to it. For example, $10 = 10$ is true; $7 < 9$ is true; $42 > 44$ is false.

But in algebra, statements often include an unknown, or letter quantity. For example: $x = 3$; $2x = 44$; or $3x - 5 = x + 7$. Write these down for your child and tell him or her that in algebra, if no operation symbol appears between a number and an unknown, as in $2x$ or $3x$, the number and the unknown are to be multiplied. Tell your child to assume that all such statements are true and that he or she is supposed to solve for the value of the unknown, letter quantity. In other words, he or she should find the value of x that makes the statement true. In the first example, there is nothing to do. $x = 3$ is exactly the right form for an answer. But the other two equations need to be simplified to solve for the unknown.

3.4 Solving Simple Statements

There are a few simple tricks for solving for the unknown in an algebraic equation, any number of which might be used in a problem. Tell your child that for any algebraic equation, he or she can

- Add the same quantity to both sides of the equation

- Subtract the same quantity from both sides of the equation

- Multiply or divide both sides of the equation by the same nonzero quantity

Next say that the general rule for solving equations (or inequalities) is that you can "do the same thing" to both sides of an equation, where "do the same thing" means one of the 4 arithmetic operations specified above.

In the equation $2x = 44$, explain that the goal is to get x by itself and that means getting rid of the 2. Since the 2 is multiplied by x, you can get rid of it by dividing both sides of the equation by 2. Doing so yields $x = 22$. That is the right form for the answer. Teach your child to recognize this form,

$x =$ ____ , because that will make it easier for him or her to figure out how to solve an algebraic equation.

Now take the equation $3x - 5 = x + 7$. Advise your child that he or she will get to the answer by putting all the numbers on one side and all the x's on the other. Ask your child: "What is the best way to do that?" If your child doesn't know, suggest adding 5 to both sides of the equation. After doing so, your child should come up with $3x = x + 12$. Now ask: "How might we get all the x's on the side opposite the twelve?" Help your child if he or she doesn't know, by suggesting that he or she subtract x from both sides. This gives $2x = 12$. Now the problem looks like the one you just solved above. To get x by itself, tell your child to divide both sides by 2 to get $x = 6$.

Give your child lots of other practice problems like this one from a textbook and ask him or her to solve for the unknown. Give guidance where necessary. These problems should be simple in that they do not contain parentheses or exponentials.

3.5 Story Problems with 1 Unknown

Ask your child to solve story problems that require solving algebraic equations with a single unknown. One class of such equations are problems involving uniform motion and that use the equation distance = rate × time or $d = r \times t$. Here are 3 examples, but give your child practice with lots of story problems of this type.

"Kip rides his bike to school, a distance of three miles. If he bikes at an average speed of nine miles per hour, how long does it take Kip to get to school?"

First, ask your child to write the nouns. These are:

9 miles per hour (This is the rate at which Kip rides his bike.)
3 miles (This is the distance to school.)
Let t be the time it takes Kip to ride his bike to school.

Attending to the verbs and statements, ask your child to write the equation governing rate, distance, and time. He or she should write: $d = r \times t$. The verb here is multiplication. Now tell your child to substitute the above unknowns into that equation. He or she should write:

3 miles = 9 miles per hour x *t*

Solving for *t* by dividing both sides of the equation by 9 yields *t* = $\frac{3}{9}$ **hour** = $\frac{1}{3}$ **hour**. So it takes Kip $\frac{1}{3}$ *hour* (or 20 minutes) to ride his bike to school.

"Sandra and Mark live at the same house, and both leave for work at eight a.m. Sandra arrives at her office at nine a.m., after traveling at an average speed of twenty miles per hour. Mark arrives at his office at eight-thirty a.m., after traveling at an average speed of fifty miles per hour. Whose office is farther from their home?"

First, ask your child to write the nouns:

20 miles per hour (This is Sandra's speed.)
1 hour (This is the time it takes Sandra to get to work.)
Let *s* be the distance to Sandra's office
50 miles per hour (This is Mark's speed.)
$\frac{1}{2}$ hour (This is the time it takes Mark to get to work.)
Let *m* be the distance to Mark's office

Tell your child to substitute the values for Sandra's trip into the equation *d* = *r* x *t*. He or she should write:

s = 20 miles per hour x 1 hour. So *s* = 20 miles.

Now tell your child to do the same for Mark's trip:

m = 50 miles per hour $\frac{1}{2}$ x hour. So *m* = 25 miles.

The answer: Mark's office is farther from their home.

If you think your child can handle it, introduce this much more difficult problem that also involves the equation *d* = *r* x *t*

"Bob and Gary race their cars, starting at the same time from equivalent positions (with Gary's car directly above Bob's) on identical circular tracks five miles in circumference, one above the other. Both cars maintain a steady speed, with Bob's car traveling at 126 mph and Gary's at 128 mph. How long will it take for the cars to arrive once again at equivalent positions on the two tracks?"

First, ask your child to write the nouns. These are the rates at which Bob and Gary are traveling, the distance of the track, and the unknown time:

126 miles per hour
128 miles per hour
5 miles
Let t be the time it takes cars to be at same position again

Once again, ask your child to write the equation governing rate, distance and time, or **$d = r \times t$**.

The tough part of this problem is figuring out what numbers to substitute for d and r, so that it will be possible to solve for the unknown t. Hint that to be directly above one another a second time, the cars will travel different distances (since they are traveling at different rates) and that you are looking for the *difference* in the distance each car must travel. Ask your child what that difference is. The answer is the circumference of the track, or 5 miles. That is the number he or she should substitute for d.

Similarly, your child should use the *difference* in speeds (2 mph) as the value of r. Now the equation becomes **$5 = 2 \times t$**. To find the time, your child needs to solve for t by dividing both sides of the equation by 2. Thus **$t = 5$ miles ÷ 2 miles per hour = 2.5 hours**.

Give your child other story problems involving constant rates of speed. After every new algebraic technique you teach your child, give him or her story problems requiring that technique in their solution.

3.6 Inequalities

Next, move on to inequalities. Tell your child that the same rules for solving algebraic equations apply to solving algebraic inequalities, with one exception: If both sides of the equation are to be multiplied or divided by a quantity headed by a negative sign, the "direction" of the inequality is reversed. That is, $<$ changes to $>$ and vice versa; $\leq$ changes to $\geq$ and vice versa.

Take the inequality **$3x - 5 < x + 7$**. Once again, your child should do the same thing to both sides of the equation. First, add 5; then subtract x. That yields **$2x < 12$**, and **$x < 6$**. This means that any value of $x < 6$ makes the statement true, so the solution is the set of all values of x less than 6. Next, change the problem to **$-3x - 5 < x + 7$**. Adding 5 and subtracting x yields:

–4x < 12, which simplifies to **x > –3**. Note that the sign switched when we divided both sides of the inequality by –4.

Give your child lots of practice solving for unknowns in various inequalities. In some of them, ask the child to multiply or divide by a negative, so that he or she practices switching the inequality sign.

4.1 Parentheses

Solving more complicated algebraic equations often involves dealing with parentheses. Tell your child that parentheses are used to indicate the order in which operations are to be performed. The calculations inside a set of parentheses are those that he or she should perform first. For example, note that **54 – (3 x 6) = 54 – 18 = 36**. By contrast, **(54 – 3) x 6 = 51 x 6 = 306**. Be sure your child understands the difference and provide several similar problems for him or her to solve to hammer the point home.

4.2 PEMDAS

Now explain that parentheses mean the same thing in algebraic expressions. For example, evaluate the following expression for **x = 6**:

$$3 \{2 [(x - 4)^2 + 1] - 10 + 5x - (x^2 - 20)\}$$

The first step is to substitute 6 for x to get a purely numerical expression, namely,

$$3 \{2 [(6 - 4)^2 + 1] - 10 + 5 \times 6 - (6^2 - 20)\}.$$

The order in which these various operations should be performed in this expression and others is:

1. First, do the operations inside parentheses, starting first with the innermost parentheses and working outward

2. Second, calculate exponentials, such as squares or cubes

3. Third, perform any multiplication and division

4. Fourth, do the addition and subtraction in left to right order

This order is captured by the mnemonic PEMDAS, for Parentheses, Exponentiation, Multiplication, Division, Addition, and Subtraction. Emphasize that multiplication and division have equal priority, as do addition and subtraction.

In the above problem, applying the PEMDAS rule is tricky, because there are several sets of parentheses. (The different shapes are used to make it easier to see the pairings of left and right parentheses.) The rule is to do the innermost parentheses first, perform all the operations inside in the order specified by steps 2, 3, and 4, and then move on to the next closest set of parentheses. Within those, perform steps 2, 3, and 4 in order. Then move out again.

In the above problem, the two closest sets of parentheses are $(6 - 4)$ and $(6^2 - 20)$. In the first, there is only 1 operation, so calculate $6 - 4 = 2$. In the second, take care of the exponential first. So $6^2 - 20$ becomes $36 - 20 = 16$. The result of these calculations is: $3 \{2 [2^2 + 1] - 10 + 5 \times 6 - 16\}$.

Next, move out to the next set of parentheses. It's $[2^2 + 1]$. According to the rules, you do the exponential first. Thus, $2^2 + 1$ becomes $4 + 1 = 5$. So the expression simplifies to $3 \{2 \times 5 - 10 + 5 \times 6 - 16\}$.

There is now only 1 set of parentheses. Still, you must first work inside that set before dealing with the 3 outside. According to the rules, you do multiplication and division first. So take 2×5 and 5×6 to get 10 and 30 respectively. This yields $3 \{10 - 10 + 30 - 16\}$.

After doing the addition and subtraction, you get simply 3 {14}. Getting rid of the outermost set of parentheses produces the final $3 \times 14 = 42$.

4.3 Factors and Terms

Here's another bird's-eye view of the same problem. Teach your child this way of looking at the problem too, because it introduces him or her to some important mathematical concepts. At the highest level, explain that the expression breaks into 2 factors: 3 times the expression inside the curly brackets. Factors are expressions to be multiplied. By contrast, terms are expressions to be added or subtracted. Teach your child the difference.

Show your child that the expression inside the curly brackets consists of 4 terms: $2 [(6 - 4)^2 + 1]$; -10; $+ 5 \times 6$; and $-(6^2 - 20)$. Explain that these should be evaluated starting from the left and moving right. The first term consists of 2 times the sum of 2 terms: $(6 - 4)^2$ and 1. These are to be evaluated in left to right order as $2 \times (2^2 + 1) = 2 (4 + 1) = 2 \times 5 = 10$. This gives us $\{10 - 10 + 30 - 16\} = \{0 + 30 - 16\} = \{30 - 16\} = \{14\}$. At the highest level we now have $3 \{14\} = 42$. So the entire expression has the value 42.

4.4 PEMDAS Part 2

Now, walk through another complex algebraic expression with your child that must be solved for a certain value of the unknown, x. The first step is always substituting that value for x. Then, the PEMDAS order is applied. Lastly, review the factors and terms of the expression with your child and solve the individual terms, from left to right, using the PEMDAS rule for each one.

Here's another example. Solve this expression for $x = 4$:

$$x \{3x - 4 (x + 2) + 2 [(x - 1) - (x^3 + 2x)]\}$$

Substituting 4 for x gives $4 \{3 \times 4 - 4 (4 + 2) + 2 [(4 -1) - (4^3 + 2 \times 4)]\}$

First do the arithmetic inside the innermost parentheses. The expression then becomes: $4 \{3 \times 4 - 4 (6) + 2 [(3) - (64 + 8)]\} = 4 \{3 \times 4 - 4 (6) + 2 [3 - 72]\}$.

Now, moving outward to the next set of parentheses, the square brackets, you get: $4 \{3 \times 4 - 4 (6) + 2 [-69]\}$. Evaluating the terms inside the curly brackets from left to right yields: $4 \{12 - 24 - 138\} = 4 \{-150\} = -600$.

Walk through as many examples as your child needs to understand the procedure. Then ask your child to solve similar problems on his or her own, providing hints along the way when necessary.

Section 5:
GETTING RID OF PARENTHESES AND FACTORING
- -

5.1 The Distributive Law

In this lesson, you'll teach your child to work with algebraic expressions that contain parentheses and in which a number cannot be substituted for the expression's unknowns. In such cases, your child will not get a single number as an answer but will find a simpler (or different) equivalent expression that still contains the letters in the original expression.

One of the most common ways of eliminating parentheses in an algebraic expression involves the distributive property. Your child probably has encountered this property but may not remember it because it isn't used much until algebra. The distributive property relates addition and multiplication in the following way: $a(b + c) = ab + ac$. In other words, it eliminates parentheses by multiplying each term inside the parentheses by the factor outside the parentheses.

To explain the distributive property to your child, give him or her a simple example of how to apply it. Take $4(3x - 4)$. To get rid of the parentheses, explain that you multiply 4 times each term inside the parentheses. So you get $4 \times 3x - 4 \times 4 = 12x - 16$. Provide other examples until your child seems to understand. Then provide practice problems for your child to solve such as:

$3(7x + 2) = \underline{\qquad}$
$x(7y + 4) = \underline{\qquad}$
$2a(x - 4) = \underline{\qquad}$
$x(x - y) = \underline{\qquad}$
$-2x(x + 6) = \underline{\qquad}$

(The answers are $21x + 6$; $7xy + 4x$; $2ax - 8a$; $x^2 - xy$; $-2x^2 - 12x$.)

The hardest aspect of using the distributive property to eliminate parentheses is multiplying two negative factors. Take the problem: $-6x(2x - 3) = -12x^2 + 18x$. Kids often get the sign of the second term wrong, incorrectly concluding, for instance, that $-6x(2x - 3) = -12x^2 - 18x$. Even when a child knows that the product of two negative factors is a positive, he or she tends to forget it when doing this more complex task. Your child is likely to need a lot of practice with this type of problem to become consistently accurate. In the practice problems you give your child be sure to insert some that require multiplying two negative factors and check your child's answers carefully, keeping an eye out for the above mistake. Keep up the practice until your child makes few or no mistakes. You will probably want to practice on several separate days to reinforce your child's consistency in this task.

5.2 Monomials and Polynomials

Explain to your child that he or she just learned to use the distributive property to multiply a "monomial" by a "polynomial." Explain that a monomial can be a constant like the number 3 or the number 15. It can be a letter unknown or variable such as x, or it can be a product of a constant and one or more variables such as $5x^2y^3$ or $12x$ or $6xy$. Please tell your child to write down several examples of monomials of his or her own choosing. (Terms like $\sqrt{x}$ and that include x in the denominator of a fraction, for instance $\frac{5}{x}$, are not monomials.)

Next, explain that a polynomial is the sum or difference of two or more monomials. Polynomials are expressions such as **3x + 1**, **5x² + x – 4**, **2xy + 2**, and **x³ + 4y + 3x**. Remind your child that each monomial in a polynomial is called a term. Two terms are like terms if they have the same unknown factors. So $6xy$ and $7xy$ are like terms, but $6xy$ and $6x^2y$ are unlike terms; $2x$ and $9x$ are like terms, but $2x$ and $2x^2$ are unlike terms. Polynomials come in different forms. A polynomial such as **2xy + 2**, with two unlike terms, is called a binomial. A polynomial like **x³ + 4y + 3x** with three unlike terms is called a trinomial. Explain that a polynomial is in its simplest form if it has no like terms.

Polynomials also have different "degrees." A polynomial's degree is determined by adding the exponents or powers of the term with the highest degree, which is the one with the most exponents. In other words, a polynomial's degree is the same as the term in the polynomial with the highest degree. For example, the degree of the polynomial **x³ + 4y + 3x** is 3. The degree of **2xy + 2** is 2 and the degree of **5x²y³ + 1** is 5. Write down various polynomials and ask your child to state the degree of each one. Using a textbook to guide you, also give your child practice adding, subtracting, and multiplying monomials if needed.

5.3 The Distributive Property Part 2—FOIL

Now, move on to simplifying more complex expressions with many terms. Tell your child that the goal in each case is to create an expression with fewer terms. For instance **3 (x + 2) + 5x = 3x + 6 + 5x = 8x + 6**. This transforms an expression with four factors and four terms to an intermediate expression with four factors and three terms and finally to an expression with two factors and two terms. Provide many other examples and practice problems, such as:

$$2(x + 1) + 8x = 2x + 2 + 8x = 10x + 2$$
$$4x(x - 3) + 5x^2 = 4x^2 - 12x + 5x^2 = 9x^2 - 12x$$
$$3(xy - 1) + 4xy = 3xy - 3 + 4xy = 7xy - 3.$$

Now show your child how to use the distributive property in problems involving two sets of parentheses, as in $(x - 4)(x + 8)$. In this case, the rule is to first multiply the two first nouns (letters or numbers) inside the parentheses. Then multiply the outer two nouns, then the inner two, and finally the last two. A good mnemonic for this procedure is FOIL for First, Outer, Inner, Last. Applying FOIL to this problem, you get $x^2 + 8x - 4x - 32$, which can be simplified to $x^2 + 4x - 32$. Give your child plenty of practice with pairs of letters and numbers in parentheses in a similar format. Using a textbook to guide you, move on to teach your child to multiply polynomials of the form $(x + 2)(x^2 + 5x + 6)$. Using the distributive property, that expression can be changed to $x(x^2 + 5x + 6) + 2(x^2 + 5x + 6) = x^3 + 5x^2 + 6x + 2x^2 + 10x + 12 = x^3 + 7x^2 + 16x + 12$. If you wish, you can then teach your child to divide monomials, binomials and other polynomials. Be sure to give the child lots of practice problems until he or she masters these techniques.

5.4 Simple Factoring

Your child also must learn to do the reverse of the above operations—that is, factoring. Factoring means taking a complex expression like the answers in the above problems and creating an equivalent expression that is a product of factors, some or all of which will be expressions in parentheses. One kind of factoring requires breaking out a common factor from 2 or more algebraic terms. In $4xy + 8y$, for instance, $4y$ is the common factor. So the correct factorization is $4y(x + 2)$. Explain this to your child and provide an example such as:

$$8x + 2 =$$

Ask your child: "Is there a common factor for both $8x$ and 2?" Your child should answer 2, since both terms can be divided by 2. Then pull out the factor 2 and ask your child what is left over to put inside the parentheses. He or she must then divide each term by that factor. This yields $(4x + 1)$. So $8x + 2 = 2(4x + 1)$. When you and your child have found the answer, ask your child to use the distributive property to get rid of the parentheses in the answer. He or she should produce the expression you started with: $8x + 2$.

Next, ask your child to solve similar problems on his or her own, those whose answers contain just 1 set of parentheses and 1 numerical quantity outside. For instance, $12x - 6$, which can be factored as $6(2x - 1)$.

Then move on to slightly harder problems like $9x^2 - 12x = 3x(3x - 4)$ or $20xy - 10x^2y = 10xy(2 - x)$. You may choose whatever examples you wish.

5.5 Factoring a Difference of Two Squares

Once your child has mastered this, move on to a more advanced kind of factoring: Factoring "a difference of two squares." A difference of two squares is just like it sounds. It's an expression consisting of one perfect square minus another perfect square. Such expressions include $x^2 - 9$, $x^4 - 36$, and $4x^2 - 81$. Factoring the first yields $(x + 3)(x - 3)$, the second $(x^2 + 6)(x^2 - 6)$, and the third $(2x - 9)(2x + 9)$.

The general idea is to take the square root of each factor and separate the roots by parentheses, using a minus sign between the terms in one of the factors and a plus sign between the terms in the other factor. Tell your child this rule and explain that the minus sign in one of the factors works in two ways. First, a negative and a positive factor is necessary to create the negative sign in front of the second square, -9 or -36 in the examples above. Second, the negative sign is necessary for the "middle terms" to cancel each other out. This will become evident if you ask your child multiply out the factors using FOIL.

Ask the child to factor these expressions:

$y^4 - 64$
$4x^4 - 4$
$z^2 - 36$

The answers are $(y^2 - 8)(y^2 + 8)$; $(2x^2 - 2)(2x^2 + 2)$ or $4[(x^2 + 1)(x^2 - 1)]$; $(z - 6)(z + 6)$. Note that the order of the two factors doesn't matter. Give your child as many of these problems as it takes for him or her to solve them effortlessly.

5.6 Factoring a Trinomial

The third kind of factoring you should teach your child is factoring a trinomial, in which the first term is of the form x^2, the second is of the form x, and the last is a real number. Give your child an example of a trinomial such as $x^2 + x - 6$. Write it down. Show that its factors are two binomials: $(x + 3) (x - 2)$. Then demonstrate that multiplying these factors yields the original trinomial, like this: $x^2 + 3x - 2x - 6 = x^2 + x - 6$.

The general rule for factoring a trinomial is to find factors for the first and last terms that together can be used to create the middle term when they are multiplied together and then added or subtracted. In the case above, the problem is reduced to finding the pair of factors for the last term—6—because the first term in each factor has to be x. At first, your child will probably have to try different pairs of factors of the final term to find two that work. Show him or her some possibilities that don't work: $+6$ and -1 as in $(x + 6) (x - 1)$ or $+2$ and -3 as in $(x + 2) (x - 3)$. Multiply each set of factors using the distributive property to show that they don't yield the original equation. For instance, $(x + 6) (x - 1)$ yields $x^2 + 6x - x - 6 = x^2 + 5x - 6$, which isn't right. And $(x + 2) (x - 3)$ yields $x^2 + 2x - 3x - 6 = x^2 - x - 6$, which also isn't right. However, the final possibility, $(x + 3) (x - 2)$, yields the original trinomial, like this: $x^2 + 3x - 2x - 6 = x^2 + x - 6$.

This is the most difficult type of factoring, so cull out many sample problems from algebra texts. Ask your child to try various factors in each case until he or she finds a pair that works. With each trial, tell your child to check that his or her answer is correct by multiplying out the factors using the distributive property. After a while, your child should be able to see ahead of time which pair of factors is most likely to work so that he or she doesn't have to try so many possibilities before landing on the right one. As with virtually all other mathematical skills, your child will probably have to practice this one on many separate occasions to truly master it.

5.7 Factoring Story Problems

After your child masters factoring, give him or her algebra story problems that require factoring. For example: "A classroom has three fewer desks in each row than the number of rows. Each row has the same number of desks. If the classroom has forty desks, find the number of desks in each row."

Ask your child to represent each unknown with a letter or an expression involving a letter. What are the two unknowns? They are the number of rows and the number of desks in each row. Tell your child to write: "Let r be the number of rows." Next, ask your child to represent the number of desks in each row with r. He or she should write: "Let $r - 3$ be the number of desks in each row." Ask your child to write an equation that relates the total number of desks to the number of rows and the number of desks in each row. The answer is

$$r(r - 3) = 40 \text{ or } r^2 - 3r = 40$$

To solve this equation, tell your child to create an expression that is equal to 0, as in $r^2 - 3r - 40 = 0$. Ask your child to factor this trinomial. The answer is $(r - 8)(r + 5) = 0$.

For this equation to be true, either $(r - 8)$ or $(r + 5)$ must $= 0$. Thus $r = 8$ or -5; r cannot equal a negative number, since there cannot be a negative number of rows in the classroom. So $r = 8$. Thus, there are 8 rows of desks and 5 desks in each row.

Give your child other story problems involving factoring, gleaning examples from an algebra textbook.

Section 6:
SYSTEMS OF EQUATIONS

6.1 Solving Systems of Equations

Next, teach your child to solve systems of equations—for instance, two equations that describe the same two unknowns. First, provide a simple example to show how this is done, such as:

$$y = 2x$$
$$y = x + 5.$$

Explain that since both $2x$ and $x + 5$ are equal to y, both expressions must also be equal to each other. Write $2x = x + 5$. Here's another way to look at what you just did: You substituted the x expression in the first equation for y in the second equation. The result is a single equation with a single unknown. Your child should be able to solve for x to find that **$x = 5$**. To find the value of y, tell your child to substitute 5 for x in either equation and solve for y.

Next, try a pair of equations involving fractions such as

$$y = \tfrac{2}{3}x + 2$$
$$y = \tfrac{5}{8}x + 10$$

Remind your child that the first step is setting the two x expressions equal to each other or equivalently, substituting the x expression in the first equation for y in the second equation. Your child should write

$$\tfrac{2}{3}x + 2 = \tfrac{5}{8}x + 10$$

Tell your child to solve that equation for x. Subtracting 2 from both sides yields

$$\tfrac{2}{3}x = \tfrac{5}{8}x + 8$$

Subtracting $\tfrac{5}{8}x$ from both sides gives

$$\tfrac{2}{3}x - \tfrac{5}{8}x = 8 \text{ or } \tfrac{1}{24}x = 8; \ x = 192$$

Ask your child to substitute 192 for x to get the value of **y; $y = 130$**. Now, test your child with two equations of this form.

$$x + y = 24$$
$$\tfrac{3}{4}x = y + 2$$

This time, your child has to solve one of the equations for y first before making the substitution in the other equation. Either equation works. Taking the first one, your child should write

$$y = 24 - x$$

Now that expression can be substituted for y in the second equation to yield

$\frac{3}{4}x = (24 - x) + 2$, which simplifies to

$\frac{3}{4}x = 26 - x$

$1\frac{3}{4}x = 26$

$\frac{7}{4}x = 26$

$x = \frac{104}{7} = 14\frac{6}{7}$

With that x value, your child should be able to find y; $y = 24 - 14\frac{6}{7} = 9\frac{1}{7}$.

Give your child lots of practice solving two equations with two unknowns until he or she can do it easily without help. Then move on to three equations, three unknowns, using a textbook to guide you if necessary. In addition, using a textbook, teach your child to solve equations such as the above using graphical methods.

6.2 Story Problems with Systems of Equations

Once your child has mastered the skill of solving for multiple unknowns in multiple equations, show your child how to solve story problems that involve this skill. Take this one: "Sam paid thirty dollars for two pounds of salmon and three pounds of cod. Julie paid seventeen fifty for one pound of salmon and two pounds of cod at the same prices Sam paid. What did Sam and Julie pay per pound for salmon? For cod?"

First, let's find the nouns. These include $30 and $17.50 and the unknowns: the price of a pound of salmon and the price of the pound of cod. As unknowns, these latter two nouns should be represented as letters. Ask your child to translate each price into a letter. The correct answer should look like:

"Let s be the price of a pound of salmon. Let c be the price of a pound of cod." Instruct your child to write those phrases on a piece of paper. Remind him or her that using the first letters of the names given in a story problem for the unknowns (unless two names start with the same letter) will prevent translation mistakes.

Now ask your child to translate the first sentence into an equation. If your child is stuck, hint that "and" means addition and that when someone buys 2 pounds of something, one must pay the price per pound twice or 2 times. Thus the amount Sam paid for 2 pounds of salmon is 2s and the amount he paid for 3 pounds of cod is 3c. Since Sam bought both for $30, translate the first sentence as:

$$2s + 3c = 30$$

In a similar vein, the second sentence translates as:

$$s + 2c = 17.50$$

Solving for s in the second equation yields: $s = 17.5 - 2c$
Substituting for s in the first equation yields:

$$2 (17.5 - 2c) + 3c = 30$$

Using the distributive property to simplify this, your child should get:

$$35 - 4c + 3c = 30$$
$$-c = -5$$

Thus, **c = 5**. They paid $5 per pound for cod. To find the price of salmon, tell your child to substitute 5 for c in either equation above. Using **s + 2c = 17.50**, you get s + 10 = 17.50, s = 17.5 − 10 = 7.5. So for salmon, they paid $7.50 per pound.

Show your child how to solve other story problems that involve two equations, two unknowns. When your child is ready, walk through a story problem with three equations and three unknowns, such as this one: "The town of Ancor is twice as old as Marton and three times as old as Frankton. The sum of Marton's and Frankton's ages is fifteen hundred. How old is Marton?"

First, let's find the nouns. These are the ages of Ancor, Marton, and Frankton. Ask your child to translate each age into a letter. The correct answer should look like:

Let A be the age of Ancor.
Let M be the age of Marton.
Let F be the age of Frankton.

Attending to the verbs, notice that Ancor is twice as old as Marton. Ask your child what "twice" means. He or she should say something like: to multiply by 2. So "twice as old a Marton" is 2M. Now focus on the phrase, Ancor is three times as old as Frankton. Ask your child to represent "three times." The answer is **3 x _____** . Next, tell your child to translate "three times as old as Frankton" Answer: 3F. The last sentence begins "The sum of Marton's and Frankton's ages . . ." Ask your child to translate this. The answer is **M + F.**

Now instruct your child to add the appropriate relations to create statements based on the above words. Ask your child to translate "is." (He or she should write "=.") Now take each sentence individually and ask your child to translate each one into a statement.

1. The town of Ancor is twice as old as Marton . . .

$$A = 2M$$

2. And three times as old as Frankton.

$$A = 3F$$

3. The sum of Marton's and Frankton's ages is fifteen hundred.

$$M + F = 1500$$

Now, you come to the question: How old is Marton?

Ask your child to translate that. The answer should be **M = _____** . So now your child should know that the point of the problem is to solve for M. Your child should be able to combine these equations in the following manner. Combining the first two equations yields **2M = 3F**, so $F = \frac{2M}{3}$. Substituting that expression for F in the last equation yields:

$$M + \frac{2M}{3} = 1500$$
$$\frac{5M}{3} = 1500$$
$$M = 1500 \times \frac{3}{5} = 900 = \text{Marton's age.}$$

Here is a harder problem that can be solved using 4 unknowns: "Martha was distributing candies at each of fifty places at her dinner party. At each place, she put either three lemon drops or five jelly beans. If she distributed 190 candies in all, how many lemon drops and how many jellybeans did she distribute? How many guests received lemon drops? How many received jellybeans?"

Have your child write down the nouns:

Let J be the number of jelly beans.
Let L be the number of lemon drops.
Let P_1 be the number of places/guests with jelly beans.
Let P_2 be the number of places/guests with lemon drops.
50 places
190 candies

First ask your child to write an equation that represents the total number of candies. If there are 190 candies in all, then **$L + J = 190$**.

Second, ask your child to write an equation representing the total number of places: **$P_1 + P_2 = 50$**.

To reduce the number of unknowns, tell your child that you need to relate P_1 to J and P_2 to L. Start with the equation relating the number of jelly beans to the number of places with jelly beans. Since there are 5 jelly beans at every place that has jelly beans, **$5\,P_1 = J$ or $P_1 = \frac{J}{5}$**.

Next, instruct your child to write an equation relating the number of lemon drops to the number of places with lemon drops. Since there are 3 lemon drops at every place with lemon drops, **$3\,P_2 = L$ or $P_2 = \frac{L}{3}$**.

Ask your child to substitute the equivalent expressions for P_1 and P_2 into the equation **$P_1 + P_2 = 50$**. The answer is $\frac{J}{5} + \frac{L}{3} = 50$. Now there are 2 equations, 2 unknowns:

$$L + J = 190$$
$$\frac{J}{5} + \frac{L}{3} = 50.$$

Solving for J in the simpler first equation yields **$J = 190 - L$**.
Substituting for J in the second equation yields $\frac{190 - L}{5} + \frac{L}{3} = 50$.
To solve this equation, have your child multiply both sides by 15 to get rid of the fractions. The result is:

$3(190 - L) + 5L = 750$, which becomes $570 - 3L + 5L = 750$. Thus, $2L = 180$ and $L = 90$. Martha distributed 90 lemon drops. Since $L + J = 190$, $J = 100$. Martha distributed 100 jelly beans. Since there were 3 lemon drops per place, 30 guests received lemon drops. Since there were 5 jelly beans per place, 20 guests received jelly beans.

Ask your child to try to solve numerous story problems with two and more unknowns, including some involving negative numbers. Give your child hints and help whenever he or she is stuck. Once your child is good at this, he or she should not have to write down every single step. That will be an advantage on speed tests when there isn't time to do so.

Section 7:
ADVANCED TRANSLATION

7.1 Nouns Revisited—Unknowns Versus Variables

In most of your discussion of algebra so far, you have taught your child to treat letters as unknowns. That is, the letter has a specific numerical value (or a few such values) that is not known originally, but will be after the problem is solved. Indeed, solving the problem requires finding a value or set of values for the unknown.

However, not all letters in algebraic equations are unknowns. Some are "variables." Explain to your child the differences between unknowns and variables, as follows:

- Unlike an unknown, which represents one or a few numerical values, a variable is a letter representing an infinity of possible numbers or values. The name "variable" comes from the fact that the value of the letter can vary.

- Unlike an unknown, the numerical value of a variable cannot be determined. It has, after all, an infinite number of possible numerical values.

- Unknowns appear in equations where 0 equals an expression with a letter, such as x, as in: $0 = 3x - 9$. In this case, note that x can have only one real value, which you do not know until you solve the equation for the value of the unknown, namely $x = 3$. Note here that "unknown" does not mean "unknowable." Indeed, it means the opposite.

- Variables, by contrast, appear in equations with two or more different letters, such as y equals an expression in x. For instance, in the equation $y = 3x - 9$, both x and y are variables that can have any of an infinity of real values, with the value of y depending on the value chosen for x or vice versa.

Show your child various single algebraic equations and, in each case, ask whether the letter or letters in the equation are unknowns or variables. Tell the child to look out for two clues.

- If he or she can solve the equation to find a numerical value or values for the letter, the letter is an unknown. If not, the letter is a variable.

- If there is just one letter in the equation, it is probably an unknown. If the equation includes two different letters, neither of which has specified numerical values, the letters are variables.

Now take the equation $y = (x - 2)(x + 1)$. Note that x is a variable with any of an infinity of real values. However, tell your child that if you substituted zero for y in that equation, x would be an unknown rather than a variable. In this case, explain that more than one value of the unknown would satisfy the equation, or make it true. In particular, for $0 = (x - 2)(x + 1)$, two values of x make the equation true, namely $x = 2$ or $x = -1$. Then tell your child that when 0 equals an expression in x where the highest power of x is 3, there will usually be three values of the unknown that satisfy the equation. For example, in $0 = x^3 + 3x^2 - x - 3$, which can be factored as $0 = (x + 3)(x - 1)(x + 1)$, the three possible values of x are $x = -3$, $x = 1$, or $x = -1$.

In general (but not always), when 0 equals an expression in x where n is the highest power of x, there will be n values of the unknown x that satisfy the equation. Give your child simple, factored equations ending in 0 and ask him or her which values of x make the equation true. Then ask whether x is an unknown or a variable. Your child should answer "unknown" in each case.

Occasionally substitute y for 0 in these equations and ask the same questions. Your child should answer that x can take on an infinite number of values, and that x is a variable.

It's important that your child knows the difference between an unknown and a variable, and many teachers and texts fail to make the distinction. If you do, your child will be better prepared to understand functional relations between x and y—described in the next section.

7.2 Verbs Revisited—Functions

Your child has probably been introduced to functions, but may have forgotten about them because it is in algebra that most students begin to work with them extensively. Explain that functions are a type of operation or "verb." They operate on a number in one set of numbers to pair it with another number in that set or another set. Tell your child that functions are often denoted by $f(x)$. The f stands for "function," a rule or sequence of operations on the input x to produce the output $f(x)$. In other words, $f(x)$ means that the function f, takes the input x and produces the output $f(x)$. Note that a function produces one output and operates on only one input, x, instead of the two inputs required by addition, subtraction, and the like. (Functions can have more than one input and output, but your child won't encounter such functions.)

Show your child a simple function such as $f(x) = 2x - 5$, where x is any real number. Explain that f says that for any value of x, there is an output value $f(x)$ specified by $2x - 5$. Explain to your child that you find the value of $f(x)$ for any value x by substituting that value for x into the equation above. So say x is equal to 1, then $f(x) = -3$. Or say $x = 10$, then $f(x) = 15$. Ask your child to create a table showing various values of x on one side and various values of $f(x)$ on the other side. Tell your child that he or she used the function $f(x) = 2x - 5$ to create the table. You might also have your child graph the function by using the x values to govern placement on the x-axis and the $f(x)$ values to guide placement on the y-axis.

Give your child other examples of functions. These include $f(x) = \sin x$, and $f(x) = e^x$.

Now write the equation $y = f(x)$. This is one that your child will encounter frequently in algebra. Tell your child that $y = f(x)$ simply defines y to be a new variable equal to the output of $f(x)$. The values for y might, for example, govern y-axis values on a graph.

Introduce the notation of $f(x) = 0$, by explaining that this is an equation stating that the output of the function $f(x)$ is equal to 0. If the function f is linear—that is, it looks like $f(x) = ax + b$ where a and b are numbers—then if $ax + b = 0$, $ax = -b$, and $x = \frac{-b}{a}$. Thus, x has one particular numerical value. So for

$$f(x) = 5x - 35 = 0$$
$$5x = 35$$
$$x = 7$$

In higher degree polynomials, x will have a greater number of possible values, dictated by the degree of the polynomial. For instance,

$$f(x) = x^2 - x - 12 = 0$$
$$(x - 4)(x + 3) = 0$$
$$x - 4 = 0 \text{ or } x + 3 = 0$$
$$x = 4 \text{ or } x = -3$$

Give your child a number of similar problems and ask him or her to solve for x. To tie this to the discussion in lesson 6.1, ask your child whether x is an unknown or variable. Of course, in equations equal to 0 or any specific number, it is an unknown.

WHERE THIS CHAPTER LEAVES OFF

Once you have taught your child about functions and the other concepts and rules in this chapter, he or she should have a good grasp of many of the fundamentals of algebra. Indeed, this chapter is designed to greatly speed your child's learning of basic algebra through its treatment of neglected, but valuable, concepts such as the difference between unknowns and variables; its novel approach to negative numbers; and its application of the language of math to algebraic equations and story problems.

You should, however, go on to teach your child omitted algebraic topics such as the quadratic formula, completing the square, properties of real numbers, graphing parabolas, and other graphic techniques. (This chapter does not cover any advanced algebra or trigonometry, topics taught later in the curriculum.) If your school organizes math classes in the middle and high school grades as integrated math, your child will also need to learn a lot of geometry, logic, clock arithmetic, statistics, and probability, among other topics. You or a tutor can teach these with help from integrated math textbooks.

Chapter 10

Math Teams and Coaching

Nothing will motivate your child to learn a lot of math more than joining a math team, a group of students who practice solving math problems and compete in regional and national contests. For students on a math team, mathematics becomes a competitive game, creating a powerful incentive to learn. Math teams are also social, and many children will do a lot of math on the team to be with their friends. In either case, a child's increased problem-solving skill will improve his or her math grades at school and scores on important admission tests like the SAT. The boost in motivation can also spill over into other academic subjects.

Not all schools have math teams, but since there are math contests for grades 2 through 12, every elementary, middle school, junior high and high school could—and should—have one. If your child's school does not, consider starting one yourself, as the coach, or encouraging another parent or teacher to do so, perhaps with some financial or other assistance from you. I spent seven years as a math team coach at the elementary and middle school levels and found the experience one of the most rewarding of my life.

What is a math team? Like a sports team, a math team is a group of kids who practice a skill and then compete to win. In this case, the skill is not passing or kicking but solving math problems. Like sports teams, good math teams practice—usually once a week in a school classroom. During practices, the coach may teach math topics to the team, or team members might solve sample math problems on their own with advice and assistance from the coach. And of course, the more the team practices, the better it gets.

Math teams can be a valuable experience for children, and not only because they teach team members a lot of math they would not learn in school. Math teams—and their noncompetitive cousins, math clubs—also provide social support for learning mathematics. When a math team wins, it goes a long way toward eliminating social rejection of students who are interested in math. A math team can even improve the math skills of everyone in the school by providing peers who can help others and by making math seem fun and important.

The competitive aspect of math teams is a special attraction for children just as it is for sports teams. But uncontrolled competition can be destructive as well. Like a coach of children's sports, a math coach must focus on improving the skills of all team members, not just the best ones who can win individually or help the team win. The coach should also teach team members to be considerate and cooperative and to develop goals that blend optimism with realism.

If you decide to coach a math team, you will give good math students a fantastic opportunity to improve their math skills and instill them with a motivation to learn they will remember for life. Many good math students—the target of math teams, given the difficulty of the contests—are not challenged by the math taught in even the best schools. By forming a math team, you can change that.

And your efforts will not go unappreciated. Informed parents know when their children's math education is lacking and will warmly welcome anyone who helps upgrade that education. The first time I coached a math team I was amazed at how supportive my team members' parents were. Indeed, parents were very enthusiastic about every math team I coached.

You don't need to be a math wizard to coach an elementary or middle school math team. If you did well in math in school, are willing to relearn some math you may have forgotten and to learn, perhaps for the first time, how to solve the more difficult problems in math contests, you have the math-related skills to be a good math coach. In addition, you must be willing and able to deal with children in a productive way. You must not show favoritism for your child. You must like children and enjoy the challenge of motivating them to learn math, cooperate with others, and handle success and failure.

Even if you do not want to coach a math team, I encourage you to read this chapter because you might like your child to join an existing team. Or maybe you'd like to pass this information on to another parent or a teacher who might be interested in becoming a coach. If you do want to coach, this chapter provides a guide to setting up and running a math team as well as tips for dealing with students, parents, and school officials.

HOW MATH TEAMS WORK

Like sports teams, math teams have two basic components: the practices and the contests. Practices, which should begin with the start of school in September, usually take place once a week in a school classroom before, during, or after school. Though different math coaches run practices differently, they generally consist of solving math problems like those that will appear on the contests, with some class-wide or individual instruction from the coach. At any given practice, a math team is often preparing for a particular upcoming math contest by learning to solve its problems from previous years.

The contests themselves are a set of problems—typically multiple choice or fill-in-the-blank—to be solved in a certain period of time, usually thirty to forty-five minutes. They are usually given in a classroom in the students' own school and administered (and often scored) by the math coach, on a particular day or days of the year. A few contests bring several or many school teams to one place, where your child can meet students with similar interests from other schools. Some math contests are given only once, while others have several rounds given on the same day or different days.

Math contests are much more difficult than other math tests, and they have a far different feel for students. Because both individual students and their teams compete against each other and other teams for good scores, kids are highly motivated to do well on them. Top scorers and teams receive certificates, medals, trophies or other awards as an additional incentive. Some contests print booklets listing the names of winners or other high scorers, which are great keepsakes for the students whose names appear in them. A math team coach can also provide his or her own awards—for instance, he or she might design certificates on a computer—to supplement those a contest provides. As a coach, I held a math-team-awards pizza party near the end of the school year.

In addition to local contests, there are at least six major national math contests for elementary and middle school students. Most of these contests include several rounds given on separate dates during the contest season, which runs from early November until mid-March. (The high school season is longer.) The middle school MATHCOUNTS contest is very competitive and only the four best team members plus an alternate participate beyond the first level of competition. In addition, there are one or two high school–level contests in which very skilled eighth graders might compete. Aside from the most competitive contests, team members might compete in contests on a dozen or more occasions throughout the school year. Almost all of these contests will be given locally and take less than an hour.

In most cases, your child will not have to try out to be on the math team, but since certain contests limit the number of entries, there may be competition among team members for those spots. In addition, a math team coach may run a more intensive practice to prepare students for the most competitive math contests. A coach will probably only invite the most skilled and motivated students to these rigorous math workouts, choosing the students based on previous performance in practices and contests or perhaps a qualifying test.

LEARN ABOUT THE CONTESTS

Since math teams revolve around the math contests, the best way to learn about math teams, and decide if you'd like to coach one, is to read and learn about the contests, which are geared toward very able math students given the difficulty of their problems. Middle school students can participate in the Continental Math League and the Math Olympiads for Elementary and Middle School Students—both of which have five contest rounds spread throughout the season—and the Math League and the American Mathematics Contest->8, which have one round each. In addition, the most skilled students can enter the new Mandelbrot Midlevels Competition, and the fabulous and richly funded MATHCOUNTS.

Elementary school students (grades 4 and up) can compete in the Continental Math League, the Math Olympiads for Elementary and Middle School Students and the Math League. The Math League holds a 6-round contest for high school students, who can also compete in several levels of contests run by American Mathematics Competitions as well as the Mandelbrot Competition, the American Regions Math League, and others.

At the end of this chapter are brief descriptions of the major nationwide math contests. I encourage you to take a look at these descriptions now, and if you have access to the Internet, to visit the web site for each contest, since those provide a wealth of additional information.

SET UP YOUR TEAM

Once you decide you'd like to coach a math team for one or more grades at your child's school, you'll need to contact the school's principal to find out if he or she is open to the idea. In your pitch, be sure to explain what math teams are along with their virtues.

In particular, be prepared to defend the decision to form a math team as opposed to a noncompetitive math club, as some educators and parents are wary of the competitive aspect of math teams. For instance, one night at a parent meeting for a New York City school at which I was coaching a very popular math team, two mothers said the school needed a separate math club for girls, because competition turned off girls. Similarly, when my daughter Kirsten volunteered as a tenth grader to coach a math team at an elementary school, the elementary school's principal said no, because she felt student competition was evil. Kirsten was eventually allowed to form a math club.

Though I have nothing against math clubs, I strongly disagree that competition is either evil or a turnoff for students, girls included. I am not at all convinced that girls are, on average, less competitive than boys. In math, girls only begin to shy away from competing with boys when they think they can't beat them, which typically begins in middle school. Girls *are* put off by male bragging, and girls want their friends with them during practices. Keep bragging down, encourage kids to bring their friends, and allow talking during most practice time, and you'll get many girls on your math team. Lots of girls joined my math teams. Some years, I had more girls than boys.

If the principal seems concerned about competition, delicately suggest that you think more students will participate in a math team than a math club, just as competitive sports teams draw more interest and attention than noncompetitive sports clubs. (How many kids would join a soccer or basketball club that just practiced and never played a game?) Point out that you will work hard to minimize the potential negative aspects of competition, such as discouragement of those who do relatively poorly and the bragging of those who do well. (See below for suggestions about how to do this.)

Aside from the competition issue, the principal's main concern may be entrusting a group of children to a parent. Be prepared to supply relevant references or recommendations to show that you are a kind, responsible person who can manage groups of children safely, maintain order, and positively influence students' personal development. If you do not have enough experience with groups of children to convince the principal to let you run a math team alone, you may need a teacher to supervise you, either temporarily or for the entire season. This may or may not be a problem for you, depending largely on whether you can find a willing teacher with whom you get along. In some cases, you may *want* a co-coach, as discussed below.

In addition, inform the principal about the school resources you will need for your math team. These include a room in the school that you can use one day per week for practices, a room in which to run the twelve to fifteen contest rounds per season, and if necessary, help covering costs.

Get Help if Necessary

If possible, I preferred to coach my math teams alone, because I enjoyed the freedom of doing things my way and didn't want to spend time coordinating with somebody else. While I very much enjoy talking to interesting people, I have generally preferred to do my research alone, teach alone, be a one-person committee, and so on. That's my personality. But you may want a co-coach with whom you can share ideas and responsibilities.

Indeed, you will need a co-coach if you are likely to have more than thirty students on your team, and might want help with more than twenty. Even if a classroom has desks for thirty students, it's easier to control cheating with fewer than twenty kids in the room. So if you think there is a lot of interest in a math team at your child's school—perhaps it's a gifted school with lots of talented kids or your math team has a history of success at the school—recruit help for the first practice, just in case.

When I coached a sixth-grade math team at my youngest daughter's middle school, a gifted school with 150 sixth graders, I predicted there would be more eager and qualified potential math team members than one coach could handle. So I recruited another coach and reserved a second room. I was glad I did: 49 kids showed up for the first two practices. In fact, there were so many kids that I needed the second coach until April, when all the contests were over. On math teams, attendance often drops significantly after the first few practices and always drops after the last contest.

If you'd like help, or think you might need it, start looking for possible co-coaches as soon as possible. You might even try to enlist the principal's aid in finding a willing parent or teacher. If you are an experienced math coach in your last year coaching at a school, consider recruiting a teacher or parent assistant coach to learn the ropes and coach the math team after you're gone.

Arrange a Practice Time

Next, decide the day and time you'd like to run your weekly practices so you can arrange to reserve a room for them. You'll need to discuss the time of your practice, which should probably last forty-five minutes or longer, with the principal. Some meeting times include: a school class period, lunchtime, and after school.

The best time to hold a general math team practice is after school, unless competing activities severely limit the number of good math students who attend. After-school practices will generally only attract serious students, and they are probably more convenient for you since you won't have to make a separate trip to pick up your child from school. What's more, classrooms are much more available after school, and practices can be longer.

I held practices and contests after school one year at a gifted middle school and had very large attendance. To help avoid conflicts with after-school activities parents might schedule for their children, I sent parents the practice and contest dates on the first day of school. I also picked the day of the week for the practice to coincide with the largest number of contest dates.

If you are a teacher or parent who doesn't work full-time, or you can take a break from work, you could also schedule practices during school. If you do that, it's best to hold them during a club period, an all-grade free period (if your math team is for a single grade) or lunchtime.

I held practices during a free period when I coached my youngest daughter's fifth-grade math team. Since students don't usually want to miss their free period, only highly motivated students came to practices. So I had the joy of dealing only with students—about thirty-six at the first practice, and about twenty later in the season—who listened attentively, asked questions, and worked hard. And for four years, I held practices during lunch recess at a middle school and had excellent attendance once I scheduled the day to avoid conflict with a very popular chorus practice.

If your team practices during a regular class period, you will get a large, more mixed group, some of whom will unfortunately attend primarily to get out of class. The first two years I coached a fifth-grade math team at New York City elementary school P.S. 87, children were excused from class for math team practices. A lot of kids came: I often had forty to fifty kids at a practice. But even with an excellent teacher helping me, keeping order was difficult, and many students fooled around and didn't learn much. Both the teacher and I felt we'd rather have coached just the twenty or so serious students who were there to improve their problem-solving skills.

So even if the principal lets you pull out children from class for math team practices, I don't recommend it. In addition to the problem of getting students you don't want at practices, your team members will be missing class, which exacts a cost to their education.

Reserve a Room for Contests

Early in the year, when you are first planning your math team, you may not yet know the dates of all the contests you want your team to enter. But you should still mention to the principal that you'll need a room to run contests, which often do not occur on the same day of the week you will be holding practices. Plan to give the principal a list of the contest dates as soon as you have them and the times you want to run the contests.

When the contest dates become available, list them along with the amount of time needed to run each one. At the elementary and middle school levels, the contests run about thirty to forty minutes, but you'll need the room for an additional ten to fifteen minutes to seat students, pass out materials, and give instructions before the contest, as well as pick up papers after the contest. If you can get a few minutes more, you can also answer questions after the contest.

If a contest date happens to fall on the same day you hold your practices, run the contest at the time practice is ordinarily held. That way, you won't have to remind students to come at some other time, and you know the room is available. For the contests falling on other days, reserve a room after school, if possible, unless some students have conflicts.

Alternatively, you might be allowed to pull students out of their regular classes for some of the contests. That's okay as long as you control who gets pulled out and can restrict the list to serious math team students. Students who participate in contests primarily to get out of class are often disruptive.

Consider Costs

The greatest cost of a math team is the coach's time, which you are donating, but there are also contest registration fees, photocopying costs, and charges for copies of old contests to use as practice materials. This adds up to several hundred or a thousand dollars a year, depending on the number and selection of contests.

Donate this expense if you can, as it can be time-consuming to try to raise money to cover math team expenses. If you cannot afford it, ask the principal or another school official if the school can help. Perhaps you could use a school photocopier or the school could pay contest registration fees and for the necessary practice materials.

If you are coaching a seventh/eighth grade team and your five-person team qualifies for the state MATHCOUNTS competition, someone has to foot the costs of traveling to and from the competition on a Saturday in March, and probably the cost for a place to stay the night before the contest. I asked parents to pay their child's share of the expenses. But if the expense is a burden for some parents, then you, the school, or a parent association may have to help.

Order Materials

Once you've received permission to form a math team, order practice and registration materials for the contests you'd like your team to enter. Peruse once again the list of contests below, visit their web sites and download, print, or order practice booklets and registration materials for the contests that seem appropriate for the age-group you are planning to coach. In addition, order any materials for local contests you learn about through your district's math education coordinator. You can find out who that is by calling the school district office or by calling other schools and asking to speak to their math coordinator or math team coach. You might also want to contact other math team coaches for general information and advice, though few do as much as I recommend.

As soon as you order materials, arrange with a teacher or administrator to get mail at the school. While your home address will work fine for the practice books and contest information, it won't for shipments of this year's contest. Contest organizers will almost always insist on mailing current contests (and answers) to a school to minimize the chances of individuals getting hold of these materials for cheating purposes.

If you are a teacher at the school, that's no problem since you already have a mailbox at the school. But if you are a parent coach, you must arrange a system to pick up mail at the school before practices and contests and at other times on weekdays. At the smaller New York City middle school at which I coached, everyone knew me and mail was held for me at the school's office. At larger schools, I had mail sent to me care of the school director or a teacher, who then either put my mail in a box in my practice room or delivered it to me in some other way.

Recruit Members

To publicize the existence of a math team and the time and location of the first practice, prepare a flyer and ask the school office to distribute copies to the homeroom teachers of the relevant grade or grades. Those teachers can then hand out the flyer for the students to read and take home to their parents. The flyer should describe the contests and practices, the wonderful problems that go far beyond the regular math curriculum, and how learning to solve these problems will greatly improve understanding of math. Make it sound exciting. The flyer should also state the dates, times, and rooms of practices and contests.

In addition, post the date, time and room for the first math team practice on school bulletin boards or walls. Ask teachers if they would remind children about the first practice on the day of, and perhaps the day before, that practice is scheduled to be held.

To recruit highly skilled math students—for whom math team is most appropriate and beneficial—ask teachers to encourage their best math students to try it. Alternatively, ask for the names of such students so you could contact them yourself.

Though skilled math students are the only ones who will be able to solve a lot of the contest problems at their grade-level, leave math team practices open to all students, and everyone who attends can participate in the many contests that do not limit the number of participants. Many of the students who find the practice problems too difficult will soon drop the math team. After a few weeks of practices, almost all the students coming to math team practices will belong there. But teach all who remain regardless of their ability. Indeed, look for opportunities to praise those who stay to learn despite being among the least skilled on the team.

MAKE A PRACTICE SCHEDULE

Using the dates of the contests as a guide, make a schedule for your math team practices. Your first practices should focus on the earliest math contests in October or November. For elementary and middle school, you'll practice for the first rounds of the Continental Math League and the Math Olympiads in early November. In addition, prepare your middle school team for the Mandelbrot Midlevels (if your students are skilled) and the one and only round of the American Mathematics Contest for grade 8, or AMC->8, later in November.

After the AMC->8 is over, the team should practice for the Math League contest for your state, which is in February for seventh and eighth graders, March for sixth graders, and April for fourth and fifth graders. The remaining four rounds of the Continental Math League and the Math Olympiads and the remaining two rounds of the Mandelbrot Midlevels extend throughout the contest season.

If your school district has a local math league, the math team must also squeeze in practices for it. I started these practices in early December since our local league—the NYC Interscholastic Math League—typically ran three rounds of contests for elementary and middle schools from January through March.

Starting in March, at the season's end, your math team can practice for next year's contests. I gave eighth graders practice on previous American High School Math Exams (now the AMC->12) and high school Math League contests. I gave sixth and seventh graders past versions of the American Junior High School Math Exam (now AMC->8) and MATHCOUNTS Warm-Ups and Workouts (problem-sets that contain problems similar to those used in MATHCOUNTS rounds) from the MATHCOUNTS handbooks for different years. In general, give the students practice problems at the next year's grade-level.

If your team participates in many contests, it will have less time to practice for each one. But practicing for one contest generally helps students on other contests as well. And the more contests your team enters, the more chances there are for kids to score well and win prizes, individually and as a team.

THE FIRST PRACTICE

When practices begin, your first job is to get contact information from all the students, because you may need to communicate with them and their parents during the year. Ask each student to write down his or her name, address, phone number, E-mail address, class or homeroom, and parents' names on a piece of paper.

At the first practice, your main goal is to show students what math team practices are like so they can decide whether the math team is for them. So after collecting contact information and making any announcements, get to work. Hand out practice problems from math contests. Choose problems for the new students that are easy as math contest problems go, but are nevertheless real math contest problems.

All math contest problems are more difficult than virtually all problems students encounter in school, so only the better math students will be able to solve more than one or two problems. Most of the other students will decide that the math team is too hard for them and drop it. This is as it should be. You won't be able to effectively teach a group of children with widely varying math skills. If you want to help many students who cannot yet handle math team problems, start a separate activity for them.

However, a few highly motivated students who solve very few problems will stick it out, occasionally for the entire year. I admire these students and make that clear to them, give them their share of help, and praise them for their progress. I have never counseled them to leave. Because there are so few of these students, you can give them their share of instruction without significantly sacrificing the instruction you give to the others. In any case, making the math team open to everyone, without an admission test, is critical to making it a socially acceptable activity at the school. You can trust the difficulty of the problems to limit the number of students not up to the challenge.

A few students will come to the first practice because they have a friend on the math team who is very good at math. Don't discourage these students, because if they stop coming to practices, so may their friends. Of course, if you have students who cause trouble you can't handle, expel them from the team.

LATER PRACTICES

There is more than one way to run a math team practice. Some coaches run them like a regular math class, concentrating on problems of the same type that they teach everyone to solve. Although I tried that during my first year of coaching for about six weeks, I eventually settled on a method that I felt students enjoyed more: Solving many different types of problems in each practice, providing more variety, and running the practices a little like the math contests themselves. Though you must find what works best for you, here is how I liked to run practices.

Usually, after any announcements, I'd begin the general practice with a five-minute explanation of a math topic many students did not yet understand. I kept these team lectures short, since most students would not listen to a long lecture from me. Almost all of my practices revolved around students solving problems from old contests.

For instance, if I used the short five- or six-problem contests, I would give them three contest rounds in a forty-five-minute practice, leaving fifteen minutes per round. Though in a real contest they'd get twenty-five to thirty minutes per round, I wanted everyone to have more than enough to do for the entire practice. At my youngest daughter's school, where practices were an hour and fifteen minutes, I gave more contests to fill the time.

After practice, I would collect their papers, grade them, and deliver them back to the students at next week's practice. In this way, each practice was an informal contest, which the students liked. Just as a good sports practice ends with an intrasquad game, so each math team practice should include some informal competition. While almost all the time in my practices was spent doing contests, I always helped individual students who asked for help and sometimes volunteered to help those who did not. I counted problems that students solved with help just as much as ones solved without help. So, although the practices included a competitive element, they occurred in a largely cooperative learning atmosphere.

Almost always I allowed students to help each other solve problems. For group work, I let the students form their own groups—which meant that friends usually worked together, and a few loners worked on their own. Each individual was graded as if he or she had done the problems alone, so weaker students received much higher scores than they would have otherwise. Nobody minded that.

Making math team an informal social occasion made it more fun, particularly for girls. I was very conscious of attracting and keeping girls on my math teams, so I tried to run practices in ways that would be fun for them. In addition to allowing teamwork and talking, I recruited girls who were strong in math by inviting them to bring their friends to math team, regardless of ability.

Occasionally I ran a practice like a real contest to prepare students for the real thing. This meant no talking. But often, unlike a real contest, I let students ask for help from me. Sometimes I held team competitions, with three or four students per team, and the same teams often competed for several weeks. The competition was fun, although often it was not completely "fair," since I didn't worry much about whether the teams were evenly matched.

That said, I always tried to minimize the potential negative effects of competition during practices—in particular, the potential to discourage or embarrass those who did relatively poorly. When I handed back completed contests from the previous practice, I kept the scores out of public view, by folding the papers, for example, or placing them facedown on a desk or table. I also emphasized that no one had to reveal his or her score, and that I would not tolerate any student pressuring another student to do so.

Along with a numerical score, I gave almost every paper a positive "rating," a word or phrase that praised each student but also revealed where he or she stood relative to the others. The ratings were: *good, very good, excellent, outstanding, math wizard, another Einstein.* I urge you to use these ratings. I got the idea and the top two ratings from the rating scale used by the Math League in their books of old contests. Sometimes I wrote the distribution of scores on the board, but finally decided it was a waste of time; the ratings did the job best. Because math team problems are much harder than math class problems, I wanted to encourage every student who came to the practice and participated productively. If a student did so badly that I felt he or she had not tried very hard, I simply left the rating blank.

These ratings were applied to contests completed during practices, as students did very little homework. In the beginning, I suggested that students work at home on problems that they had solved incorrectly or had omitted in papers I had handed back. Only a few students actually did this. Still, it is worth doing. The only time students in the general practices did significant math team homework was when I funded a five-month homework contest for seventh and eighth graders that carried monetary prizes. There were three prizes for each grade, given to the three seventh graders and three eighth graders who had correctly solved the most homework problems from June until November 1, above a designated minimum. Many students participated in that and solved a lot of math problems.

INTENSIVE PRACTICES

For the four years I coached a math team for grades 6 through 8, I ran a long, intensive after-school practice for highly skilled math students in addition to the weekly general math team practices. I got the idea for these practices from the director of the chorus my daughter Kirsten had joined in sixth grade. The director, Jo Morris, established three levels of chorus based on members' ability and commitment, with the higher levels practicing more and being expected to achieve a greater level of skill than the lower levels.

Similarly, I established this higher level math team for about eight students who were both able and willing to do the work necessary to compete at the top echelons in math for their age. The practices, which ran for two and a half hours one or two days a week at my apartment, prepared students for the chapter (local), state, and national levels of MATHCOUNTS and, with lower priority, the American High School Math Exam (now called American Math Contest->12).

At a minimum, every child in the intensive practices had to have passed or currently be learning first-year algebra. Other than that, I based my selection of students—mostly seventh and eighth graders and a few talented sixth graders—on their performance during previous math contests. Although MATHCOUNTS is limited to seventh and eighth graders, it is wise to train some sixth graders in preparation for next year. Invite a few sixth graders to join the intensive practice in September and invite others when the eighth graders leave after state MATHCOUNTS in March.

Some math team members turned down my invitation to come to the intensive practices, but no one I had not invited ever asked to come. That's not to say it can't happen, but it's unlikely that lots of unqualified children will clamber to do extremely difficult math for two and a half hours at a stretch and hours of homework each week. If, however, you somehow end up with more eager-and-able students than you can handle in this practice, limit the number using objective criteria—say, by taking only the top so-many scorers on a qualifying test. Alternatively, you could temporarily take more students than you want and use homework and test performance to winnow down the group.

Running Intensive Practices

My intensive practices generally focused on MATHCOUNTS, the most difficult and competitive math contest for middle school students. So after giving the kids a chance to snack and solve problems they'd missed in previous sessions, with my help or that of another student, I devoted the bulk of each intensive practice to MATHCOUNTS contests the students had not yet worked on that year.

The team practiced all the different parts of MATHCOUNTS. Often they'd start with a "Sprint Round," thirty problems to be done in forty minutes, followed by a "Target Round," pairs of problems done in six minutes. Next, they'd do a "Team Round," in which teams of four students work together on ten problems for twenty minutes. For these rounds I'd pick four of the top five team members for one team, and the others, with help from me, would form the other. Sometimes, they'd pair off for a fast-paced oral "Countdown Round." Lastly, I would give out new homework assignments and the students would go home around 6 P.M.

I started in early September with the oldest chapter-level MATH-COUNTS contests, proceeding to more recent years as the sessions passed. Then I would shift to state-level MATHCOUNTS contests. (The four MATHCOUNTS levels are school, chapter, state, and national.) When I had some team members for whom chapter-level contests were too easy, I gave them national-level contests to do instead. When the state contests began, all students did them.

In October and November, just before the American Junior High School Math Exam (AMC->8), I gave prior years' versions of that contest to do for homework under test conditions. I also devoted one or two intensive practices to the more advanced American High School Math Exam (AMC->12) in January and February and told students to work on that test at home.

After the state MATHCOUNTS contest in March, my eighth-grade students left the intensive practices (except for those who qualified for nationals and so practiced for that), and I invited new sixth or seventh graders into the group. At that point I sometimes assigned everyone MATHCOUNTS Warm-Ups and Workouts. Other times I assigned Warm-Ups and Workouts to new students only, along with chapter MATHCOUNTS tests, while the more advanced students did national MATHCOUNTS contests or previous versions of the American High School Math Exam.

In contrast to general practices, the intensive math team practices involved an enormous amount of homework every week. For homework, students solved problems they'd failed to solve on practice MATHCOUNTS and other contests. They did MATHCOUNTS Warm-Ups and Workouts as well as practice versions of the American Mathematics Contests at home under contest conditions. Generally, the students would hand in these assignments at the start of every intensive practice. I even gave summer homework assignments, which many of these students completed.

My intensive practices were for middle school kids. Such practices could also be part of an elementary school math team, but implementing them could be more difficult for younger children. First, a coach of an elementary school team is more likely to have to deal with a disgruntled parent who wants his or her child to attend the intensive practices, even though the child does not want to attend them or didn't qualify for them. (Parents exert more control over the lives of younger children; older kids demand more independence and thus block some parental interference.) Second, elementary school students may have more trouble getting to the practices since most cannot travel on their own.

SELECTING TEAMS

In many of the math contests, such as the Continental Math League, the Math League and the American Mathematics Contests, an unlimited number of kids can compete. The Math Olympiads permits as many as 35 students per team, and if you have more than that, you can pay to register a second team.

Some of the contests, however, such as the chapter and state MATH-COUNTS and the high school Mandelbrot contest, limit team size to a small number of students (four or four plus an alternate). To pick a team for those meets, use an objective competition so that you are not accused of favoritism, especially if you have a child on the team.

To select your chapter MATHCOUNTS team, I recommend using the school competition plus two or more old state competitions. The much harder state contests are better indicators than the school-level tests of who will do well at the higher levels of MATHCOUNTS. Indeed, on easy tests that many team members can ace, relatively poor problem-solvers may even outscore your best problem-solvers simply because the more skilled students happened to make more careless mistakes.

RUNNING CONTESTS AND PREVENTING CHEATING

In addition to selecting teams to compete in math contests, you as the coach also must run all or many of the contests. Each contest packet will contain explicit instructions for how to run that contest, which you should read and follow. However, in general, you will need to

- Rearrange desks or tables and chairs to reduce students' ability to see each others' papers—for example, spacing students as far apart as possible—and when the room is crowded, put your best students in the places where it is most difficult for others to see their papers

- Ask students to go to the bathroom before the test starts

- Instruct students to use backpacks, coats, and other objects to block others from seeing their answers

- Pass out scrap paper and pencils for those who need them

- Pass out the contest and answer sheet facedown or closed

- Tell students to write their names on the back of the contest or answer sheet, even if there is a place for names on the front

- Read contest instructions

- Tell students not to talk during the contest and to keep their eyes on their own paper

- Explain that you cannot answer any questions during the contest—including what anything means—except to pronounce the name of a word or symbol that is reproduced unclearly

- Tell students to raise their hand if they need more scratch paper or another pencil

- Ask if there are any questions before the contest begins

- Write the time the contest begins and the time it will end on the board and say, "begin"

Aside from taking such practical steps to ensure a contest is run fairly and smoothly, do your best to instill values in math team students that are incompatible with cheating on math contests. A coach can only do a little to instill positive values in his or her students, but that little is worth doing. During the season, I told students repeatedly that cheating was unfair to others and that winning by cheating is an act of self-delusion that hurts a person's self-worth. I made it clear that I felt cheating was unacceptable by announcing that I did not want to see anyone looking at another student's paper during a math contest. I also monitored the room carefully during contests, walking around so that everyone felt my presence and glaring at students who were whispering or whose eyes were wandering.

I sought to prevent cheating before it happened, because I never felt comfortable punishing or publicly embarrassing any student I suspected of cheating. There is no system for dealing with cheating in math contests, and it is difficult to prove someone cheated in a contest by looking at a neighbor's paper. I couldn't bring myself to play witness, prosecuting attorney, judge, and jury by myself. I never disqualified students who talked during a math contest, because I could tell it was almost never associated with cheating. Almost all the talking during contests occurred between less-skilled math students who had given up and were bored. I didn't want to drive these students away from math team.

Of course, the coach must never cheat. Never open contest materials and look at the questions before running the contest. For some contests, you must open the materials to make enough copies for the students. In those cases, take pains to copy them without reading the questions to avoid consciously or unconsciously using that information to prepare students for the test. And be careful not to leave answers where students can see them.

COMMUNICATING WITH TEAM MEMBERS, PARENTS, AND THE SCHOOL

Though you will be communicating extensively with your team at practices, that does not ensure that students remember details such as the date and time of the next contest or whether to bring a calculator to it. Nor does it inform parents or other students and teachers about the activities and achievements of the math team. So you must find additional ways of communicating with parents, students, and teachers.

Sending a notice home with each team member is the easiest way to tell parents about upcoming contests. Also use those notices to provide information about which contests allow or require calculators, how to obtain previous contest problems or other relevant practice materials, and anything else you might want parents to know. However, children often fail to bring home notices from school or fail to give them to their parents, so this is not completely reliable. It also won't reach the parents of students who aren't at the practice at which you hand out the notice. So hand out the notices every week to math team members starting weeks in advance.

You can mail notices if you have everyone's address, but addressing envelopes is tedious. I used the mail primarily to communicate with parents of students involved in the intensive MATHCOUNTS practices. I wanted to enlist their aid in getting their children to do the homework, to notify them of the Saturday MATHCOUNTS meets so they would not make competing commitments for their children, to explain the costs of the state MATH-COUNTS contest, and to recruit people to drive to state MATHCOUNTS.

When I coached at the Computer School, a public middle school in New York City, I called team members the night before each contest to be sure they would be at the right place at the right time. It produced the desired results but was time-consuming. I also had to call parents to get permission to take their children to the NYC Interscholastic Awards Ceremony and to invite parents to come.

The Computer School had a monthly newspaper published by a parent. In my second year coaching there, I started writing a column for each issue called "Math Team News" that described upcoming contests, reported how the team had done in past contests, and named the top-scoring individuals. It also stated the day of the week and the room in which the math team practiced and that all students were welcome to come. For a time I included a math team problem and the solution to last month's problem.

This publicity helped increase interest in the math team among both students and parents, recruited additional students to practices, communicated future contest dates to parents, and relayed our accomplishments, which provided additional recognition to the students who had done well. If your school has a newspaper and you have the time, writing an article about the math team as often as you can is worthwhile.

INTIMIDATION AND MOTIVATION IN MATH

The competitive aspect of math teams motivates children to practice math, as they all want to compete successfully. Indeed, competition is an underused tool for motivating students to work hard in academic subjects. Just as kids' physical health would be much worse without competitive sports, their academic health is suffering because educators shy away from competition.

Even so, competition is not a cure-all, and coaches need to try to combat aspects of competition that can hurt morale. One problem can be intimidation. Students often become intimidated when peers solve a math problem or understand a math concept faster than they do. This may happen fairly often even to highly skilled students, causing them to question their own mathematical ability. Intimidation often causes students to stop learning mathematics before they should.

So I strove, on the one hand, to socialize math team members not to put down others on the team and, on the other hand, to persuade team members not to be intimidated by put-downs or others' successes. I emphasized that they could, usually rather easily, learn how to solve all the problems they had not solved correctly in math contests or practices.

I tried especially hard to discourage bragging and put-downs to keep girls on my team, as unfriendly, competitive behavior tends to especially annoy girls. I tried to create goodwill among my students by talking to them individually outside of math team practices. I complimented students when they got a good score or a greatly improved score on a contest, and I told those who put down others that their behavior was immature. I think I was more successful at building confidence and motivating students than I was at socializing braggers, but the kids who bragged the most made enormous progress in math, which I hope increased their self-confidence to a point where they felt less need to brag.

With math team, as with all education, the emphasis should be on the value of work for academic achievement rather than on innate ability, which we can do nothing to change. At the same time, genetic factors play a role, so it is wrong to think that hard work can make anyone the best mathematician in the world. That kind of unrealistic thinking leads to unhappiness.

It is rational to accept that we have limits, but it is equally rational to realize that we can never know precisely what those limits are. Thus, I offered students a philosophy of life that I felt was a good blend of realism and optimism. I told them to aim a little higher than what they thought they could accomplish, but to be happy with what they did accomplish even if it was less than they'd aimed for.

The Major Math Contests

Here are descriptions of the major national contests for elementary and middle school students with some high school contests for advanced students. Bear in mind that this list, while extensive, is not exhaustive. In particular, please ask the math education coordinator for your school district whether there are any local math contests appropriate for the students you'd like to coach.

Except for MATHCOUNTS, which restricts participants to grades 7 and 8, all other math competitions permit students of any grade at or below the specified grade-level to compete. In general, however, a student cannot compete in more than one grade-level of a given contest or league in the same year. One exception to this rule: A student at or below eighth grade may participate in both AMC->8 and one of the higher level AMC contests.

- *The Continental Math League* has math competitions for grades 2 through 9. This contest has five monthly rounds, starting in November, for grades 4 to 9 and three rounds for grades 2 and 3. A round consists of six problems to be solved in thirty minutes. (There is also a high school contest with four eight-question rounds.) Any number of students can take the tests. Each student gets a score and the team score for each round is the sum of the six highest individual scores. A month or so after each round, coaches receive lists of the teams scoring highest in that round, of the cumulative scores of every team, and of the country's highest individual scorers, along with other scoring data.
  http://www.li.net/~majorbar/cml/
  Or contact:
  Continental Mathematics League
  P.O. Box 2196, St. James, NY 11780-0605
  Phone: 631-584-2016
  E-mail: Quartararo@xoommail.com

- *The Math League* provides math contests for grades 4 through 8 and high school. The fourth through eighth grade contests consist of one thirty-minute round of thirty to forty multiple-choice questions. The seventh and eighth grade contests are given in February, followed by the sixth grade contest in March and the fourth and fifth grade contests, which may be given anytime after April 15. Though the same contests are given nationwide, teams compete within a state or regional Math League, such as the New York Math League or the New England Math League. Team scores for grades 6, 7, and 8 are the sum of the best five individual scores for each team. The grade 4 and 5 Math League contests are strictly intramural competitions; scores are not reported or compared across schools.

The high school contest consists of six thirty-minute, six-question rounds given each month from October through March. Team scores for each round are derived from the top six individual scores and both individuals and teams from different schools compete against each other. There is a homeschool division for each Math League contest. Homeschoolers can't win anything, but can compare their scores to those of the winners in their grade.

http://www.mathleague.com/

Or contact:

Math League Press

P.O. Box 720

Tenafly, NJ 07670

Phone: 201-568-6328

Fax: 201-816-0125

E-mail: comments@mathleague.com

- *The Math Olympiads for Elementary and Middle School Students* includes two competitive divisions, one for seventh and eighth graders and the other for fourth, fifth, and sixth graders. In each division, school teams of up to 35 students compete in five monthly contests of five problems each, given from November to March. Awards are given to both top-scoring individuals and teams, scored by adding the ten highest individual scores, taken after the fifth contest.

    http://www.moems.org

    Or contact:

    Math Olympiads

    2154 Bellmore Ave.

    Bellmore, NY 11710-5645

    Phone: 516-781-2400

    E-mail: moes@i-2000.com

- *The American Mathematics Contest->8* (formerly the American Junior High School Math Exam) is a twenty-five question, forty-minute multiple-choice exam for students in grade 8 or below. (Homeschool students age fourteen or under are also eligible.) This one-round contest given on a Tuesday in late November is the second most difficult math contest for middle school children, exceeded only by MATHCOUNTS.

    Students who score well on the AMC->8 are invited to participate in the recently developed AMC->10 or the AMC->12, formerly the American High School Mathematics Exam. However, an invitation is not required for younger students to compete in these contests.

    http://www.unl.edu:80/amc/

    Or contact:

    Titu Andreescu, Director
    American Mathematics Competitions
    University of Nebraska-Lincoln
    Lincoln, NE 68588-0658
    Phone: 402-472-6566
    Fax: 402-472-6087
    E-mail: titu@amc.unl.edu

- *MATHCOUNTS* is probably the most educational, challenging and exciting math contest available for seventh and eighth grade students. Each fall, local MATHCOUNTS coordinators distribute to all schools in their area a handbook with 300 practice problems and solutions along with registration information. Coaches then use the handbook to prepare students for up to four levels of MATHCOUNTS competitions, each of which can last almost three hours and includes four main parts

    - A Sprint Round of thirty questions, to be completed in forty minutes

    - A Target Round with four pairs of questions, and six minutes to complete each pair

    - A Team Round, in which the team works together for twenty minutes to solve ten problems

- A Countdown Round, in which pairs of mathletes (top scorers from the previous rounds) challenge each other in oral competition

The first MATHCOUNTS competition, held in January, is the intramural school competition. It is open to all interested seventh and eighth graders, and its typical purpose is to help the coach select the four students who will compete both individually and as a team at one of 500 regional "chapter" meets held across the country in February. (However, team selection is at the coach's discretion.) Winning teams then progress to the more difficult state contests in March. The state's four top individual scorers earn an all-expense-paid trip to Washington, D.C., to represent their state at the rigorous national finals in May.

http://mathcounts.org/

You may also contact the MATHCOUNTS Registration Office at:

P.O. Box 441

Annapolis Junction, MD 20701

Phone: 301-498-6141

E-mail: math@pmds.com

The MATHCOUNTS Foundation can be reached at:

1420 King Street

Alexandria, VA 22314

Phone: 703-684-2828

Fax: 703-836-4875

E-mail: mathcounts@nspe.org

- *The American Mathematics Contest->10 and 12* are 25-question, 75-minute multiple-choice exams open to students in grades 10 and below (AMC->10) or grades 12 and below (AMC->12). The AMC->10 is a new contest inaugurated in 2000 and the AMC->12 is the new name for the American High School Math Exam. Both also accept homeschool students with age cutoffs of 16 and 18 respectively.

These tests, held on the same day in February, are very difficult math exams, especially for younger students. Students take one or the other, not both. Top scorers on the AMC->10 (top 1 percent) and AMC->12 (score of 100 or higher) qualify for the even higher level American Invitational Exam (AIME). The very highest scorers are invited to take the USA Math Olympiad

(USAMO). These higher level exams and the Mandelbrot A contest are perhaps the only high school math contests more difficult than the AMC->12. For both AMC tests, questions are ramped in difficulty starting with easier questions and ending with difficult ones. Tests are scored to severely punish incorrect answers compared to omissions: Correct answers earn 6 points, omissions earn 2 points, and incorrect answers earn 0 points.

Thus, if a student wants a score of 100 on the AMC->12 to qualify for the AIME, one possible strategy might be to answer exactly fifteen questions. That will yield 20 points from omitted questions and another 84 points if the student gets fourteen of his or her fifteen answers correct. An alternative strategy would be to answer seventeen questions, which would qualify the student for the AIME if the student errs on no more than two questions.

Brochures for the AMC->10 and 12 are mailed to schools each fall. But registration forms and other information about these tests (as well as the AIME and USAMO) can also be found at:

http://www.unl.edu:80/amc/
Or contact:
Titu Andreescu, Director
American Mathematics Competitions
University of Nebraska-Lincoln
P.O. Box 81606
Lincoln, NE 68501-16066
Phone: 402-472-6566
Fax: 402-472-6087
E-mail: titu@amc.unl.edu

- The *Mandelbrot Competition* is a high school–level math contest with two divisions: the more advanced A Division or less advanced B Division. (Students choose to take either Mandelbrot A or B, but schools may enter a team in each division.) In both divisions, students compete in four rounds that take place from October through March. Each round contains a forty-minute individual test of seven short-answer questions and a team test, in which four students chosen by the coach work together on proofs for 40 minutes. Both Mandelbrot A and B are very difficult tests, even for gifted high school students, and are probably too challenging for middle school students.

http://www.mandelbrot.org/
Or contact:
Greater Testing Concepts
P.O. Box 380789
Cambridge, MA 02238-0789

■ The *Mandelbrot Midlevels Competition* is a recent addition to the Mandelbrot repertoire designed for eighth graders and advanced seventh graders, but open to any student who has not yet completed the eighth grade. Instead of four rounds, the Midlevels competition contains three rounds, which take place from November through March. Each Midlevels round consists of a forty-minute Individual Test of ten short-answer questions, from which students choose six, and a forty-minute Team Test, in which a four-student team works together to answer discussion questions on a particular subject. The subjects of the Team Tests are provided at the beginning of the year, so that students may prepare beforehand—a unique and educationally desirable feature. Students will gain a deeper understanding of a smaller number of math topics than in MATHCOUNTS. The two contests complement each other nicely.

http://www.midlevels.org/
Or contact:
Mandelbrot Midlevels
P.O. Box 382805
Cambridge, MA 02238-2805
E-mail: contact@midlevels.org

Ideas for
Better Schools

A merica expects too little of its children, and those low expectations
are all too apparent in our educational system. People respond positively to respect and to confidence in their abilities. The more we
treat our children with respect and make it clear we believe they deserve it,
the more they will work hard to live up to our expectations.

American educators could do much better in this regard. First, they
must set higher educational goals for children, and that means specifying a
rigorous curriculum and requiring all students to pass it. Children should
also be given the power to pace their own progress through the curriculum,

to accelerate when they are able, catch up with their classmates after an absence or personal crisis, and obtain additional instruction and school time when that is needed. Schools need to better allow for differences in rates of learning, and I will describe a wonderful system for accomplishing this, one that motivates children of many levels to learn and is fairer and more effective than tracking.

The educational system should not just *allow* for individual differences, but celebrate them, giving each child a chance to explore, develop, and show off his or her talents and special interests as adults can in the broader society. Schools today place too little emphasis on anything aside from traditional academic subjects, a system that leaves many children without much to feel good about. But if, along with traditional academics, schools supported the development of a greater variety of talents or interests, more children would feel good—even excited—about coming to school. And this feeling would spill over to their attitude toward learning in general.

Schools should embrace the fabulous diversity of human beings, treating children as unique individuals, and take advantage of a powerful source of human motivation: the desire to shine in one's own way.

A SPECIFIC CORE CURRICULUM

The first step toward giving our children the tools to succeed is for each school system to adopt a detailed, ambitious core curriculum for each grade and subject area. These curricula would specify the knowledge and skills every child is expected to acquire, and would be written for both required and major optional courses. To assure that the core curriculum was taught effectively, the school system should test it near the end of each school year.

As Eric Hirsch writes in his courageous and enlightening book, *The Schools We Need and Why We Don't Have Them*, a specific core curriculum, as opposed to a vague one, would let teachers at each level know what knowledge their students had been taught so they can build upon it efficiently. Teachers would thus be free to challenge students without fear of confusing them with topics they can't yet grasp or boring them with material they already know. Teachers would also be far less likely to accidentally omit important subject matter.

For their part, children would be expected to learn a large number of facts, concepts, and principles. It should not be an easy curriculum, and there should not be fuzzy descriptions of the core knowledge that make it difficult to test whether a child has or has not learned that knowledge.

Opponents of such an approach contend that the facts one needs to know are changing so fast that education should focus not on facts but on higher-order thinking skills that allow students to quickly look up or deduce the knowledge they need. In most cases, this argument rings hollow. The spelling and the meaning of words change very little over a lifetime; grammar and the principles of good writing also remain fairly constant. Some historical "facts" may change due to new information or interpretation, but not enough to invalidate most of what was learned in school. Some political, economic, and geographical facts change over decades, but much geography remains constant, and understanding the changes that do occur requires knowing how the world used to be. Knowledge of great works of literature, music, and art is useful even if opinions about them change over time.

The facts and ideas taught in standard mathematics classes remain true and very useful, even with changing opinions about their application. And while most scientific fields have undergone a revolution in my lifetime, the scientific theories and facts I learned in school were essential to my ability to understand new ones.

In addition, neither deduction nor looking up information can substitute for knowing a lot of facts, concepts, and principles. To be widely useful, deduction requires knowledge; it amplifies factual knowledge rather than substituting for it. It is also not practical to look up most of the knowledge needed to make decisions in life. Retrieving information from the brain is far faster than finding it any other way, including via the Internet, and will remain so until brain-computer integration is far more advanced than it is today. Making decisions, planning, problem solving, and creative thinking depend far more on knowledge stored in the brain than on knowledge one looks up. In any case, one must use one's brain to process any knowledge obtained elsewhere, so specific facts must inevitably be learned.

Finally, there are precious few higher-order thinking skills to fill the K–12 curriculum once it has been emptied of facts. Cognitive psychologists have repeatedly demonstrated that such thinking skills are almost always restricted to a specific body of knowledge and work effectively only when a person has knowledge on which they can operate.

CORE CONTENT

The specific knowledge our children are required to learn should be divided into six core areas:

- Reading and Literature
- Writing (including grammar, spelling, typing, and penmanship)
- Mathematics
- Science
- Social studies
- Arts (including visual arts, music, performing arts, competitive speech, and physical education)

Writing should be a separate subject, not combined with literature in the English department. After all, writing is important in many realms aside from literature. In addition, good writing instruction requires writing specialists. While I have known a few excellent writing teachers in schools, writing almost always gets short shrift from teachers whose main interest is literature. Frequently these teachers are neither very interested in, nor skilled at, teaching writing.

Colleges across the country have learned this lesson and established separate departments or programs to teach writing courses. Elementary and secondary schools should follow this model, hiring good writing teachers to fill each writing department.

Hiring writing teachers is the first step toward improving writing instruction. The second is to recognize that effective writing instruction requires students to rewrite many times, with the teacher reading and making comments on each draft. This is extraordinarily time-consuming for the teacher. The number of students in a writing class should be much lower than in other classes to make them effective.

Along with a separate writing department, schools should establish a separate writing requirement. High schools might, for example, require three years of writing classes and middle schools two years, while separately requiring students to take a certain number of literature courses.

Another subject schools should feature more prominently in their core curricula is statistics. Units on statistics should be included in the curricula of science, math, and social studies classes, as statistics is absolutely essential to a person's ability to interpret trends, findings, and events in our society. Lack of statistical knowledge has made misinterpreting the world's news astoundingly common, and that has caused countless people to make ill-informed political and personal decisions.

In the media, and sometimes even in scientific papers, statistical analysis of data used to draw conclusions about important social or scientific issues—from the impact of video games on violence to the importance of dietary fiber in preventing disease—is often absent or incorrect. Reporters usually gloss over supporting data because it is hard to explain or understand, often replacing it with compelling personal anecdotes. Readers are persuaded by anecdotes, whether in the media or in ordinary conversation. Few miss the hard data.

To intelligently manage everyday life—from what to eat and how to vote to whether to own a gun—people need to understand that anecdotes do not constitute evidence and they need to understand the kind of data that does. The ability to interpret and use data is basic knowledge that should be supplied in school. If all children were schooled in statistics, our society would have a common language through which people could accurately analyze data and draw conclusions about social issues and prescriptions for health, among other things.

MORE DIRECT TEACHING

In addition to providing specific fact-focused curricula, schools should train their teachers to teach this material. In math and science, teachers should not rely heavily on the "discovery approach," advocated by Standards math proponents, in which students are asked to rediscover much of the information they need to know in the course of solving problems or doing experiments.

As discussed elsewhere in this book, the discovery method is impractical as a means of teaching more than a tiny fraction of what a student needs to learn. Thus, almost all of the math and scientific knowledge students should learn must be taught directly by teachers. Effective direct teaching does not mean just listening to a lecture. It involves answering questions posed by the teacher and administering tests to be sure students are paying attention and properly associating new and old knowledge.

That said, there is a place for guided discovery in the classroom, in which a teacher gives lots of hints to aid the discovery process. My children once took a fascinating physics class in elementary school in which they rolled balls of different masses down ramps of various lengths and timed their descent. The kids could discover that the time it took a ball to roll down a ramp of a given length was independent of the mass of the ball. Such discovery exercises are valuable for children if they are done infrequently, say, once or twice a year in math classes and somewhat more often in science classes, to give children a sense of what math or science research is like.

TAILORED ADVANCEMENT

In addition to challenging students with its content, our schools' curricula should be structured to give students more control over their own progress through school. Schools should permit each student to advance through each major school subject at a pace determined by that student's skill and motivation in that subject at each point in time. Each student should advance to the next level in each subject after, and only after, having mastered the material taught at the previous level based on a test or evaluation.

Students should not be promoted just because they attended class regularly or to keep them in the same class as their friends. And tracking students based on a onetime evaluation of their skill, such as an IQ-type test, is not ideal either. Instead, students should control their progress through school at many stages as they either master, or do not master, each level of a course of study. Such a system would not only be fairer than tracking, but would also improve education. Because every student in a class would be at the same level, a teacher's instruction could maximally benefit all of them.

ACCELERATED REVIEW MASTERY (ARM) SYSTEM

I invented something I call the Accelerated Review Mastery (ARM) system, to accomplish these goals. It is a practical way of individualizing the rate of learning within the ordinary whole-class method of instruction. I think it is an ideally American approach to education, in which setting high goals and working hard to accomplish them result in greater achievement.

It starts in first grade and is designed for course sequences that span several years. In this system, each half-year term of a course sequence is divided into two parts. The first part is a creative review of the material taught during the previous term (using a different approach, say, or new examples) and the second part covers new subject matter. At the end of each term, students are tested on their understanding of both the reviewed and new curricula, using objective tests where possible (though in some subjects, written compositions or other subjective evaluations will be more appropriate).

To pass a term and advance to the next, a student must have mastered the reviewed material only. Without exception, any student who does not demonstrate such mastery must repeat the term. If a student also demonstrates mastery of the new curriculum, the student skips the next term and advances to the term beyond that.

The required core sequence would extend the longest in math—at least into first year algebra and perhaps beyond—and in writing. Shorter core sequences would be required in literature, science, and social studies to allow more student choice in these areas, which provide more diversity in what students can productively study.

This system enables enormous variety in the rate of progress of different students through a school subject. For example, a student who consistently masters all levels of a subject's curriculum the first time (meaning he or she never needs the extra half term of review) will proceed through the subject at twice the normal rate. A student who sometimes needs the review and sometimes doesn't, progresses at a rate somewhere between normal and twice normal. A student who studied on his or her own could request an additional test at the end of a term to justify promotion to a higher level in that subject. This option could help an occasional student advance in a subject at more than twice the normal rate. For children who underachieved in the past, this provides an extra opportunity for them to catch up to intellectual peers.

A student's rate of progress can vary as motivation and learning rate change, something not possible with tracking. For instance, a student who must repeat a term or more can, if motivation and skill allow, catch up later by skipping terms. In this way, a serious personal problem that slows up a child's progress in one or more subjects for a year or two can be compensated by faster progress later. If this happened at a transition to middle school, a child could probably advance to the new school with his or her age group if middle schools offered some upper elementary level courses.

In this way, each student's progress is always in that student's hands based on his or her achievement in each subject. Progress is not determined by a one-time score on a verbal or math aptitude test, or by the opinion of a teacher or administrator. Such one-time placements, made in the course of tracking students, can be not only out of date and inaccurate, but also discriminatory against certain ethnic groups and social classes if subjective judgments or discriminatory tests are used.

The ARM system is much fairer. It mixes students who differ in ability, motivation, class, and ethnicity in the same classes to the extent that they are represented in the school. And the best (and worst) teachers teach that entire mix of students, grouped only by their readiness for the material. No teacher can use his or her clout to teach only the smartest kids.

What's more, ARM eliminates the difficulty of teaching students at different levels in a subject in one class. With ARM, everyone in a class has mastered the prerequisite material, maximizing teaching efficiency and minimizing differences in student performance in a class. Teachers will not dumb down their instruction for slow students, understanding that students who don't master a course in the time allotted will simply repeat it— without the current stigma attached to "failing" a grade. When students repeat a course, their final grade would be their last grade, so a personal crisis need not affect the permanent record. In this way, difficult honors and AP courses can be open to all students who have satisfied the prerequisites without compromising the level of the course.

The ARM system also helps motivate students. It rewards all students who get a score above a reasonable mastery criterion, with the highest levels of achievement resulting from consistently meeting this criterion. This encourages all students to learn, not just the smartest ones.

IMPLEMENTING ARM

An elementary school could try out the ARM system in one subject, such as math, devoting one period to it. For just that period, a student would leave his or her regular classroom for his or her math class, which would be taught by the school's regular teachers. In general, first-grade teachers would teach the lowest levels of math and fifth- or sixth-grade teachers would teach the highest levels. As some students advanced beyond the highest math classes taught at the elementary school, some teachers could learn to teach more advanced classes, new part-time teachers could be recruited, or advanced students could be sent to a middle school for math.

To fully implement the ARM system, however, an elementary school would have to abandon the model of a single teacher who teaches all subjects to a class of students of about the same age. That's because in the ARM system, any one student is likely to be at different grade-levels in different subjects and in class with kids of different ages. So like middle school and high school students, elementary school kids would go to different classes throughout the day based on their skill levels and interest rather than their ages.

Such a system is not unprecedented for elementary schools. My two eldest children attended a school called Eastside Elementary in Eugene, Oregon, in which children of different ages mixed in the same classes. Students still played primarily with others their age, but they also had chances to meet and socialize with older and younger students. What's more, they got to experience different teachers. While that may take a little adjustment for the youngest ones, it means that no child gets stuck with a teacher he or she doesn't like for an entire school year, something that can leave a child unhappy, lacking in self-confidence, and with a bad attitude toward school.

It also means better instruction, not only because all children in a class would be caught up to the same level, but also because each teacher can be a specialist in a subject, be it writing, math, science, or social studies. Math instruction, in particular, would improve greatly in elementary school if it were taught by special math teachers since many regular elementary school teachers are ill-equipped to teach it.

Of course, having many teachers during a school day means teachers won't get to know each child as well as they would if they had only one group of students. But getting to know each child well is not necessary for most children to get a good education. A teacher cannot, after all, adjust his or her presentation to the personality of any one child. And even with many classes, a teacher can glean enough about student personalities to encourage the shy students to participate and keep pushy kids from dominating a discussion. He or she will also notice behavior problems and deal with them accordingly, perhaps with advice from other teachers or the child's parents.

In any case, the advantages of the ARM system outweigh the difficulties of multiple teachers for each child. ARM is a system that treats everyone equally, is educationally efficient, does not separate students who fail certain courses from their friends in all subjects, gives students who slip plenty of second chances, and allows students to accelerate up to twice the normal rate through the curriculum.

To maximize these benefits, every hard-working student should be allowed to stay in school for as long as it takes for him or her to accomplish his or her educational objectives. This is the best way to provide equal educational opportunity—better than assigning everyone thirteen years of public education no matter what their ability, motivation, and personal circumstances. The benefits for children modestly below average in academic ability could be enormous. Some kids who couldn't otherwise go on to college would be able to do so, and those who sought employment after high school could get more interesting jobs than they could otherwise. Considering the amount of money spent on special education, providing extra schooling for this far greater number of students seems well worth the expense.

EVERY CHILD HAS A GIFT

A principal at one of my children's schools espoused a beautiful educational goal. She said that every child has a gift, and it is the school's job to discover that gift and develop it. I strongly agree with this philosophy, realizing that a child's gift need not be a traditional school subject, but almost any skill or ability. If all American educators thought this way, school children, especially those not exceptionally skilled in traditional school subjects, would be more confident, happier, and more motivated to work hard in school.

I believe every person is born with a strong desire to gain expertise in specific areas that distinguish him or her from others. Large differences between people in knowledge and skill in different areas have contributed enormously to the success of our species. Human productivity has been greatly amplified by a system in which people with different areas of expertise perform particular tasks very efficiently for the benefit of the group. This system, which improves with time, has lifted our standard of living to what it is today.

The human brain is well suited to specialization. In a large part of the brain called the cerebral cortex, billions of nerve cells represent specialized knowledge by modifying their structures and connections in any of countless ways depending on a person's experience. In the cortex of a mathematician, for instance, more cells are devoted to mathematical knowledge, while that of a doctor is dominated by medical knowledge and a teacher's brain has much of its space devoted to education.

But while the world of work encourages people to specialize, schools by and large do not. Instead, they focus on helping children obtain the essential base of knowledge that all educated adults have. This is important, but by exclusively focusing on traditional academic skills, our educational system enables only a small group of kids—those with high academic IQ's—to be successful. Although one academically gifted child might be better than another at writing or math and vice versa, school skills tend to travel together so that the same small group of kids tends to come out on top every time.

In the larger world, however, the totality of useful knowledge and skill is far greater than any one person can learn, so each person masters a different tiny fraction of it, and thus stands out in his or her own way. Thus, many more adults can be "winners" in the world of work, family, and community than children who can now be "winners" in school. Schools could and should change that by providing children with broader opportunities to succeed, without shifting their focus from traditional academic subjects.

First, educators should give children more choice about what they learn. U.S. schools usually limit course choice, either explicitly or by requiring lots of specific courses. But students as young as third grade should be allowed to choose what they study during a small part of their school day, perhaps 1 of 7 or 8 class periods. During this period, children might choose a special course or independent study guided by parents, teachers, or librarians.

Students engaged in independent study might, for instance, go to the library where they could consult books or use a computer to search the Internet, asking a librarian or parent volunteer for help when needed. They might store their data on a school computer system and on backup disks they could take home. As children get older, they should be allowed to spend a greater and greater fraction of the day exploring or learning about a subject of their choosing. In this way, a child would have an opportunity to display his or her special interests in a school setting, and find success that would help motivate the child to learn and improve his or her attitude about coming to school.

Second, educators should encourage and support school-based extracurricular activities such as art, music, drama, and athletics; also student government, a school newspaper, and many clubs and academic teams. A friend of my daughter was a spectacular soccer player, but a less spectacular student. He was a behavior problem in school, but I often wondered whether he would have been had the school had a soccer team on which he had been a star. I doubt it. He was not socially immature or emotionally troubled outside of school. As a soccer player, he made an early transition from ball hog and prodigious goal scorer to a consummate team player. Like everyone else, he wanted to be admired by others for his talents, and though he received the appropriate admiration through the community soccer league, he did not in school and so had to seek attention there by causing trouble.

To give as many children as possible a chance to shine, educators in a school should also seek out and encourage children to participate in a variety of contests—from math and science fairs to music contests, spelling bees, and writing competitions for poetry, stories, or essays. The more contests, the more potential winners. School officials could provide information about local and national contests as well as holding school-wide contests, say, for the best student reports on independent projects.

Schools should also celebrate achievements with awards ceremonies at the close of each semester. Such ceremonies should honor not only students with the best grades, but also those who win contests, who are stars on sports teams, or in concerts and plays, and who are working on creative independent projects. In this way, every child could become a winner in something.

COMPETITION AND COOPERATION

Indeed, encouraging students to enter various kinds of contests is one way schools could use competition productively as a way of motivating children to achieve. Many educators think of competition as an adversary of cooperation. It is not. In the broader world, the competitive free-enterprise system is not only a very successful way of taking advantage of the specialization of labor, but also a brilliant example of human cooperation. It happens on a global scale spanning hundreds of different countries and billions of individuals.

And it happens effortlessly. As economist Paul Samuelson explained in his introductory economics textbook, the amount of milk delivered to New York City each week will closely agree with the amount New Yorkers will buy, without any government explicitly deciding on this amount. The same applies to other types of products.

Competition serves cooperation well by creating incentives for individuals to align their interests with their abilities. Any other system erodes motivation to achieve, as the failure of communism as an economic system demonstrates. In the same way, injecting some controlled competition into the school system could help motivate children to excel.

SCHOOL DISCIPLINE

Schools could learn another lesson from the larger society: the policy of removing from society those people who endanger or disrupt the life of others. In the adult world, that means putting criminals in jails or corrective institutions. In school, it should mean removing from regular classes children who imperil the learning of others.

Disruptive students are significantly inhibiting learning in American classrooms. Indeed, the harm done by such students to the education of their classmates is a serious problem whose social cost is probably far greater than that of juvenile crime. Though the primary responsibility for discipline rests with parents, schools must help correct the problem by putting disruptive students in separate classes where they cannot interfere with the learning of other students. This step—one advocated by the late

Lessons from Japan

In hunting for ways to improve U.S. schools, American educators would be well advised to look to their colleagues in Japan. Extensive live and videotaped observations of math teaching in the U.S. and Japan shows that math classes in Japan are more efficient, devoting more class time to math learning and less time to interruptions and transitions between activities. In addition, ratings of teaching effectiveness done by expert teachers indicate that American math instruction during class is substantially inferior to that in Japan. Why might this be?

First, the salaries and social status of teachers relative to other professions is much higher in Japan than in the United States. These incentives attract more intelligent, motivated, and ambitious individuals to the teaching profession. In Japan, the competition to be a teacher is so fierce that only one-fifth of the 200,000 applicants who take a difficult certification exam each year obtain teaching positions.

Second, Japanese teachers receive most of their teacher training in on-the-job apprenticeships, whereas American teachers are taught in schools of education with little apprenticeship training. In the first year of teaching, Japanese teachers learn from master teachers who take a year off from regular teaching to be mentors. After that, other teachers in the school effectively mentor new teachers and each other. There is much less mentoring in the U.S. Many teachers must learn how to teach largely on their own.

Third, Japanese teachers spend more time in the school outside of the classroom than American teachers. As a result, Japanese teachers have more time to prepare their lessons and discuss teaching methods with colleagues.

Fourth, in Japan, from first grade on up, *every* teacher has a subject specialty.

Albert Shanker, former head of the American Federation of Teachers, in his newspaper columns—would greatly improve the learning of the vast majority of American children. It should be taken regardless of the relative quality of the classes for disruptive students, though, of course, these students should be educated as effectively as possible and be returned to regular classes when they are no longer disruptive.

Although Japanese students are not taught exclusively by specialists until middle school, the math specialists in Japanese elementary schools serve as resource teachers for other teachers who teach math. Japanese learn from each other by participating in two types of committees: grade-level and subject matter. When a grade-level committee meets to discuss the math lessons they will teach, a math specialist is there to provide advice. When all the school's math specialists meet, they exchange tips, which they then pass on to the nonspecialist teachers. By contrast, U.S. elementary teachers are rarely well trained in math or math instruction and receive very little, if any, ongoing help from specialists.

Fifth, there is a national math curriculum in Japan. This means that a teacher is assured that every child in his or her class was taught the same information the prior year. And because math teaching is more effective in Japan, students master previous material much more thoroughly than American students, and require much less review.

Finally, Japanese teachers (and parents) instill a high value on learning, respect for teachers, and cooperation with other students. By contrast, many U.S. students lack motivation, some to the point of being severe discipline problems who disrupt the learning of everyone in class.

We pay a steep price for not paying and training our teachers better, and for not giving them the respect, preparation time, and mentors to perform optimally in the classroom. Poorly trained math teachers with little time to prepare their lessons teach poorly, and it is no wonder that many American kids have trouble with math. We clearly have a lot to learn from the Japanese. But we can do even better than the Japanese, if we institute a good American system of acknowledging individual differences that allows students to proceed through the math curriculum at their own rate.

GIVE CHILDREN THE RIGHT TO VOTE

We are not a complete democracy, because we deprive one quarter of our citizens of the right to vote, namely, those under eighteen years of age. At this point, hardly anyone thinks that's wrong, just as 2,000 years ago hardly anyone thought slavery was wrong or, 200 years ago, few Americans believed denying women and slaves the right to vote was wrong. The reason children don't have voting rights is presumably because they are too inexperienced or immature to vote intelligently, and therefore likely to echo the votes of their parents. But we don't exclude adults for being stupid, poorly educated, or excessively influenced by others, so it is logically and morally inconsistent to deny the right to vote to children for these reasons.

Some might argue that there are lots more children than adults who lack the qualities to vote responsibly, dangerously increasing that fraction of the voting population. But I believe otherwise.

At birth, all citizens should be given a vote to cast. Citizens eight years or older cast their own votes. Citizens younger than eight have their votes cast by their parents or guardians. This obviously increases the political power of parents with children under eight. This is morally right, because the interests of children should be represented in proportion to their number. Allowing parents to vote for all children under eighteen would be more democratic than the present system.

What would be the greatest political changes to result from giving children voting rights? We'd get more financial support for education, libraries, after-school programs, parks, playgrounds, recreation centers, food and medical care for children—all poorly funded today because our government is not a government of all the people.

And if eight- to seventeen-year-olds voted for themselves, they would be much more motivated to learn about current events, government, economics, history, geography, education, local issues, and other social studies topics. Many more young people would read newspaper articles on local, state, national, and foreign news and policy. They might even want to educate themselves about statistics, graphs, and areas of science relevant to understanding issues that bear on what or who to vote for. There is nothing like giving a child adult power and responsibility for making that child want to learn information relevant to exercising that power and fulfilling that responsibility.

As children begin to view themselves as eager learners, they will be more motivated to learn about an even broader variety of topics. Children will pay more attention in class and read more, expanding their vocabulary and broadening the range of books and periodicals they can enjoy.

In addition to the tremendous value of the additional knowledge, giving children the right to vote will make them more likely to establish a lifelong habit of educating themselves about the issues on the ballot and of voting. Teachers and parents could see to it that students registered to vote and that they were informed on at least some issues. What better time to establish a habit of conscientious citizenship than during childhood?

Giving children the right to vote is not only right, it would also vastly improve the health, education, happiness, and sense of responsibility of our children and the adults they will become.

Math Learning Resources

isted below are a large number of math-learning resources referred to in this book. Those I have used or skimmed to determine suitability often include my comments. However, I am not intimately familiar with all of the listed sources.

Note that there may be later editions of some of these resources with some differences in content, and other particulars, given the delay between this writing and the time you read this. The grade-level indicated for a book or other resource is the grade-level the publisher attaches to it—typically one based on the nonhonors math curriculum in which algebra is delayed until ninth grade.

MATH TEXTS AND WORKBOOKS

The best math texts are those that include a large number of problems of many types and levels of difficulty and for which you can purchase a manual with solutions for at least half the problems. You'll need solutions to all of the problems if you or your child's tutor can't figure out the remaining solutions. In this appendix, "solutions" means that all the important steps in getting the answers are shown; "answers" means that only the final answers are given. Books that include answers or solutions in the back make it more difficult to prevent cheating than those whose solutions come in a separate volume. Use books with answers in the back to teach honesty or tear out the answer pages.

For texts without a student solutions manual, try to get a teacher's solutions manual or answer key. For any kind of solutions manual, you'll probably have to ask the publisher explicitly, as they are often not advertised. Explain that you will use this only for home teaching, not to help your child cheat on homework. In *Books In Print*, or other book lists, a solutions manual often has the same title as the text, but a lower price. A teacher's edition may be denoted by TCH instead of STU for a student's edition.

Many of the publishers listed below have web sites and other contact information listed below under Publishers in Book Sources. Others may be purchased using online bookstores and other information in Book Sources or included with the description of the book.

K–8

Filano, Dr. Albert E., K. E Possler, and Barbara K. March. *Mathematics: Skills, Concepts, Problem Solving*. Continental Press, 1998 and 1999. These are more traditional workbooks that include more examples of each problem type than *Get Ahead in Math*. Excellent when a child needs additional practice problems. Available from Kindergarten (Level A) to Grade 8 (Level I), with teacher's guides. Grade 7 and 8 focus on algebra, according to Continental Press. May be purchased on-line.

Giles, Dr. Robert and Fred Remer. *Get Ahead in Math*. Continental Press, 1998. These workbooks are wonderful, provided a parent or tutor discusses each problem with the child (even those answered correctly) to be sure the child understands all the underlying concepts. Available for Grade 2 (Level A) through Grade 8–9 (Level G). There is also a teacher's guide for each level. Continental Press lists these workbooks as "Test Preparation" books on its web site. May be purchased on-line.

Pre-Algebra

Martin-Gay, K. Elayn. *Prealgebra,* Second Edition. Prentice Hall, 1997. Paperback. ISBN 0-13-242470-3.

Poole, Barbara. *Basic Mathematics.* Prentice Hall, 1994. Paperback. ISBN 0-13-342569-X. There are 6,260 problems. Solutions to most odd-numbered word problems.

First-Year Integrated Math

Bumby, Douglas R., Richard J. Klutch, Donald W. Collins, and Elden B. Egbers. *Integrated Mathematics, Course 1.* Glencoe/McGraw-Hill, 1995. Student edition: ISBN: 0-02-824566-0, Teacher's Annotated Edition: ISBN: 0-02-824567-9. Answers to odd problems. Highly Recommended.

Dressler, Isadore and Edward P. Keenan. *Integrated Mathematics Course 1,* Third Edition. AMSCO School Publications, 1998. ISBN: 0-87720-228-1 (Softbound) 0-87720-230-3 (Hardbound).

First-Year Algebra

CORD Algebra 1: Mathematics in Context. Comprehensive student edition. Center for Occupational Research and Development Staff. Globe Fearon Educational Publishers, 1998. ISBN: 0-538-67121-1. To order, call: (800) 848-9500.

Second-Year Integrated Math

Bumby, Douglas R. Richard J. Klutch, Donald W. Collins, and Elden B. Egbers. *Integrated Mathematics, Course 2.* Glencoe/McGraw-Hill, 1996. Student Edition: ISBN: 0-02-824906-2, Teacher's Annotated Edition: ISBN: 0-02-824907-0. Answers to odd problems. Highly Recommended.

Dressler, Isadore and Edward P. Keenan. *Integrated Mathematics: Course II,* Third Edition. AMSCO School Publications.

Geometry

CORD Geometry. Center for Occupational Research and Development Staff. Globe Fearon Educational Publishers, 1999. ISBN: 0-538-68127-6. To order, call (800) 848-9500.

Gerver, Robert, Chicha Lynch, David Molina, Richard Sgroi, and Mary Hansen. *South-Western Geometry: An Integrated Approach*. South-Western Educational Publishing, 1998. Student Edition: ISBN: 0-538-67122-X.

Third-Year Integrated Math—Algebra and Trigonometry

Keenan, E. P. and Gantert, A. X. *Integrated Mathematics: Course III*. Second Edition. AMSCO School Publications, 1991. ISBN 0-87720-277-X. No answers. Highly Recommended.

Modeling

Mathematics: Modeling Our World. Course 1, COMAP Inc. Staff. W. H. Freeman, 2000. ISBN: 0-7167-4153-9.

Mathematics: Modeling Our World. Course 2, COMAP Inc. Staff. W. H. Feeeman, 2000 ISBN: 0-7167-7-4155-5.

Mathematics: Modeling Our World. Course 3, COMAP Inc. Staff. W. H. Freeman, 2000 ISBN: 0-7147-4158-X.

Mathematics: Modeling Our World. Course 4, COMAP Inc. Staff. W. H. Freeman, 2000, ISBN: 0-7167-4115-6

These books, for grades 9, 10, and 11, are designed as an alternative to the traditional first 3 years of high school math. I would use them as a supplement. This math-modeling approach teaches a lot of math and computer programming not taught in the more established approaches, but it probably leaves out topics included in traditional texts. COMAP stands for the Consortium for Mathematics And its Applications.

Precalculus

Cohen, David. *Precalculus: A Problems-Oriented Approach*, Fifth Edition. Brooks/Cole Publishing, 1997. ISBN 0-314-06921-6. Answers to many problems. Excellent text. Student Solutions Manual available.

Cohen, David. *Precalculus with Unit-Circle Trigonometry*, Third Edition. Brooks/Cole Publishing, 1998. ISBN 0-534-35275-8. Same coverage as other Cohen precalculus text, but a different order for presenting trigonometry. Student Solutions Manual available—see next entry.

Cohen, David, prepared by Ross Rueger. *Precalculus with Unit-Circle Trigonometry Student's Solutions Manual*, Third Edition. Brooks/Cole Publishing, 1998. ISBN 0-534-35277-4.

Calculus

Anton, Howard. *Calculus with Analytic Geometry*. Fifth Edition. John Wiley & Sons, 1995. ISBN: 0-471-59495-4.

Larson, R. E. and R. P. Hostetler. *Calculus*, Alternate Third Edition, D.C. Heath & Co., 1986. ISBN 0-669-09569-9. Answers to odd problems.

Stewart, James. *Calculus*. Fourth Bk and CDROM Edition. Brooks/Cole Publishing, 1999. Hardcover ISBN: 0-534-35949-3.

Advanced Math (College)

Analysis

Marsden, J. E. and M. J. Hoffman. *Elementary Classical Analysis*, Second Edition. W. H. Freeman & Co., 1993. ISBN: 0-7167-2105-8.

Rudin, W. *Principles of Mathematical Analysis*, Third Edition. McGraw-Hill, 1976. ISBN 0-07-054235-X.

Proofs

Cupillari, Antonella. *The Nuts and Bolts of Proofs*. PWS Publishing Co., 1989. ISBN: 0-534-10320-0. First-semester calculus level. Complete solutions to all problems. Easier to understand than Solow, because organized around 2 types of proofs. Includes various types of proof problems.

D'Angelo, John and Douglas B. West. *Mathematical Thinking: Problem Solving and Proofs*. Prentice Hall, 1997. ISBN: 0-13-263393-0.

Eisenberg, Murray. *The Mathematical Method: A Transition to Advanced Mathematics*. Prentice Hall, 1995. ISBN: 0-13-127002-8.

Solow, Daniel. *How to Read and Do Proofs*, Second Edition. John Wiley & Sons, 1990. ISBN: 0-471-51004-1. Complete Solutions to odd-numbered problems. This book analyzes types of proofs much more deeply than Cupillari and is more original, but it is therefore a little harder to understand.

Math Study Strategies

Schiavone, Peter. *How to Study Mathematics: Effective Study Strategies for College and University Studies*. Prentice Hall, 1998. ISBN: 0-13-906108-8.

OTHER MATH BOOKS

Problem and Solution Books

In addition to textbooks, you can buy books of solved math problems for any level. These books are often very inexpensive, though it may be difficult to coordinate their use with a textbook.

Barron's Regents Exams and Answers Sequential Math Course I.
Barron's Regents Exams and Answers Sequential Math Course 2.
Barron's Regents Exams and Answers Sequential Math Course 3.

Barron's Regents Exams are updated every year. If you live in New York, get the latest edition. Otherwise, it doesn't matter. Although these exams are only given in New York State and are designed for an integrated math curriculum, the Barron's books provide excellent practice for the usual algebra, geometry, advanced algebra and trigonometry courses too.

Blyth, T. S. and E. F. Robertson. *Algebra Through Practice: A Collection of Problems in Algebra with Solutions*: Books 1, 2 & 3, Vol 1. Cambridge University Press, 1985.

———. *Algebra Through Practice: A Collection of Problems in Algebra with Solutions*: Books 4, 5 and 6, Vol 2. Cambridge University Press 1985.

Grimmet, Geoffrey and David Stirzaker. *Probability and Random Processes: Problems and Solutions*. Second Edition. Oxford University Press, 1992. Paperback. ISBN: 0198536658.

Ogden, James R. *Algebra and Trigonometry Problem Solver*, Revised Edition. Research & Education Association, 1990. Paperback. ISBN: 0878915087.

Schmidt, Philip. *3000 Solved Problems in Precalculus*. McGraw-Hill, 1988, Paperback. ISBN: 0070553653.

Shakarchi, Rami. *Problems and Solutions for Undergraduate Analysis (Undergraduate Texts in Mathematics)*. Springer Verlag, 1998. Paperback. ISBN: 0387982353.

Schaum's Outline Series.

McGraw-Hill. Highly recommended. This series contains lots of high quality problems with complete solutions in many different areas of math and science. Here is a small sample of the books available:

Bronson, Richard. *Differential Equations*. 1994.

Mendelson, Elliott et al. *Calculus*. 1999.

Moyer, Robert E., Frank Ayres, Jr. *Trigonometry*. 1998.

Rich, Barnett. *Elementary Algebra*. 1993.

Rich, Barnett, Philip A. Schmidt. *Geometry: Includes Plane, Analytic, and Transformational Geometries*. 1999.

Safier, Fred. *Precalculus*. 1997.

Spiegel, Murray R., John J. Schiller, and R. Alu Srinivasan. *Probability and Statistics*. 2000.

Spiegel, Murray R. *College Algebra*. 1997.

How to Solve Math Problems

Lehoczky, Sandor and Richard Rusczyk. *The Art of Problem Solving*. Vol. 1 (grade 8–10) and Vol. 2 (grades 10–12++). To order, contact Mu Alpha Theta at matheta@ou.edu or (405) 325-4489. I highly recommend these books for anyone participating in math teams at the middle school (Vol. 1) or high school level (Vol. 2) or for those wanting to solve hard multi-step problems at these levels.

Wickelgren, Wayne A. *How to Solve Mathematical Problems*. Dover Publications, Inc., 1995, ISBN: 0-486-28433-6. A slightly corrected republication of *How to Solve Problems: Elements of a Theory of Problems and Problem Solving*. W. H. Freeman & Co., 1974, which is no longer in print. Elegant theoretical analysis of problem-solving methods and why they work, but they are very abstract, high level methods. They are applied primarily to recreational math problems requiring knowledge of arithmetic and some elementary algebra and geometry. To solve more advanced math problems, you'll need a book like *The Art of Problem Solving* that contains problem-solving methods geared toward particular problem types.

Logic and Other Recreational Math Problems

Gardner, Martin. *Entertaining Mathematical Puzzles*. Dover Publications, Inc., 1986.

Jacoby, Oswald and William H. Benson. *Mathematics for Pleasure*. Fawcett Publications, Inc., 1970.

Phillips, Hubert, S. T. Shovelton, and G. Struan Marshall. *Caliban's Problem Book: Mathematical, Inferential, and Cryptographic Puzzles*. Dover Publications, Inc., 1961.

Fixx, James F. *Solve It! A Perplexing Profusion of Puzzles*. Doubleday, 1991.

Fox Dunn, Angela, Ed., *Second Book of Mathematical Bafflers*. Dover Publications, Inc., 1983.

Friedland, Aaron J. *Puzzles in Math & Logic*. Dover Publications, Inc., 1970.

Gardner, Martin. *The 2nd Scientific American Book of Mathematical Puzzles & Diversions*. Simon and Schuster, 1961.

———. *The Scientific American Book of Mathematical Puzzles & Diversions*. Simon and Schuster, 1959.

———. *The Unexpected Hanging and Other Mathematical Diversions*. The University of Chicago Press, 1991.

Kaplan, Philip. *Posers: 80 Delightful Hurdles for Reasonably Agile Minds*. Harper & Row, 1963.

Silverman, David L. *Your Move: Logic, Math and Word Puzzles for Enthusiasts*. Dover Publications, Inc., 1991.

Wells, D. G. *Recreations in Logic*. Dover, 1979.

BOOK SOURCES

Publishers

These publishers of K–12 (and some college) math texts and workbooks have sales policies that are congenial to learning at home. When you can't purchase on-line from the publisher, you can order by phone, through a bookstore, or from on-line bookstores. Some K–12 math publishers (not listed) make it very difficult for anyone other than a teacher or school official to purchase their books. If you want to obtain materials from such publishers, ask an educator to help you. You might also find them in a library or a bookstore catering to teachers.

AMSCO School Publications http://www.amscopub.com/ 315 Hudson Street, New York, NY 10013, Attention: Order Department, Phone: (800) 969-8398 or (212) 886-6565, Fax: (212) 675-7010. Teacher's manuals (answers) must be sent to a school address or require proof that you are a certified teacher or homeschool teacher.

Barron's Home Page http://www.barronseduc.com/main.htm On the home page choose School house. Then under Regents Exams choose

Math 1, 2, or 3 for books with 10 prior New York State Regents Math tests and solutions for Course 1 (first-year algebra), Course 2 (geometry), and Course 3 (second-year algebra) and other preparation books and software.

Brooks/Cole Publishing http://www.brookscole.com/ 511 Forest Lodge Road, Pacific Grove, CA 93950, Phone: (800) 354-9706. Ask about the availability of student solutions manuals. Brooks/Cole does not mention them in their online catalog even though they publish them.

Continental Press http://www.continentalpress.com 520 East Bainbridge St., Elizabethtown, Pa 17022, Phone: (800) 233-0759, Fax: (888) 834-1303. Very good K–8 workbook and textbook series. See above.

Houghton Mifflin Company http://www.hmco.com/ 222 Berkeley Street, Boston, MA 02116, Phone: (617) 351-5000 or (800) 225-1464. The School Division has an on-line store. The College Division—which starts with elementary algebra texts—includes book descriptions, but you cannot order on-line. There are often student solution manuals available.

Key Curriculum Press http://www.keypress.com/ 1150 65th St., Emeryville, CA 94608, Phone: (800) 995-MATH, Fax: (800) 541-2442. Upper elementary through high school math. Answer books available.

Prentice-Hall Mathematics http://www.prenticehall.com/list_ac/b7-5.html Upper Saddle River, NJ 07458. Phone: (800) 282-0693, Fax: (800) 835-5327. Middle school, high school, and college math texts. Look particularly under Developmental Math, Precalculus, and Advanced Courses.

Saxon Publishers http://www.saxonpub.com 2450 John Saxon Blvd., Norman, OK 73071, Phone: (800) 284-7019, Fax: (405) 360-4205. Saxon math books are high quality, and teacher's manuals with answers are available, as are a very helpful set of placement tests to help you determine which textbook your child needs.

South-Western Educational Publishing http://www.swep.com/ Thomson Learning, Attention: Order Fulfillment, P.O. Box 6904, Florence, KY

41022-6904, Phone: (800) 354-9706. Fax: (800) 487-8488. On-line, choose "shop," and then "consumer catalog."

Can't Find a Publisher? Try These Sites

AcqWeb's Directory of Publishers and Vendors: http://www.library.vander-bilt.edu/law/acqs/pubr.html

Education Publishers: http://www.library.vanderbilt.edu/law/acqs/pubr/educhtml

Publishers' Catalogues Home Page: http://www.lights.com/publisher/

On-line Book Searches

Bottom Dollar http://www.bottomdollar.com/

Dealtime http://www.dealtime.com/ The successor to Asces, this is the smartest book-finder for determining which bookstore on its list will sell you a book for the lowest price including shipping (but not taxes). Search by title, author, keywords, or ISBN.

On-line Bookstores

A1Books http://www.a1books.com

AllDirect.Com http://www.alldirect.com/

Amazon.co.uk http://www.amazon.co.uk

Amazon.com http://www.amazon.com

Barnes and Noble.com http: www.bn.com

BIG WORDS http://BigWords.com/store/

AddALL http://www.addall.com/

Powell's Bookstore http://www.powells.com/ The best on-line used bookstore. New books too.

MATH AND EDUCATIONAL SOFTWARE

Free Math Software and Shareware

Macintosh Shareware: http://www.passtheshareware.com/mac.htm

Windows Shareware: Including hardware driver updates, program reviews, MP3 utilities, and more: http://www.passtheshareware.com/

XyAlgebra: Download at http://mathO.sci.ccny.cuny.edu/xyAlgebra/ This outstanding program, which teaches and tests understanding of first-year algebra, was developed by my college roommate, John Miller, a math professor at City College of New York. All basic algebra classes at the City College of CUNY are taught using xyAlgebra, which runs under Windows 3.1 with 4 MB or Windows '95/'98 with 8 MB. Where the web page asks for your institution and department, just provide your name and address.

Software Reviews

MacWEEK: http://www.macweek.com/

Macworld Online: http://macworld.zdnet.com/

ZDNet: http://www.zdnet.com/

Software: Where to Buy

MicroWarehouse: http://www.warehouse.com/

PC & MacZone: http://www.zones.com/

PC Connection: http://www.pcconnection.com/

SmarterKids: http://www.smarterkids.com/

Software Companies

Computer hardware and software are improving so rapidly that I won't recommend specific programs. But here are web sites of educational software publishers and, in the next section, sites where you can find software reviews. You can also type the name of a math program into any web search engine to find reviews of the product.

Broderbund Software, Inc. http://www.mattelinteractive.com Point on the link for Broderbund to pull up choices in the bubble.

EDMARK Corporation http://www.edmark.com/

Future School http://www.futureschool.com/ A video and 122 CD-ROM's on the K–12 math curriculum.

GAMCO http://www.gamco.com/

Key Curriculum Press http://www.keypress.com/catalog/products/software/Prod_GSP.html The Geometer's Sketchpad: outstanding software for learning Euclidean, coordinate, transformational, analytic, and fractal geometry.

Knowledge Adventure http://www.knowledgeadventure.com/home/

The Learning Company http://www.mattelinteractive.com/ Point on the link for the Learning Company, to pull up choices in the bubble.

Tom Snyder Productions Educational Software http://www.teachtsp.com/index.shtml

MATH CONTESTS AND CONTEST PROBLEM BOOKS

Find a large list of math contests at: http://www.davidson.edu/academic/math/davis/cmc/ssGuideToMathGps.html

Contests: Intermediate to Advanced

American Math Competitions (AMC->8, 10, and 12): http://www.unl.edu:80/amc/ Titu Andreescu, Director, University of Nebraska-Lincoln, P.O. Box 81606, Lincoln, NE 68501-16066. Phone: (402) 472-6566, Fax: (402) 472-6087, E-mail: titu@amc.unl.edu. Individual copies of prior year's contests for grades 8, 10, or 12 and below, including solutions, cost $1 per contest year. Order by phone or mail. Download an order form from the web site or ask to have one sent to you. American Math Competitions also sells copies of the American Invitational Math Exam (for those who make the honor roll on the AMC->10 and 12), USA Math Olympiads (a test for the top scorers on the AIME), and the International Math Olympiads. Ask them to send you a brochure of their high school materials.

The Continental Math League: http://www.li.net/;slmajorbar/cml/ P.O. Box 2196, St. James, NY 11780-0605, Phone: (631) 584-2016, E-mail: Quartararo@e-mail.com. Math team coaches can register their school in leagues from grades 2–9. Homeschools may also be allowed to compete. Anybody may order books of prior contest problems from this address. The available books, for $20 each, are: *Best of CML Grades 4–9 1980–1989, Best of CML Grades 2–3 1990–1995, Best of CML Grades 4–6 1990–1995, and Best of CML Grades 7–9 1990–1995.*

Math League Press: http://www.mathleague.com/ P.O. Box 720, Tenafly, NJ 07670-0720, (201) 568-6328, Fax: (201) 816-0125, E-mail: comments@mathleague.com. Math team coaches can register for contests at this address or web site, and anybody can order books of prior contest problems and solutions (click on "contest books"). Homeschools can order and take this year's contest, but cannot officially compete in it. Contest books are available for grades 4, 5, and 6; grades 7 and 8; high school; and algebra 1 students. There are 3 volumes for each level. For instance, for grades 4, 5, and 6, volume 1 contains contests for the school years 1979–80 to 1985–86, volume 2 contains contests from 1986–87 to 1990–91, and volume 3 contains contests from 1991–92 to 1995–96. Each volume costs $12.95 plus $3.00 shipping per order. Prices decrease for 11 or more copies. Credit cards are accepted. Order by phone, mail, or through their web site.

Mandelbrot Midlevels Competition http://www.midlevels.org/ P.O. Box 382805, Cambridge, MA 02238-2805, E-mail: contact@midlevels.org. The individual and team competitions are designed for eighth graders and advanced seventh graders. From the problems on the web site (this contest is new), the contests appear to range in difficulty from Chapter to National level MATHCOUNTS. The high school Mandelbrot contest allows an adult coach to register teams of four or more students without a school registering, so the Mandelbrot midlevels might also.

MATHCOUNTS http://www.mathcounts.org/ MATHCOUNTS Registration Office, P.O. Box 441, Annapolis Junction, MD 20701, Phone: (301) 498-6141, E-mail: math@pmds.com. MATHCOUNTS is a lavishly funded and wonderful math contest limited to students in grades 7 and 8. MATHCOUNTS problems are my favorite. They come in an enormous range of difficulty, and motivate middle school students to learn more algebra and geometry. Click on "MC Store" to see what coaching materials are available for purchase. They include a book called *The All-Time Greatest MATHCOUNTS Problems* and sets of 300 practice problems called Warm-ups and Workouts from various years that coaches receive in the annual School Handbook. There are also Competition Sets, which include instructions, problems, and answers from various upper-level MATHCOUNTS contests. Complete solutions for some contest problems are also available for separate purchase. Order by printing the web site's order form or by contacting Sports Awards Co., 4351 N. Milwaukee Ave., Chicago, IL 60641, Phone: (800) 621-5803; in Illinois: (773) 282-8060. Visa and Mastercard accepted.

Math Olympiads for Elementary and Middle School Students (MOES) http://www.moems.org/ 2154 Bellmore Ave., Bellmore, NY 11710-5645, Phone: (516) 781-2400, E-mail: moes@i-2000.com. MOES holds contests for fourth through eighth graders. Contests are open to any accredited school or homeschool association that does not discriminate on the basis of race, color, national origin, or gender. An excellent problem book is also available by George Lenchner called *Math Olympiad Contest Problems for Elementary and Middle Schools*. It contains 400 wonderful problems at the 5th to 7th grade level written over 16 years for the Olympiads. Problem-solving strategies are discussed and illustrated. It includes a section with hints for solving each problem, and one with detailed solutions for each problem. Credit cards are not accepted. You must order through the mail. The order form is available through the MOES web site. (Click on "Ordering Items.") Or call for instructions on ordering.

Contests: Very Advanced

American Regions Mathematics League (ARML) http://www.armlmath.org/ President: Mark Saul: msaul@compuserve.com. Corresponding Secretary: Kristee Sallee,ksallee@visto.com. ARML is an annual national mathematics competition. High school students form teams of 15 to represent their city, state, county, or school and compete against other teams from the United States and Canada at one of 3 sites: Penn State, the University of Iowa, and the University of Nevada-Las Vegas

Mandelbrot Competition http://www.mandelbrot.org/ Greater Testing Concepts, P.O. Box 380789, Cambridge, MA 02238-0789, E-mail: info@mandelbrot.org. This is a very challenging high school contest with 2 divisions, A and B. B is easier than A. Schools may enter one or both divisions, each of which contain both individual and team contests. Students under 20 not affiliated with a participating high school, such as homeschool students, may also enter a team provided the team has at least 4 students and is sponsored by an adult acting as the coach. Make arrangements through Greater Testing Concepts. On the home page, you will find a link to "Register" for this year's contest and a link to "Resources," which include previous contests and solutions that may be purchased by anyone.

USA Mathematical Talent Search (USAMTS) http://www.nsa.gov:8080/programs/mepp/usamts.html USA Mathematical Talent Search, COMAP, Inc., Suite 210, 57 Bedford Street, Lexington, MA 02173. Individuals register for this very difficult, proof-oriented, high school–level contest. It's open to anyone, and it's free. There are 4 rounds of 5 problems. Unlike most contests, which are short speed tests, students have a month to complete each round, something like math research. (Asking for help is prohibited, however.) Students' solutions are evaluated by a group of mathematicians at the National Security Agency. A copy of the evaluations, showing scores and possible commendations, are sent to the student after each round. When my daughter Kirsten participated in this contest in eighth grade, she received lots of encouragement from contest organizers.

Contests: International
Australian Math Trust Publications List http://www.amt.canberra.edu.au/amtbooks.html This contains a list of numerous books of prior contests. To order, write or fax: AMT Publishing, Australian Mathemat-

ics Trust, University of Canberra ACT 2601, Australia, Phone: +61 2 6201 5136, Fax: +61 2 6201 5096.

Canadian Mathematics Competition http://cemc.uwaterloo.ca/CMC English.html Faculty of Mathematics, University of Waterloo, Waterloo, Ontario N2L 3G1, Phone: (519) 885-1211, extension 2697, Fax: (519) 746-6592, E-mail: cmc@math.uwaterloo.ca. Canadian Math competitions are open to U.S. schools. Homeschools must contact the office above. Except for the most advanced Descartes contest, individuals cannot register for contests. Individuals *can* order reprints of prior contests and solutions and the *Problems, Problems, Problems* series of practice problems and solutions at grade-levels from 7–12.

National Mathematical Olympiads http://www.fmf.uni-li.si/~math comp/MathOlympiads.html Leads to sites for various countries.

MATH AND SCIENCE RESEARCH CONTESTS

Intel (formerly Westinghouse) Science Talent Search http://www.intel. com/education/sts/ Science Service, 1719 N Street, NW Washington, D.C. 20036, Phone: (202) 785-2255, Fax: (202) 785-1243, E-mail: webmaster@sciserv.org. This is the premier science and math research competition for U.S. high school seniors. Research papers are due in early December. Ideally students should find an adviser and begin their project a year or more in advance.

Intel International Science and Engineering Fair (Intel ISEF) http://www. sciserv.org/iisef/ Science Service, 1719 N Street, NW Washington, D.C. 20036, Phone: (202) 785-2255, Fax: (202) 785-1243, E-mail: webmaster@sciserv.org.

High School Math Project Ideas http://www.columbia.edu//umk1/

TUTORING SCHOOLS

Kaplan Score Centers http://www1.kaplan.com/score/view/area/ 1,2288,690,00.html Phone: (800) 49-SCORE. Score offers three types of services: Assessment, Independent Learning (Advantage Program), and Personal Training. They will assess your child's achievement level and needs in: Math 1–10, Reading K–10, Writing 5–10. You can then arrange for instruction outside of Score. The Advantage Program uses interactive multimedia instruction with a teacher available to answer questions in: Math K–8, Reading K–8, Writing 5–10, Spelling and Science. In Personal Training, a teacher designs an individualized lesson plan and personal instruction for each student in either 1 or 2 of these areas: Math 1–10, Reading K–10, Writing 5–10. Both the Advantage Program and Personal Training include an initial assessment, and both have guarantees of achievement.

Sylvan Learning Centers http://www.educate.com/homepage.html Phone: 1 (888) EDUCATE. Sylvan offers instruction in K–12 math, reading skills, literature, writing, study skills, and SAT and ACT test preparation. They promise an initial individual skills assessment, an individualized study program involving classes with an average student-teacher ratio of 3 to 1, self-paced learning, objective assessment of progress, and even a guarantee of achievement in basic math and reading skills.

TEST PREPARATION AND COLLEGE INFORMATION

Barron's Home Page http://www.barronseduc.com/main.htm Test prep books and software for a variety of tests including the ACT, SAT1, SAT2, and Advanced Placement, California and New York Regents tests.

College Board Online http://www.collegeboard.org/ *How to Prepare for High School Entrance Examinations-SSAT/ISEE*, Eighth Edition, Peters, Max and Jerome Shostak. ISBN: 0-8120-9725-4, Barron's Educational Series. A comprehensive test-prep book geared to a high school entrance exam. It is also moderately useful for preparing for the Johns Hopkins Institute for the Academic Advancement of Youth fifth and sixth grade Talent Search Contests.

Kaplan SAT1, PSAT, & ACT Test Prep Centers http://www.kaplan.com Phone: (800) KAP-TEST.

Peterson's http://www.petersons.com/

Princeton Review Test Prep Centers http://www.review.com/ Phone: (800) 2REVIEW. SAT1, PSAT, & ACT, but also SAT2, GRE, LSAT, GMAT, MBE, MCAT, TOEFL, USMLE.

TESTS AND ANSWERS

Texas Education Agency http://www.tea.state.tx.us/student.assessment/release.htm Old competency tests.

Texas Business and Education Coalition http://www.tbec.org/ Practice tests.

Princeton Review's Homeroom http://www.homeroom.com/

Test Professor.com http://www.testmasters.net/ Math competency for various levels in many states.

ACADEMIC SUMMER CAMPS AND DISTANCE LEARNING PROGRAMS

General Listings

Advisory List of International Educational Travel and Exchange Programs. Council on Standards for International Educational Travel, 3 Loudoun Street SE, Leesburg, VA 20175, Phone: (703) 771-2040.

Center for Talent Development Educational Program Guide http://ctdnet. acns.nwu.edu Northwestern University, 617 Dartmouth Place, Evanston, IL 60208, Phone: (847) 491-3782, E-mail: kmp607@lulu. acns.nwu.edu. See web site or ask for information on academic summer programs.

Directory of Student Science Training Programs http://www.sciserv.org/ stp/ A very valuable directory describing hundreds of U.S. summer math and science programs.

Peterson's Summer Camps and Programs—Academics: Mathematics http:// www.petersons.com/ Terrific listing of an enormous number of summer math programs. You can also access listings of other summer programs from here.

Peterson's—Distance Learning On-line Listings and Books http://www. petersons.com/ On-line listings of distance learning programs and books of such programs available for purchase on-line.

Summer on Campus: College Experiences for High School Seniors. Available in bookstores or from College Board Publications, Box 886, New York, NY 10101-0886.

Summer Opportunities for Kids and Teenagers. Available in bookstores, from Peterson's Guides, P.O. Box 2123, Princeton, NJ 08543-2123, Phone: (800) 338-3282, or on-line at "Peterson's—Pre-College Books" http://www.petersons.com/

Talent Identification Program (TIP) http://www.tip.duke.edu/index. html Duke University TIP, 1121 West Main Street, Suite 100, Durham, NC 27701, Phone: (919) 683-1400, E-mail: info@tip.duke.edu. Ask for the Educational Opportunity Guide listing academic programs and other information. TIP also provides on-line information on educational programs in the U.S. and abroad.

Yahoo! Summer Programs http://dir.yahoo.com/Education/K__12/ Programs/Summer__Programs/ Includes a link to the Peterson's site and others.

Yahoo! Distance Learning http://dir.yahoo.com/Education/Distance__ Learning/K__12/ Great resource for K–12 distance learning programs for children of all ages and abilities.

Especially for Gifted Students

Center For Talent Development (CTD) at Northwestern http:// ctdnet.acns.nwu.edu CTD-MTS, Northwestern University, 617 Dartmouth Place, Evanston, IL 60208, Phone: (847) 491-3782, E-mail: kmp607@lulu.acns.nwu.edu CTD runs the Midwest Talent Search (MTS) for students in Illinois, Indiana, Michigan, Minnesota, Ohio,

North Dakota, South Dakota, and Wisconsin. To participate in MTS, you must score among the upper 5 percent on a nationally normed achievement test. Those who score well in MTS (which uses the SAT or ACT tests) qualify for academic summer programs at Northwestern and other colleges. Summer programs are available for students from grades 7–12. Distance learning options include "LetterLinks," honors courses in math, social sciences, and the humanities for students in sixth through twelfth grade.

Center for Talented Youth (CTY) or Institute for the Academic Advancement of Youth (IAAY) http://www.jhu.edu:80/~gifted/registration/CTY The Johns Hopkins University, 3400 North Charles Street, Baltimore, MD 21218, Phone: (410) 516-0337, E-mail: iaay.programsinfo@jhu.edu. Talent search contest for grades 2–8 for those scoring among the top 3 percent on an ability test. Even for math wizards, talent searches are competitive. About half of those participating in the search qualify for summer camps or distance learning programs. The summer camps offer a broad range of courses including math and science. One of my children took a very good writing course. CTY's distance learning is largely the same as EPGY's, though it includes somewhat fewer college-level math and physics courses. IAAY has an extensive series of writing tutorials starting in sixth grade and culminating with preparation for the AP English Language and Composition exam. CTY also offers academic summer camps for a broader group of seventh graders and above who score well on the SAT but do not fall in the upper 3 percent.

Computerized Database of Summer Programs for Gifted and Talented Students Sandra Berger, The Council for Exceptional Children, 1920 Association Drive, Reston, VA 22091, Phone: (800) CEC-READ.

Education Program for Gifted Youth (EPGY) http://www-epgy.stanford. edu/ EPGY, Ventura Hall, Stanford, CA 94305-4115, Phone: (650) 329-9920, E-mail: epgy-info@epgy.stanford.edu. K–12 math courses including first-year calculus and college courses in linear algebra, multivariate calculus, differential equations, number theory, and logic. They offer C-level AP introductory physics courses, college physics courses, and writing courses including preparation for the AP exam in

English Language and Composition. To enroll, students must score in the upper 15 percent on an ability test. For the writing courses, students must also submit a writing sample.

Gifted & Talented Resources http://www.nhptv.org/kn/vs/special7.sht Lists lots of useful sites for gifted and talented education.

Talent Identification Program (TIP) http://www.tip.duke.edu/index.html See above for additional contact information. TIP accepts students from 16 states in or bordering the South. Like IAAY, TIP runs a talent search competition for seventh graders. High scorers qualify for its academic summer programs or distance learning courses. Students can also attend academic programs in England, Italy, and Germany. Ask for the Educational Opportunity Guide.

DISTANCE-LEARNING COURSES

K–12 Courses
Dept. of Distance Education—University of Nebraska http://dcs.unl. edu/disted/ College, high school, and review courses in middle and elementary school math.

Escondido Tutorial Service http://www.gbt.org/

The Willoway CyberSchool http://www.willoway.com/

College Courses
Department of Distance Education—University of Nebraska See above.

International Center for Distance Learning http://www.icdl.open.ac.uk/

New Jersey Institute of Technology Distance Learning http://www.njit. edu/DL/

Stanford Online http://stanford-online.standord.edu/

Western Governors University http://www.adec.edu/vuniv/wgu/wgu. html

FREE ON-LINE TUTORING

Questions and Answers

Algebra Online http://www.algebra-online.com/ Resources for learning algebra including a short list of books, answers to algebra problems or topics of your choice, and to previously posed questions.

Ask Dr. Math http://www.forum.swarthmore.edu/dr.math/dr-math. html Ask Dr. Math any question in K–college math. If this Swarthmore college site doesn't have the answer on file, send an E-mail.

The Online Math Tutor http://www.fliegler.com/mathman.htm Ask any question involving K–12 math.

Help with Specific Topics: K–11

These web sites offer free instruction in various math topics.

A+ Math http://www.aplusmath.com Receive flash card practice for basic arithmetic facts, or practice in long addition, subtraction, multiplication, and division. There is a homework helper and a bingo-type game for these problems and more.

Amazing Mathematical Object Factory http://www.schoolnet.ca/vp/ECOS/ Learn about combinations, permutations, partitions, and the number of subsets of a set.

DAU Math Refresher http://www.cne.gmu.edu/modules/dau/math A quick review course covering many topics from middle school through high school math, including elementary calculus with instruction, examples, exercises, and tests on each topic. Each learning center is depicted as a stop on a subway line. There are not enough exercises for a beginner, but what is there could be useful. I only explored a tiny part of this site, and I found a few mistakes, but overall, I liked what I saw of this ambitious project.

Education 4 Kids http://www.edu4kids.com/

Flash card Addition, Subtraction, Multiplication, and Division Practice http://www.edu4kids.com.math/ Choose what you want to practice and this site generates questions such as $4 + 7 = ?$; it corrects your answers and keeps score.

Geometry: Euclid's Elements http://aleph0.clarku.edu/~djoyce/java/elements/elments.html Read all 13 of these classic books on the web.

Knowledge Adventure Features for Parents http://www.education.com/features/parents/

Math Den http://www.actden.com/ A very large and valuable collection of challenging middle school and high school math problems with complete solutions, not including calculus. About 140 problem sets of 20 problems each are divided into 4 levels. If you register, the site keeps a record of the sets you've done and your scores.

Professor Freedman's Math Help http://www.mathpower.com Professor Ellen Freedman is a highly skilled web site designer. Very lively site with music and games. There's some math instruction in algebra and pre-algebra and some motivational advice plus links to other math sites. But don't count playing the terrific games or listening to the music as math learning.

Help with Specific Topics: Advanced

Analysis Course at the University of Nebraska at Lincoln http://www.math.unl.edu/~webnotes/home/home.htm Text, proof problems, and solutions for a course in real analysis, a tremendous resource for anyone wanting to learn this topic—essentially a free distance learning course. The author of this outstanding resource is John Lindsay Orr of the Department of Mathematics and Statistics. If you learn from this web site, please send him E-mail to thank him for his very substantial contribution to math education.

Integrator http://www.integrals.com/ Type in a mathematical expression and let Mathematica find its indefinite integral for you. This is great for checking your calculus homework—but not for doing it! That's not the way to learn, and no conscientious teacher would accept an answer without the intermediate steps in any case.

Linear Algebra and Precalculus Tests http://www.math.vanderbilt.edu/ ~msapir/cgi-bin/visit.cgi Some test problems for courses in linear algebra and precalculus are available for those who are not Vanderbilt students. For a fee, you can obtain complete course materials.

Topology http://www.math.niu.edu/~rusin/known-math/index/54-XX.html Not a course, but contains instruction, lists good texts, and contains many pointers to other topology sites.

University of Michigan Math Scholars http://www.math.lsa.umich. edu/~mathsch/ Has links to the on-line courses called Graph Theory & Enumeration, Chaos & Fractals, and the Nature of Infinity.

Free Math Education Archives

These web sites provide links to many additional math education web sites.

The Alive! Education Network http://www.alincom.com/educ/index.htm Several subjects including math.

AskERIC Lesson Plans: Math http://ericir.syr.edu/Virtual/Lessons/ Mathematics/index.html

Canada's SchoolNet: Learning Resources http://www.schoolnet.ca/home/ e/resources/ Many subjects including math.

Federal Resources for Educational Excellence—Mathematics http://www. ed.gov/free/s-math.html

Fred Worth's Math Resources http://www.hsu.edu/faculty/worthf/ hs5.html#math

Go Education http://infoseek.go.com/WebDir/Education?tid=670 Choose "Fields of Study" for sites relevant to many subjects.

Go Education: Fields of Study: Math http://www.infoseek.com/Topic/ Education/Fields_of_study/Mathematics/K_12_math?tid=13090

K–12 Math Teaching Materials http://archives.math.utk.edu/ k12.html Includes lesson plans for teaching a huge variety of math facts, concepts, principles, and procedures.

Internet Mathematics Library http://forum.swarthmore.edu/library/ very broad collection of math resources.

Internet Public Library: Mathematics http://www.ipl.org/ref/RR/static/ sci5000.html

Math Archives http://archives.math.utk.edu/tutorials.html A listing of college math courses, some containing lectures, tutorials, problems, and solutions.

MATHCOUNTS Math Archive http://206.152.229.6/Other__ Sites/Sites.html

Math Resources http://forum.swarthmore.edu/math.topics.html A listing of a gigantic number of math education texts, problems, and solutions for K–12 math and beyond. Sites were selected from a larger set included in the Math Forum.

Mathematical Atlas—Encyclopedia of Areas of Mathematics http://www.math.niu.edu/~rusin/known-math/index.html Covers many areas of math and contains lots of information.

Mathematics Resources on the Internet http://mthwww.uwc.edu/wwwmahes/files/math01.html Math education and a lot of other math links.

Searchopolis http://www.searchopolis.com/ Archives for many subjects including math.

Teams Distance Learning: Math Resources http://teams.lacoe.edu/documentation/places/math.html

Wadsworth Math and Science Archive http://education.wadsworth.com/edsites/mathsci.html

ADVANCED SUMMER MATH AND SCIENCE PROGRAMS

Caltech Physics 11 Summer Research Program For information and an application, high school juniors or their teachers should write in early September to: Physics 11 Summer Research Program, Professor Thomas Tombrello, Chair, Division of Physics, Math, and Astronomy,

California Institute of Technology, 1200 East California Blvd., Pasadena, CA 91125. This summer research program invites about 8 high school students, primarily juniors, for 10 weeks of physics research supervised by Tombrello and other Caltech faculty and graduate students. Students selected for this program receive a free room in a Caltech dorm, free round trip air transportation to and from Caltech, and a $3,000 stipend. Selections are based on students' ability to solve theoretical modeling problems. My daughter Kirsten participated in the program in 1998. She made astounding progress on 2 research projects, learned an enormous amount of advanced math and physics, and decided to pursue a career in math research.

Hampshire College Summer Studies in Mathematics http://www.hampshire.edu/offices/specprog/hcssim.shtml Natural Science Department, Hampshire College Amherst, MA 01002-5001, Phone: (413) 559-5375, E-mail: dkelly@hampshire.edu. Six weeks, $1,882, secondary school students. Topics include rings, randomization, topology, symmetry, mathematical logic, map coloring, complex numbers, limits, number theory, chaos, and fractals.

PROMYS http://math.bu.edu/INDIVIDUAL/promys PROMYS, Department of Mathematics, Boston University, 111 Cummington St., Boston, MA 02215, Phone: (617) 353-2563, E-mail: promys@math.bu.edu. Six weeks, high school students, $1,500, financial aid based on need. Number theory and, for more experienced students, abstract algebra.

Research Science Institute (RSI) at MIT http://www.cee.org/rsi/index.shtml The Center for Excellence in Education, 140 Park St. SE, Suite 200, Vienna, VA 22180-4627. To apply, contact Ms. Maite (pronounced "My-tay") Ballestero, Director of Administration, Phone: (703) 938-9062, E-mail: maite@cee.org. Six weeks. No cost for those selected except transportation to and from MIT and spending money. Admits 50 U.S. and 25 International high school students—except high school seniors—with high ability in science and math. Lectures, discussion, and research supervised by faculty and graduate students in the Boston area. Students often work on projects to submit to the Intel (formerly Westinghouse) competition. This is an outstanding experience, but competition for the 50 slots is keen.

Ross Young Scholars Program http://www.math.ohio-state.edu/ross/index.html Department of Mathematics, The Ohio State University, 231 W. 18th Ave., Columbus, OH 43210. Professor Ross at (614) 292-1569 or aer@math.ohio-state.edu. Professor D. Shapiro at (614) 292-5894 or shapiro@math.ohio-state.edu. Eight weeks, $2,100, ages 13–18. First-year students take a course in number theory.

ALTERNATIVE SCHOOLING

Fred Worth's Home School Resources http://www.hsu.edu/faculty/worthf/hs.html

Homeschooling Books and Publications http://wwwœ.home-ed-press.com/HSRSC/hsrsc__02bks.html

Homeschooling Information http://www.dimensional.com/~janf/home-schoolinfo.html

Homeschooling Links http://www.eduplace.com/parents/hslinks.html

Homeschool Resource Guide http://members.home.net/ct-homeschool/guide.htm

Sudbury Valley School http://www.sudval.org/ 2 Winch Street, Framingham MA 01701, Phone: (508) 877-3030, Fax: (508)788-0674, E-mail: SudVal@aol.com. This site contains information on similar schools in other locations and sells literature about their school's educational philosophy and on starting your own school.

COMPUTER MATHEMATICS

Logo http://www.atlantic.net/~caggiano/logo/logo.html Logo is a great first programming language for children. This site has links to other Logo sites, books on Logo, and Logo projects.

MATLAB from Mathworks http://www.mathworks.com/ MATLAB is the finest numerical mathematical programming language. You can define various useful functions and use them in new programs without having to load them yourself, because MATLAB finds them on your disk drive and integrates them in your current program. MATLAB's syntax is easy to use and understand. It is not a symbolic mathematical programming language, but you can purchase "toolboxes" that integrate symbolic mathematics and variable precision computation into MATLAB. With these toolboxes, MATLAB users can easily combine numeric and symbolic computation without sacrificing speed or accuracy.

Maple from Waterloo http://www.maplesoft.com/ A symbolic programming language that is considerably easier to learn than its competitor, Mathematica. Symbolic mathematical languages are more difficult to use than numerical languages.

Mathematica from Wolfram Research http://www.wolfram.com/ Three of my children wrote successful programs in Mathematica in physics, economics, and mathematics. Mathematica is very complex and difficult to learn because of its arcane syntax and alternative user interfaces designed to permit many different approaches to programming. However, there is a wealth of books and programs applying Mathematica in a wide variety of fields, and there is no doubt that Mathematica is a powerful symbolic programming language.

GENERAL EDUCATION SITES AND RESOURCES

Especially for Parents

Books to Build on: A Grade-By-Grade Resource Guide for Parents and Teachers. Hirsch, Jr. E. D. and John Holdren, Editors, Delta Books, 1996. Paperback. ISBN: 0385316402.

National Parent Information Network http://www.npin.org/

The New York Times Learning Network http://www.nytimes.com/learning/

Parent Soup http://www.parentsoup.com/

Teach Me to Read. Winters, Mary K. Doubleday, 1959, Grade K–2. Excellent test of whether your child has reached the "whole word level," which is usually what "reading readiness" means.

Other

American Federation of Teachers http://www.aft.org

American School Directory http://www.asd.com/

Class Struggle—What's Wrong (and Right) with America's Best Public High Schools. Mathews, Jay. Times Books, 1998. ISBN:0-8129-2447-9. www.randomhouse.com. Ranks the top 230 public high schools on the total number of AP tests given divided by the number of graduating seniors in 1996. All public high schools with more than 200 graduates in 1996 that selected no more than half their students based on academic criteria were included in the study, as were some smaller schools. A high ranking indicates that the school encourages students to strive for high academic goals. Mathews found that many elite high schools in wealthy school districts restrict honors classes to a tiny fraction of the brightest students and actively discourage many qualified students from taking these courses.

National Council of Teachers of Mathematics http://www.nctm.org/ Access the 1989 and 2000 Standards from here.

National Education Association http://www.nea.org/

Barwise, J. "An Introduction to First-Order Logic." In K. J. Barwise, ed. *Handbook of Mathematical Logic*. North-Holland Publishing, Amsterdam, 1977, 5–46.

Benjamin, Arthur and Michael B. Shermer. *Teach Your Child Math: Making Math Fun for the Both of You*. Lowell House, Los Angeles, 1996.

Corbett, A. C. "Retrieval dynamics for rote and visual image mnemonics." *Journal of Verbal Learning and Verbal Behavior*. 1977, 16, 233–246.

Dehaene, S. *The Number Sense: How the Mind Creates Mathematics*. Oxford University Press, New York, 1977.

Dossey, John A. "A Comparative Analysis of American and Japanese Assessments of Eighth Graders." Dept. of Education: Office of Educational Research and Improvement, 1977. NCES 97-885.

Gallencamp, Charles. *Maya, The Riddle and Rediscovery of a Lost Civilization*. David McKay Company, New York, 1976.

Gates, A. I. "Recitation as a factor in memorizing." *Archives of Psychology*, vol. 6, no. 40, 1917.

Gelman, Rochel and C. R. Gallistel. *The Child's Understanding of Number*. Harvard University Press, Cambridge, Mass. 1978.

Hartocollis, Anemona. "Math Teachers Back Return of Education in Basic Skills." *The New York Times*, April 13, 2000.

Hartocollis, Anemona. "The New, Flexible Math Meets Parental Rebellion." *The New York Times*, April 27, 2000.

The 1994 High School Transcript Study. U.S. Department of Education, National Center for Education Statistics, U.S. Government Printing Office, Washington, D.C., 1994.

Hirsch, Eric Donald, Jr. *The Schools We Need and Why We Don't Have Them*. Doubleday, New York, 1996.

Kulik, J. A. "An Analysis of the Research on Ability Grouping: Historical and Contemporary Perspectives." *Ability Grouping Research-Based Decision Making Series*. No. 9204, University of Michigan, Ann Arbor, 1992.

Malone, Hermione. "Go Figure. Some Parents Wary of New Approach on Math." *The Boston Globe*, December 3, 1999.

Mathews, Jay. *Class Struggle—What's Wrong (and Right) with America's Best Public High Schools*. Times Books, 1998.

Mosteller, F. "The Tennessee Study of Class Size in the Early School Grades." *Future of Children*. 5: (2), summer-fall 1995, 113–127.

Mosteller, F., R. J. Light, and J. A. Sachs. "Sustained Inquiry in Education: Lessons from Skill Grouping and Class Size." *Harvard Educational Review*. 66: (4), winter 1996, 797–842.

Newell, A., J. C. Shaw, and H. A. Simon. "The Processes of Creative Thinking." In Gruber, H. E., G. Terrell, and M. Wertheimer (Eds.) *Approaches to Creative Thinking*. Atherton Press, New York, 1962. 63–110.

Perkins, David. *Smart Schools: Better Thinking and Learning for Every Child*. The Free Press, New York, 1992.

Polya, George. *How to Solve It*. Doubleday, New York, 1957.

Polya, George. *Mathematical Discovery*. Vol. 1, Wiley, New York, 1962.

Polya, George. *Mathematical Discovery*. Vol. 2, Wiley, New York, 1965.

Polya, George. *Mathematical Discovery*. Combined paperback edition, Wiley, New York, 1981.

Samuelson, Paul A. *Economics*. Tenth Edition, McGraw-Hill, New York, 1976.

Schoenfeld, Alan H. *Mathematical Problem Solving*. Academic Press, San Diego, 1985.

Simon, H. A. and A. Newell. "Human Problem Solving." *American Psychologist*, 26, 1971, 145–159.

Stevenson, Harold. Personal communication.

Stevenson, Harold W. and James W. Stigler. *The Learning Gap: Why Our Schools Are Failing and What We Can Learn from Japanese and Chinese Education*. Touchstone, New York, 1992.

Sykes, Charles. J. *Dumbing Down Our Kids: Why American Children Feel Good About Themselves but Can't Read, Write, or Add*, St. Martin's Press, New York, 1996.

Third International Mathematics and Science Study-4. "Pursuing Excellence—A Study of U.S. Fourth-Grade Mathematics and Science Teaching, Learning, Curriculum, and Achievement in International Context." U.S. Dept. of Education, National Center for Education Statistics, U.S Government Printing Office, Washington, D.C., 1997.

Third International Mathematics and Science Study-8. "Pursuing Excellence—A Study of U.S. Eighth-Grade Mathematics and Science Teaching, Learning, Curriculum, and Achievement in International Context." U.S. Dept. of Education, National Center for Education Statistics, U.S. Government Printing Office, Washington, D.C., 1996.

Third International Mathematics and Science Study-12. "Pursuing Excellence—A Study of U.S. Twelfth-Grade Mathematics and Science Achievement in International Context." U.S. Dept. of Education, National Center for Education Statistics, U.S Government Printing Office, Washington, D.C., 1998.

Useem, Elizabeth L. "You're Good, but You're not Good Enough," *American Educator*, fall 1990, 24–27 and 43–46.

Useem, Elizabeth L. "Getting on the Fast Track in Mathematics: School Organizational Influences on Math Track Assignment." *American Journal of Education*. May, 1992, 325–353.

Wickelgren, Wayne A. *How to Solve Problems: Elements of a Theory of Problems and Problem-Solving*. W. H. Freeman and Company, New York, 1974. (Now reprinted as: *How to Solve Mathematical Problems*, Dover, New York, 1995.)

Winters, Mary K. *Teach Me to Read*. Doubleday, Garden City, NY, 1959.

Yablun, Ronn. *How to Develop Your Child's Gifts and Talents in Math*. Lowell House, Los Angeles, 1995.

Index